UNSTUCK

A Strategic Approach to Living the Life You Want

PHILIP OWENS
Copyright © Philip Owens 2019

Unstuck – A Strategic Approach to Living the Life You Want

Published by Dean Publishing
Po Box 119
Mt Macedon, Victoria, 3441
Australia
www.deanpublishing.com

Copyright © Philip Owens 2019

All rights reserved. No part of this publication may be reproduced, stored in a retrieval system or transmitted in any way or by any means, electronic, mechanical, photocopying, recording or otherwise, without the prior written permission of the author.

The information provided in this book is designed to provide helpful information on the subjects discussed. This book is not meant to be used, nor should it be used, to diagnose or treat any physical, emotional or psychological medical condition. For diagnosis or treatment of any medical problem, consult your own physician. The publisher and author are not responsible for any specific health or psychological needs that may require medical supervision and are not liable for any damages or negative consequences from any treatment, action, application or preparation, to any person reading or following the information in this book. References are provided for informational purposes only and do not constitute endorsement of any websites or other sources. Neither the publisher nor the individual author(s) shall be liable for any physical, psychological, emotional, financial, or commercial damages, including, but not limited to, special, incidental, consequential or other damages. Our views and rights are the same: You are responsible for your own choices, actions, and results.

Cataloguing-in-Publication Data® National Library of Australia
Author: Philip Owens
Title: Unstuck – A Strategic Approach to Living the Life You Want
Edition: 1st edn
ISBN: 978-1-925452-12-9

DEDICATION

This book is dedicated in three ways:

In a professional sense, this book is dedicated to Dr Michael Yapko, whose lifetime of work in strategic thinking in therapy inspires and informs everything that I do in helping others.
Thank you, Michael.

In a personal sense, it is dedicated to my wife Nicole, and my boys Alexander and Cameron. The love and support of my family is the rock on which I build everything that I do.
Thank you for everything.

And it is dedicated to you, the reader – on your own path to becoming unstuck. This book is dedicated to you as a resource: to help you a little further along your path.
Thank you for trusting me to be your guide.

This book is also **Interactive!**

To learn more from Philip about how to get Unstuck and set yourself free — go to: **deanpublishing.com/books/philowens** for free videos, audios and much more.

Table of Contents

Dedication iii
Foreword vii
Chapter 1: Are You Stuck? 1
Chapter 2: The Nature of Your Problem 7
Chapter 3: You Can't Always Get What You Want 21
Chapter 4: Compared to What? 35
Chapter 5: Setting Goals That Work Long Term 51
Chapter 6: The Behaviour That Gets You Stuck and
           Learning Your Way Out 69
Chapter 7: What Drives Your Problem? 105
Chapter 8: Diving Below the Waterline: Into the Conditional Field 117
Chapter 9: Self-Awareness: Exploring What Lies Beneath 135
Chapter 10: Identity – Who Are You? 151
Chapter 11: Sticky Labels 179
Chapter 12: Deciding How to Decide 191
Chapter 13: Discriminations That Matter 213
Chapter 14: Deeper Discriminations 221
Chapter 15: You Are More Than You Know 245
Chapter 16: Moving On: Becoming the Next Version of You 259
Afterword 267
Free Resources for You 269
Acknowledgements 271
About The Author 273

PHILIP OWENS

Foreword

One of the best pieces of advice ever provided, in my opinion, came from the French poet and author, Antoine de Saint-Exupery, perhaps best known for having written the charming tale of *The Little Prince*. He insightfully said, "A goal without a plan is just a wish," thereby highlighting one of the many challenges associated with trying to live a full and satisfying life. As any clinician is likely to tell you, people usually know *what* they want. Typically, they just don't know *how* to go about getting what they want. How can you take a step in the right direction to make your life better when either you don't know what that step should be or when you simply don't feel courageous enough to take it?

It's not easy to *form* a realistic plan and delineate the specific steps needed to bring that plan to a successful fruition. It's not easy to *stay* with a plan that doesn't provide instant success, and it's not easy to flexibly *adjust* plans when it becomes clear the original plan isn't working and, worse, isn't very likely to work. Yet, these are essential skills to develop when you want your life to reflect the ambitions of your dreams.

In writing *Unstuck*, Philip Owens has taken his substantial experience as a clinician and coach and, combined with his uncommon good sense, identified some of the most common ways people have for getting stuck in some area(s) of their lives. In so doing, he then provides readers with ample no-nonsense advice that can help them get the stagnant parts of their lives moving again. He is careful to point out that you as a person aren't the problem; instead, what keeps you stuck is *how* you go about trying to solve the problems you face. What a powerful – and empowering message! There is a contagious optimism that comes from such statements, and Owens not only feeds the optimism that says you are capable of more but, he does much more than that; he shows you *how* to convert that optimism into meaningful *action*. He is quite right in his assertion that what you think and feels matter, but so do the actions that you take.

Owens has a quality of clarity in his approach to life that is inspiring and to his great credit he shares it generously in this book. He helps readers define goals, anticipate obstacles, avoid getting sidetracked by irrelevant and paralyzing feelings of doubt and keep the focus on attaining desired outcomes. He does this through his elaboration of key principles of good problem solving, illuminating case examples that highlight how the principles apply, thought-provoking questions to nudge your thinking in a more helpful direction, and structured exercises to help build valuable skills for making better choices. After all, as Owens emphasizes, the quality of your life is a direct reflection of the quality of the choices you make.

This is a valuable book that requires attention to details and a willingness to experiment with new possibilities. Philip Owens has provided readers with a strong combination of insightful concepts and practical methods for moving from mere wishes to actual successes. He really can help you get "unstuck!"

Michael D. Yapko, Ph.D.

Clinical psychologist and author of *Keys to Unlocking Depression* and *The Discriminating Therapist*

Chapter 1

Are You Stuck?

We all get stuck. It is part of life's journey.

Welcome to *Unstuck*.

This book will help you move on in your life. It will create a whole new way to approach challenges and overcome them with ease.

There are many self-help books offering one single 'answer' to *all* your problems. Unfortunately life is never really that simple or easy. Two people can appear to have the same problem but what helps them become unstuck can be entirely different.

Rather than defining yourself by your problems, with *Unstuck* you will learn:

- That you are far more capable than you think.
- That you are more powerful than any label you give yourself.
- That you can be independent of your problems.
- You can build a breakthrough framework for problems to be seen as 'processes' that neither define or limit you.
- How to better respond to stress and anxiety.
- How to remove internal obstacles and create momentum in your life.

I have worked extensively with people in my clinic and in the professional and coaching realm. There are many similarities in the issues we all face. More importantly, there are simple, common methods that each individual can immediately use to become unstuck and move forward.

I have seen people suffering from chronic depression, anxiety, fears and phobias, relationship issues, professional roadblocks, trauma and crises that have become unstuck. Yes, it is possible! And you can too.

So, how can someone who has been suffering depression for decades suddenly start to become unstuck? Or someone with anger issues suddenly learns calmness?

Because behind every problem is an understandable process that can make things SHIFT.

Get Unstuck

There are important exercises throughout each chapter that are designed to deepen your learning and insight. Doing these exercises can be simple, but feedback has shown that taking the time to do them can be a really powerful tool to help you on your journey to becoming unstuck. I encourage you to grab a notebook and do the exercises or download the workbook from the website **www.gettingunstuck.com.au**—it's free.

There are also supportive audios you can listen to via www.mindsetmaestro.com.

Taking action by doing the exercises is a great way to move forward. Let's kick off with something to get us rolling:

Unstuck Exercise #1: Do you need this book?

1. Think about where you're stuck in your life.
2. Now, identify one or two obstacles preventing you from getting what you want. It might be something 'big' like depression or anger, or something small yet annoying, like lack of discipline or motivation.

Have you thought of something? Good. Now…*stop* it! That's right. Just—
Stop it!

Take a moment and check what happened. Are the obstacles gone? If they have, stop reading now. You're done!

But if those obstacles are still there, then the rest of this book is for you.

Many self-help books spend 300 pages proposing various ways to do the exercise you've just completed—gain awareness of your problem and pledge to change it. I promise you that you're in for something different. There isn't a secret mantra or recipe for enhancing your life within this book. There's no need for you to trust in some special outside power. Instead, this book puts *you* as the leader. *You* gain understanding of what it *really* means to be stuck and why it's not only OK but entirely normal. This helps *you* discover new personal solutions that empower *you*. This book helps *you* 'unstick yourself' in new and often exciting ways.

But it's up to you to take action.

I will share with you why sometimes taking action is ridiculously easy, and other times hard. Often when we believe action will be difficult, we don't try. However, taking action is often less difficult than we imagine.

For almost the entire population of the planet, 'Unstuck Exercise #1' is *not* helpful. Simply being told to 'stop it' or 'do this or that' is not enough. In fact, it is often harmful. Sometimes it comes with an implied undertone that you 'should' be able to stop, start or do what the expert is telling you. And because at this point—you can't; there must be something 'wrong' with you, right? It also removes your choice, control and personal power over your experience. It suggests that you need to rely on some external wisdom or guru for answers.

There are no demands here. I simply invite you to recognise where you're stuck and be open to the possibility of learning something that may help. Try to release the need to beat yourself up, or berate the amount of effort you've put in to resolving it. That's why you're here now – to learn a new way of seeing yourself and finally resolve the issues that plague you.

Have You Been Applying the 'Insane Approach'?

Einstein has been attributed to saying that the definition of insanity is 'doing the same things over and over and expecting a different outcome.' Unfortunately, when it comes to where we are stuck in our lives, we usually apply that approach. We keep battering against our issue with the same methods that haven't worked in the past in the hope that things will be different in the future.

Simply put: **If you knew how to move past your problem, you would have already.**

I can guarantee that you're an expert in your problem. If you could have resolved it, you would have. Period. You've probably been navigating the world as best you can whilst being stuck with your problem or unresolved issue. This in itself is often overlooked – the massive effort and strategies used to manage 'being stuck' whilst having to navigate the rest of your life. It's not easy.

Imagine for a moment if we could find a way to break the 'insanity cycle'. That there was a different way to move forward. Imagine if you no longer had to deal with your current problem. That you could move ahead with your life without having to struggle to manage it. Would that be a massive relief? Would you smile?

So, let's approach the common elements within every problem. Let's challenge your thinking around it. Here's a quick roadmap. Let's:

- Recognise where you're stuck.
- Define precisely what *stuck* means.
- Discover what's missing or needs to change.
- Create a new path forward.

Are you ready?

The Path from Stuck to Unstuck

This approach is designed and focused on one thing only: to move you from stuck to unstuck.

Learning the truth about being stuck will help you remain unstuck in the future. Once you have read the entire book, it will be a helpful resource to dive into if you ever worry about getting stuck again.

Whilst it is OK to skim through the exercises or do them in a superficial way – the true value comes when you take your time with them. I would suggest taking time after each exercise to ask yourself what you've noticed or learned from doing it. Reflection is an important part of the process.

What If It Gets Too Much?

Any time you're challenged in your life, you have a range of options. Naturally, as you face problems, they may trigger some unpleasant thoughts and feelings.

If this becomes overwhelming, then put the book down and reach out to a real person. It may be a family member, a spiritual counsellor or friend. Reaching out and asking for help is not a burden on these people, it's a gift you give them by allowing them to help.

There may be times when they're not able to help with your problem; but what they do offer is human connection, care and understanding. These are vital ingredients to feeling less alone in your problem.

If you're not comfortable with reaching out to someone that you know, there are a number of great organisations, such as Lifeline and other phone-based counselling services specifically trained to provide confidential help and support.

It's important to know that support is available anytime you need it.

Before you begin, let's have a shared agreement that if things get too tough, you *will* reach out and speak to someone directly – even if only for comfort. Then, only when you're ready—resume your journey to being unstuck.

Someone Like You

Throughout the book, you will read a number of real-life cases offered as examples. Each case is real; however, names, ages and details have been changed. Confidentiality is critical. It is likely, however, that you may recognise 'someone like you' in this book. As human beings, we are more similar in our experiences than different. However, whether you are a first-time reader or past client, I can assure you that no specific client or case can be identified.

Ready to go? Let's begin the life-changing journey of getting *unstuck* — once and for all!

Chapter 2

The Nature of Your Problem

Clients often ask me, "But Phil, why me? Why did this happen to me?" This is a natural question to ask, especially during or after a life-altering situation or when you feel there's no way forward. This question cannot always be answered. In fact, it's this question that often keeps people stuck. Can I suggest that perhaps a better question to ask is "How do I?" This question offers forward momentum, whereas 'Why me?' often has no valuable answers.

Learn What Stuck Is

Think of a situation where you want an outcome but are unable to achieve it.

Do you want to be happy; rich; have an amazing relationship; get a promotion or manage stress and anxiety better?

When you want to have, achieve or experience something and you can't have or get it—then you feel stuck.

That is the definition of stuck.

So, if the question stops being 'Why me?' and becomes 'How can I make that shift?' We now have a way forward. Let's delve a little deeper.

Going from stuck to unstuck can happen in three different ways:
1. You could change the goal.
2. You could change the way to go about getting the goal (your behaviour)
3. You could change the 'rules' and beliefs you have that drive your behaviour (from the unconscious programming of your mind)

Creating small changes in one or all of these levels may be enough to help you get unstuck. Sometimes it is the smallest shift – in the right place – that can make all the difference.

Unstuck Exercise #2: Can I make a shift?

Ask yourself the following questions:
- If I'm not getting the goal or result I want, can I somehow modify it to make it achievable?
- Could I change something that I am *doing* to achieve a different result?
- What are the rules, beliefs, strategies and boundaries I set for myself?
- Do these mental 'rules' make my goal reasonable or even possible?
- Could understanding my personal conditions/beliefs/rules/strategies allow me to change my approach so the result may become possible?

What did you notice as you as you challenged yourself with these questions? Did one particular area leap out to you as worthy of deeper exploration?

Unstuck Exercise #3: Three ways to positive change

Take some time to reflect on where you're stuck. Answer these questions as clearly as you can:
- What outcomes do I want? What do I want to achieve?
- Which behaviours are useful in helping me achieve this? Which behaviours are not helpful?
- What beliefs do I have that prevent me from getting what I want? What beliefs would serve me better?

Take time to get to know yourself better through these questions. Sometimes we hit roadblocks and want answers but miss the need to reflect before we can find the key that opens the lock. Taking time to do this is often the best thing you can do to move forward.

Getting unstuck requires change

There's so many books on 'how to change' that it can all be very confusing. However, change – with the right tools, support and framework, is what humans are great at. Including you!

At some point in your life, there was something you couldn't do. You may have felt stuck, frustrated and even angry. But over time you learnt something new and were able to adapt. Let's take reading as an example. Reading isn't a skill we're born with; we acquire it through *learning*. This learning involves making sense of symbols on a page to create meaning. At one point, you may have been stuck seeing odd shapes without meaning. But over time, through practising this skill, it became seamless and natural. You moved from stuck to unstuck.

That's because something you began *doing* changed you from being a non-reader to a reader.

What if this was also true for your current issue or problem?

History proves that change and adaptation are what humans do best. But if you don't know what exactly to change or you don't have a good process for change – then you're likely to remain stuck and frustrated.

Imagine for a moment that getting unstuck was simply a matter of learning something new.

A learning that would help you do something different.

So, are you ready to change?

Unstuck Exercise #4: The specificity test

Take a moment and answer the following questions honestly and completely. Consider where you're stuck:

1. What specifically do you want to change?
2. How specifically are you going to change it?

Review your answers. If you have great answers to both questions, then it's unlikely that you're stuck. If you've struggled to answer these questions (which is incredibly common)—then you may be stuck.

The common answer for those stuck usually is 'I don't know'. And that's completely OK because that's what happens when we face a challenge we can't yet overcome.

Unstuck Exercise #5: The revealing factor of why you're stuck

Take a step back and consider a circumstance where you're *not* stuck – where you perform well. It may be something that you love doing or just seem to do well.

- Describe your goal – what result did you set?
- How do you do it? Is there a process, or specific triggers you use to get your result?
- How did you get good at it?
- What beliefs do you have about it, and about yourself?

Unstuck Exercise: #5b: Repeat with a twist

- Run the exercise again and replace the thing that you're good at, with the current issue you face.

What did you learn from this exercise? In particular, what was the difference between the two cases? You may notice that when we're stuck, we often have a blind spot (lack of clarity) about being able to answer these questions.

Most people have blind spots. But often it's a just matter of 3 things.
1. The way you set up your goal
2. The behaviours you use to reach your goal
3. The conditions, rules and beliefs you place on yourself

Consider what it might be like to make a small shift in one of those areas. Perhaps it could completely change your experience.

Pause. Read the last paragraph again. It implies something subtle but incredibly powerful.

Do you get that it's not *you* but HOW you've been going about it?

Yes, you have the power to change many things about your experience, about how you do things.

I learned this frame of reference from leading psychologist Dr Michael Yapko. His approach helps people shift from 'there's something wrong with me' to 'there's only something wrong with what I'm doing'. The changes are miraculous. I invite you to perhaps cut yourself a break and explore how this could apply to you and your circumstance.

Awareness Changes Everything

The process of changing often happens through the first step of self-awareness. This is usually half the battle we all face in adapting, learning and change.

Self-awareness can be uncomfortable because it forces us to look in the mirror and take stock. It may make you reflect on painful times or notice problems that still persist and cause you distress. It may take some courage but if you stick with this book – and remain open to talking straight with yourself – then positive change will be inevitable.

I invite you to always start from the core assumption that '**It is not you; just how you've been going about it'.** From this stance, self-awareness can simply be an opportunity to *observe* what's happened in your life without guilt or shame. It's simply about seeing patterns that may need to change to achieve your desired outcomes.

Fixed or Flexible?

Some things in life are fixed (the parents you have, where you were born) whilst others are entirely flexible (your attitude, your feelings). When we become stuck, we can often believe that where we are stuck is absolutely fixed. If this belief develops, it shifts us further away from exploring possibilities that may emerge if it were more flexible. When you hear yourself say fixed sentences like "I can't", or "I always" then perhaps you could consider hearing them as 'rigidities'. These rigidities may not be true, but they will certainly keep you stuck. Be curious to how you view your issue, what you believe is fixed and what may be flexible. Because if it's flexible, wouldn't it be much easier to change?

The Courage to Look

Let's be candid about something—if change were easy, perhaps you would have already done it. Change doesn't have to be difficult but it does require a certain measure of courage.

The definition of courage is simply 'feeling the fear and taking action anyway'. Nothing more. You can't exactly predict where and if you'll hit discomfort or fear in your **Unstuck Exercises, but I guarantee that if you have courage, the benefits to your future can be substantial.**

The other guarantee is—if you don't do anything different, you can't expect a different outcome.

I encourage you to call yourself out when you *know* you're lying to yourself. I also want you to acknowledge when you're being too tough on yourself and cut yourself a break. Trust in the processes of this book. You may be surprised what you discover and what changes occur.

The Real Problem

At this point, many people often say, 'Oh yes, but all this stuff is true for everyone else, my problem is different. I'm different.'

Consider your fingerprint. As unique as your fingerprint is, every human on the planet has one. How about your genetics? This must be unique too, right? Yes, except everyone has their own genetics and life experiences.

So, whilst you are unique, you also are not. Consider the following:
- Why are you stuck where you are, while others are not?
- Why do others get stuck or have problems that you don't?
- How did others get over the same problem you have and never look back?

Unstuck Exercise #6: Who else?

Write down a list of some of the ways you are stuck.
- For each entry in your list, write down people you know who have the same issue.
- Look down the list again. Can you identify someone who overcame the problem? It might be a close friend, someone in your life, or a celebrity you read about in a magazine.

What did you learn?

As people do this exercise, many often reflect on a few things that you may also realise:

1. You're not alone. Whilst you are unique, there are lots of people that are unique too.
2. Whatever your problem is, someone has probably learned to overcome it, tolerate it, or turn it into an advantage.

3. Whatever it is that you want, either someone else has achieved it, or no one has at all.

The Structure of Stuck Is Common

When you stand as an individual and look at where you're stuck, it seems so unique. However, when you see the same problem described over and over again, you begin to understand the structure and nature of the actual problem itself.

Although each story is different, the structure that sits behind each issue is completely common, and often highly predictable.

Rather than dwell on *why* your situation is unique (things like how it began, its intensity or duration – which are all highly-specific to your unique circumstance), what if we looked for a recognisable pattern within the problem itself?

For example, if a client shares their persistent anxiety issue, I already have a fair idea of the structure of their problem without knowing their unique specifics. This is the same for depression or addiction as well.

Regardless of how you detail your story, it almost always conforms to a fundamental structure and series of processes that can be understood and modified.

In fact, there are certain elements that are always present. For example, if you didn't care about the future, would it be possible to be anxious?

Let's look at some common examples.

Bernie has anxiety. If you're like Bernie, then perhaps you worry about things that might happen in the future. You go over and over it, even to the point of interrupting your sleep or interfering with other things in your life. You might keep asking yourself 'What if' style questions. Then, when the thing you worried about doesn't happen, you say 'Phew! That was lucky' and find something else to worry about.

Doris presents with depression. If you were like Doris, then perhaps you can't help but think about things that happened in the past, and because those things were so bad, you know that the future is going to be bleak too – maybe even bleaker than the past. Maybe you've decided that it's not even worth trying because things won't be good regardless of what you do.

So, if each problem has similar underlying structures – even though their context, story, impact and severity may be different – what if we could work with the structure? And in doing so, regardless of the unique elements, the issue would no longer keep you stuck?

Imagine if you could do this without ever needing to rehash your story. Does that sound like something you'd prefer? If you had that ability, would you change?

This seems like a bizarre question. If you had the ability to change, why would you *not* want to?

Ripple Effects

Sometimes change can lead to a series of 'ripple effects'. This can happen to individuals and the groups in which they belong (such as families). For example, imagine how children can change for the better when a parent overcomes a drinking problem and their violent behaviour in the household stops.

Often, we simply can't see the impact our changes will make. Sometimes the ripples create wonderful additional outcomes, and sometimes they change circumstances in more challenging ways.

One example might be a woman who chooses not to change the disempowering family dynamic because the idea of a family breakdown is more painful than her need to feel safe. For her, based upon her beliefs and priorities, the cost of the change (breaking up the marriage) might just outweigh the benefit of stopping the abuse she suffers.

From the outside, it may seem 'crazy' as a choice but based on her beliefs, rules, experience and self-belief this may be the way she perceives the change, or lack thereof.

In this case, working with this person at the level of their beliefs and 'rules' may be important so she can reshape these beliefs and expectations and create a different understanding of the outcome and what it means.

Often moving forward can lead to additional gains or losses in life. Being *aware* of what gains or losses may allow you to approach it with a clearer sense of what is it means for you, and what is at stake.

Unstuck Exercise #7: Check the ripple effect

Ask yourself:
- If I were to become unstuck, what additional things might I gain or lose in the process?
- What ripples might be created into the lives or circumstances of those around me?
- Knowing what they are, am I willing to accept them as part of the moving forward process?

What did you notice doing this exercise? Did you find both gains and losses in your change equation?

It's not reasonable to believe that anyone wants to remain stuck in their current circumstance is causing them massive distress. Understanding the ripple effects from any change can assist in finding different ways to getting unstuck.

Being stuck in one place does not mean being stuck everywhere.

Sometimes the place we're stuck becomes such a major focus that we overlook all the other areas in our lives where we are skilled, capable and doing great. It's normal to do this. We often discount what's easy for us, even if it's difficult for others. Inevitably this means we are more likely to focus on our challenges instead of our strengths. This can sometimes dominate our thinking.

It's often valuable to take a breath and consider what's actually going right in your life., Recall the valuable skills you have. Appreciate that you have more capabilities and skill than you probably realise.

Consider Thommy. He was so frustrated by his inability to meet a suitable partner that it was dominating his thoughts, interfering with his sleep, and ruining his chances when he went on a date because he was always second guessing himself. When I invited Thommy to step back and have a look at the good stuff in his life, he discovered that he had a great group of friends, he was doing well at work, and he had enjoyable hobbies and fairly active social calendar. Thommy was able to notice that he was actually good at making friends and being a good friend.

Reframing his 'urgent' partner search regarding finding and building a slightly different type of friendship—something he was already good at—allowed Thommy to see his situation in a different way. Thommy allowed himself to appreciate his skills and broaden his focus – and not only see his problem. Thommy had a great time over the next 6 months making friends with a whole lot of new people and entered a steady relationship shortly after.

Maybe you're doing better than you think?

Life can be messy sometimes. No matter happened before, the circumstances that we face are not those that we've somehow scripted, but they're what emerges from living life the best we can.

Our circumstances are really outside our control. There is no script or rule book. Circumstances emerge, and stuff happens. Good things can happen to bad people, bad things can happen to good people – and everything in between.

We have no control over circumstances. We cannot change the weather, what someone does or thinks, or what will happen tomorrow. All we have is our ability to respond to the circumstances—whether good, bad or something in between. Whilst we cannot control what happens—we can control how we respond.

Yes, you can't change the weather, but you can decide to wear snow gear. You can't change what someone says to you, but you can choose how you respond to what they say. You cannot know what will happen tomorrow, but you can be prepared to choose a response when things emerge.

There's no formula for what has happened or will happen to people in life. I often marvel at people who have been through horrendous situations and simply found a way to cope. Their choice to respond in the best way they could at the time takes incredible courage and effort.

The truth is this:

Sometimes doing the best you can in your current circumstance is exactly that – *the best that you can.*

In new and novel circumstances, you cannot know what your response will be, until that is after you've done it. But whatever action you choose, it is likely to be the best option you could come up with at the time. That's It. You won't know what that specific thing is until you are confronted with it. The first time you are ever exposed to a new circumstance, you don't have a rulebook to follow.

In life, we often face new situations and – without thinking – we tend to rely on old habitual patterns. The behaviours that may have once been appropriate in one circumstance, however, may be problematic when applying them to other circumstances.

For example, in the boxing ring, Billy might know that he can win with an uppercut to the jaw. However, it's not an effective strategy at the office with his manager or at home with his wife. Therefore, Billy has to adapt his trained responses into a different set of behaviours in other circumstances to be successful.

Learned behaviours are often used across a range of circumstances – some of which are appropriate, some of which are not. When these are used in inappropriate situations, these learned behaviours are often seen as 'problems' (Think of Billy and his great upper-cut punch). Even though somewhere, and at some time, it may have been an effective strategy or the best that you could do.

So, what if we 'tuned up' those responses? What if you could take what works for you, modify and sharpen it to create responses that help get you a better outcome?

Remember, it's not you, just how you have been going about it.

The process of learning

Question: If you have done something once, can you do it again? What if you have done something multiple times – in fact, more times than you can remember or count – could you repeat it?

There are no prizes for guessing that the answer to this should probably be 'yes'.

There's been two things in your life that you've done countless times, more times than you can even remember. These two things are: adapt and learn.

Consider that you were born unable to hold this book, born unable to read. Even born without the language and vocabulary to make sense of what we are talking about here. The truth is, you have changed and learnt throughout your whole life. Along the way, no matter how many steps or attempts it took you, you learned to hold a book, focus your eyes, decode the symbols and interpret the meanings of the words on the page. How awesome is that!

Think of all of the other things in your life that you have learned. So many things that perhaps you don't even pay attention to them.

Learning Is Your Friend

And here it is. The heart of getting past every issue that you've ever had.

If you're open to learning, then you can learn your way out of where you're stuck and learn your way into a new future.

You are a learning machine; only stuck because of what you haven't learned yet. That's right. Wherever you are right now, we can extinguish old patterns and learn new ones. We can learn new rules, select valuable behavioural pattern and completely rearrange the way you move forward in your life.

You can't go back and change the past but you can change the way you live today, tomorrow and in the future.

It's not where you start but what you do from here. If you're willing to accept this view, then you can change your life in a moment. This moment, if you choose to.

By understanding that we're always actively making choices and each choice brings an element of known and unknown consequences, we begin to move from stuck into the terrain of unchartered possibility.

Possibility can be a very exciting place.

Stop Beating Yourself Up

If you've been doing the best you can with the circumstance that you've got, then that was really the best you could do with what you'd learned to that point.

Take a moment to appreciate that. Perhaps see yourself with empathy; as I do with everyone that I work with. Perhaps it is time to stop beating yourself up about being stuck, and instead start exploring the possibility that there might just be another way to go about it, and perhaps get a whole lot better outcome.

Unstuck Exercise #8: Through the ages

Find somewhere to lie or sit comfortably. For this exercise, allow yourself to read each statement and then take time to experience it. Perhaps close your eyes, imagine, or let your thoughts and feelings flow.

Are you in a comfortable place? Here are the ideas to experience.

- Imagine you were born at the age you are now. You are fresh and new with no habits, learnings or understandings. Everything in the world around you has no meaning. No threat, no implication, no importance. Everything is simply interesting and curious. Take some time to experience what it would be like to be in that state.
- Imagine now that you're rapidly growing through childhood and adolescence. As you transition across life's stages, you learn things. However, you do not learn what have learnt in your life to date; you learn other things. You learn good things, valuable things, and curious things. You create ways of seeing the world that make you feel happy, peaceful and strong. Take some time to experience what it would be like as if this is true.
- Imagine that version of you fusing into who you are now. All the new, valuable lessons, meanings and interpretations replacing the patterns and processes that have been holding you back. The things you learned that were once valuable but are no longer so, are replaced with different ways to see the world, and different ways to respond. Take some time to experience what this would be like. What would be different.

What did you notice or learn from doing this exercise?

Chapter 3

You Can't Always Get What You Want

People are often quick to complain when they're not getting what they want. A lot of distress and unhappiness arises when people don't get what they think they should or could have.

Some people are unhappy because they're not getting what someone else has got.

Imagine if you're stuck simply because you haven't been able to *properly* evaluate what you have, what you should get, and what you want?

Unstuck Exercise #9: What do you want?

Write a list of the things you want. These might be material things, experiences, feelings or successes. Ask yourself: 'What do I actually want?'

Take time to consider each question below.
- How did you decide specifically that you wanted that?
- How did you determine that it would be valuable to you?
- How did you define when you would have it—that is, when 'getting it' is achieved?
- How do you know that you're capable of getting it?
- What cost are you prepared to pay in order to get it?

What did you notice as you answered these questions?

Once again, when stuck it can be difficult to answer these questions clearly. 'I don't know' is a common answer.

But what if *how* you planned your goals could actually move you ahead? Would you try it? Let's take a look.

Goals and Outcomes – What are they exactly?

Goals can be defined as imaginary targets we set and want.
Outcomes are what we get from the efforts and strategies we use as we work towards our goals.

If you set a goal and take action, you'll most likely create an outcome. The outcome is what *comes out* of the effort and strategies you use. Hence the word 'outcome'. The outcome has everything to do with the action you take and not so much with the goal you set.

For example, my *goal* is to run a marathon; I decide to train a lot to reach my goal. My training strategy produces a range of different *outcomes*. These include weight loss, enhanced fitness, new friends at the running club – or even an injury.

Whilst the goal is a *target*, the outcome is the *result* you get from doing.

Setting goals and taking action creates outcomes. These can be predictable things such a learning new skills or unpredictable things such as new opportunities that emerge.

No goal is ever achieved without effort and strategies.

Consider Marie. She sets herself a New Year's resolution to drop two clothes sizes but Marie's goal will not happen unless she does something about it. Simple, right?

Goals without action are simply dreams.

Where we get stuck is when the goal:
   – is impossible to achieve regardless of the actions you take
   – is not congruent with other things in your life
   – is poorly formed
   – has no clear strategy or actions
   – has little commitment or effort from you

Check your goals with the above criteria that lead goals to fail. If your goals pass the test, then you're probably getting what want and feel satisfied and not stuck. If your goal created expectations that you have either met or exceeded, you most likely also feel satisfied.

But if your outcome is less than you expected, it may be that your goal is failing at one of the above hurdles. In relation to that goal, it would be no wonder if you were quite dissatisfied. It's a common recipe. The goals that we set and the expectations we place on them set the level of satisfaction we experience. When expectations cannot be met, we end up dissatisfied – and this is a key element in feeling stuck.

Unstuck Exercise #10: Check your expectations

Are there things in your life that you are dissatisfied with? List them on a piece of paper
- What are your expectations for each item?
- Where did that expectation come from?
- How do you decide each expectation was reasonable?

What did you notice as you completed this exercise?

You may have noticed that whilst you can describe your expectations, it can be challenging to identify where they come from. This is often because expectations get created either unconsciously or based on something non-specific, such as feelings or intuition. If you have no logical basis for your expectations then how you *feel* about what you're doing is open to being influenced by your mood or the internal rules you unconsciously set.

Dissatisfaction as a Driver

Sometimes being dissatisfied with the outcome can act as a powerful motivating tool. Appropriate dissatisfaction can help us take action and get things done. But if our expectations are either too high or too low, then the outcomes are often too much of a stretch. Inevitably, we become frustrated with the outcomes (or lack thereof) which leads to suffering.

If you feel stuck because you're not reaching your goals, ask yourself the questions:

- Was the goal I set achievable?
- Was the goal reasonable?
- How did I decide on the expectations I set around this goal?
- How did I decide on which behaviours and strategies to use for this goal?
- When did I decide what a 'completion' or 'pass' was for this goal?
- How did I judge the outcome I achieved versus the goal that I set?

Consider Mischa. She was invited to attend a large self-help seminar conducted by a very well known 'guru'. Mischa reported that the seminar played rock music as people entered and the crowd was whipped up into a frenzy. Following this, they were asked to write down 'Big Scary Goals'. Later, Mischa came to see me because she felt like a failure, she hadn't been able to start on the goal, let alone complete it.

Mischa is a perfect case of what can happen at these popular seminars. There's often a focus on goal-setting and a strong crescendo of excitement and motivation. People get pumped and are ready to achieve and succeed. Until days later when the emotion settles, and they're stuck with massive goals to fulfil and an inability to complete them.

Though goal-setting has its place, pumping people full of motivation without checking if their goals are possible, or if they have the skillset to achieve them, isn't helpful. Rather than 'helping' people, these programs often set people up for huge disappointment. This same seminar also gave Mischa the wonderful buying 'opportunity' to really excel in life; the platinum level training course at a price she couldn't afford with the 'gift' of being able to get unstuck. Thankfully, Mischa was realistic enough to question this offer. She reflected on and answered all the above questions. She realised that setting outlandish goals was not only a recipe for disappointment but it made her feel bad about herself. It reinforced her feelings of being stuck and made her internal dialogue and feelings of low self-worth run rampant.

This is often where people get stuck. They set goals with unrealistic expectations.

The good news is: when you set goals with appropriate expectations you can rapidly move beyond dissatisfaction and disappointment.

What now? The first step is creating goals that are possible and relevant to you.

The Right Goals For You

How can you know that the goal is right for you? It's easy because the right goal for you is:

- ✓ Specific and possible for you to achieve in your current circumstance.
- ✓ A goal where you're prepared to make an effort to achieve your outcome.

If your goal is not specific, it can be difficult to achieve. Specific goals are easy to spot because the desired outcomes they produce can be measured.

I've often heard people say, 'I want to be a millionaire by the time I am thirty'. This goal provides a point in time where this person's wealth can be assessed. They can then determine if they were successful or not in their pursuit.

But some goals are vague and poorly defined. For example, 'I want to be rich' is vague. What does rich actually mean and when is it measured?

Someone who sets 'get rich' as their goal may find it difficult to achieve due to the *lack of specificity*.

What's more difficult is when the goal is comparative; for example, 'I want to be richer than my father-in-law'. In our society, comparative goal-setting is a massive driver of behaviour – but it often leads to enormous dissatisfaction, distress and unhappiness. Breaking this ineffective pattern of goal-setting can bring immediate relief.

Even when a goal is specific, it may not be realistic to achieve in your current circumstance.

Some goals are simply not possible for anyone. Sometimes goals will be challenging for you even if others easily achieve them and vice-versa. We don't all start at the same place or have access to the same resources. We don't set the same value regarding what price we're willing to pay to reach that goal.

If my goal was to flap my arms unaided and fly, it wouldn't happen. You, me and everyone else on the planet simply cannot do this. This goal is not possible for anyone to achieve.

A 200cm tall basketball player has a reasonable chance of being able to slamdunk a basketball unaided, but someone under 140cms in height would probably find it impossible.

Be clear on the fact that some goals that are appropriate for others may not be appropriate for you. This is the joy of the unique skills and capabilities of individuals. If our goal is appropriate then we have the chance to turn it into a valuable outcome.

Is your goal a priority?

It is also useful to look at the priority of your goal. And the investment.

What if your goal was to graduate as a doctor? For starters, you'd have to go to medical school – which would mean looking at options on how to get in. You would have to do a lot of work and study just to get in the door. For some people, this is easy, while for others it's more difficult.

Some people will sacrifice everything for that chance. Others, however, may like the idea of becoming a doctor but consider going out with their friends more important. There's nothing wrong with either approach to life; however, one is more likely to lead you toward your outcome of becoming a doctor. If you don't make your goal a top priority or sacrifice the investment of time, effort and money, then how can you expect that this is a reasonable goal to achieve?

Being realistic about what can be achieved for *you* is critical.

The goal in context to the bigger picture.

People often set goals as the 'finish line' without understanding 'what next'. In truth, when we achieve a desirable outcome, there's still opportunity in our lives to achieve more. This happens because each goal we pursue creates outcomes, such as learning a new skill to help us achieve future goals.

If our goal is just a 'finish line' then there's nothing beyond it.

If this happens, the goal then fails to fit into a bigger picture of what we want in our lives; we can even achieve the goal but feel lost and empty. If we achieve goals we think are important to us, but in reality, they're not – then there's little true pleasure or satisfaction for us to receive through that achievement. This often happens when we set a goal to please someone else.

Consider Ted. He worked his whole career looking forward to his retirement. That was his finish line. The big day arrived. Ted gave his speech, had the cake, said farewell to his work colleagues and went home. He had no idea of the 'what next' and became despondent and depressed shortly after. Having such a big finish line without understanding it in the context of his life meant that when Ted got to the finish line, the image of what he thought it would be like did not match his reality.

If Ted's goal had been to reach retirement as part of a bigger plan of his life, he could pat himself on the back and reflect more positively on his work life. He would be engaged in his 'bigger picture'.

Consider Reece. He set himself the goal of getting 50,000 Instagram followers. He put considerable effort into creating all sorts of material to reach this goal. When he got his 50,000 followers, he had a 'so what' moment. He felt that what he had done was actually meaningless. He had set himself a big goal and achieved it, but he really didn't know what for.

Meaning at the heart of every goal

You can make each goal meaningful and valuable by aligning it to your deeper purpose. Therefore, fulfilling each goal becomes part of your bigger purpose.

For Ted, retirement is now a step to create a wonderful future with his lifetime partner full of travel and adventure For Reece; it could have been about building a tribe of like-minded people.

You can find meaning and purpose in even the smallest tasks, but only when you align them to what is important to you.

If helping others makes you feel good and is aligned with your personal values, then spending Christmas Day volunteering in a soup kitchen can be incredibly satisfying. If you don't value that, then the goal will probably just be a chore.

Unstuck Exercise #11: Goals and you

1. List your current goals.
2. For each goal, rate out of 10 how much joy each one gives you.
3. For each goal, rate out of 10 how important that goal is to you.
4. For each goal, rate out of 10 how easy is it for you to spend your energy pursuing that goal.

What did you learn about the current goals you have? Do they inspire and excite you or are they just hard work?

Setting Purposeful Goals

What gives you meaning? It seems like a simple question but it is one of the most challenging. Take time to understand what *really* drives you. What 'lights you up' and gives you pleasure? This is the cornerstone in defining goals that matter to you. When your goals are aligned to your purpose, and your purpose is the basis of your goal-setting, you become congruent, and the possibility of finding your authentic self truly emerges.

Are you doing things that matter?

In the 'real world,' there's a lot of stuff that needs to get done. Life doesn't stop. Taking care of the routine tasks may seem to be chores (and they probably are), but they are important. Why? Because they often provide the foundation to achieve better outcomes. You may not like your work, and it may feel like a chore, but it allows you to pay your bills and save money so you can then fulfill a greater dream of taking the family overseas.

Vacuuming the rug, putting the bins out or tidying your workspace doesn't seem like big goals to set. For most people, they are annoying chores, but they're chores that need to be done to create the opportunity or environment for more valuable things. They are also part of the responsibilities of being a member of a household, a community and a family. They are important contributions that you make toward the greater good, yet often they're overlooked to focus on more exciting goals.

Finding Purpose

Purpose is the 'true north' on your personal compass. No matter which way you face, the needle swings and shows you which way you have to move toward your true north. When you are aligned with your purpose, actions seem meaningful and worthy of your time and effort because you're moving toward your 'true north'. Often, doing things in line with your purpose is energizing whilst doing things against your purpose can seem quite draining.

Consider Ali who works in a refugee legal service. She is passionate about the plight of refugees and working in legal service is incredibly meaningful to her. To Ali, all the mundane office tasks have incredible meaning. She puts in extra hours and accepts a lower wage than she could get from another employer. She achieves things for her boss that she wouldn't do for herself because of the meaning she puts on what she does and the engagement with her work.

Now, think of Basil. He works for a large firm in the city. He thinks his boss is an idiot, and their department boss even worse. Basil took the job because it paid a little more than his last role. He has no real connection to what the company does, and he feels disengaged from the customers. He struggles to clock-in on time and in the afternoon, he's constantly watching the clock to go home. Basil doesn't really like what he does but does it anyway.

Consider how Ali and Basil would describe their work lives to you. Do you think Ali feels more energised and engaged with what she does than Basil?

Doing something meaningful and purposeful creates engagement and positive energy. It's why organisations are attempting to define their 'purpose' and help their employees view what they do as meaningful. Meaning and purpose drives engagement, commitment and profits.

What would you say is *your* purpose? What are the things that give you energy? Why are they important to you? These questions are a bit like asking, 'What is the meaning of life?' However, I encourage you to take time to discover what is important to you.

Unstuck Exercise #12: Finding your purpose

1. Start with a large blank sheet of paper.
2. At the top of the page, write the answer to this question: What gets you out of bed in the morning? When you have done this, draw a line under it.
3. Below the line, write: 'Why is that important to me?' Write your answer under that line. When you are done (it may be one word, a sentence or a few sentences) draw a line under that answer.
4. Look at this answer and repeat the process, asking yourself 'Why is that important to me?'
5. Continue asking this question for each new answer until you feel that the answer is emotionally relevant and powerful for you. Take your time. Remember, it is what is important to YOU that matters.
6. At the end of this process, write down a 'statement of purpose' to summarise what you've discovered.

For example, here is Tom's list after having completed the exercise:

I get out of bed to go to work.

I work to make money.

Money gives me freedom.

I want to able to make my own decisions.

I hate feeling powerless.

I love feeling I have some control over what happens to me.

Control means I feel strong and capable.

Purpose statement: *My purpose is to challenge myself and find new ways to feel in control in unfamiliar circumstances.*

Here is Rachael's list:

I get out of bed to help my customers.

I love helping my customers make great choices.

I love the feeling of helping others.

Helping others means I feel valued and meaningful to them at that important time.

Feeling valued makes me feel validated like I deserve to be here.

Deserving to be here makes me feel like I belong. This is what I want to feel.

Purpose statement: *My purpose is to feel valued by being deeply important to others as I serve them.*

Your lists and statement of purpose are unique to you. But if you take the time, you will know when it gets 'real'.

Consider Rachael and Tom. Think about how doing the same activity can have a completely different meaning to them. If they both had to sell a big piece of equipment to a customer, Rachael would likely see it as helping her customer get the very best product for their needs. Tom, however, would likely see it as his ability to control the way a big purchasing project turns out.

They can both strive for the same goal, but for different reasons.

When they do things that align with their personal purpose – and at a deeper level, to fulfil a personal or social need – they feel great. If they were to do things aligned with other people's goals, they wouldn't feel so engaged. In fact, they would probably struggle to do the task at all.

Yes, every goal you set serves your bigger purpose and gives what you do meaning and motivation.

Doing things that satisfy someone else's goal, rather than your own, is almost like 'purpose slavery'. When you are simply 'working for the man' it can be draining and meaningless. However, you can also 'work for the man' in a way that satisfies your purpose and suddenly you can feel very different about the work that you do.

Purpose from a different perspective

Another way to look at purpose is to ask, "What impact do I want to have on the world?" If you were to imagine that you could have an impact on the world by doing things, what would it be? It may even be an impact that you want to have on one or a small number of people in your community. Something like 'I want to find ways to help the local indigenous community reach full employment', or 'a world where everyone has access to education'.

Sometimes our purpose can be found by looking at the impact that we want to make. It could even be 'I want to raise my kids, so they face the world with courage and empathy for others'.

Unstuck Exercise #13: My impact

Consider the impact you want to make.

Perhaps start with the statement 'Imagine if'… and describe what you would LOVE to create.

If creating that impact was your 'purpose', what would your goals now look like?

What did you notice doing this exercise?

Purposeful goals:

Once you discover your purpose, you'll have a sense of your 'true north'. As you go through your life, it is completely normal for your purpose to be updated or modified. Reframe your goals so they 'fit' this true north. This often stimulates motivation and makes your goals meaningful and easier to reach.

Unstuck Exercise #14: Align with your purpose

Go back to the list of your current goals.
1. Do each of these goals serve your 'true north'?
2. If not, how can you reword that goal so that it becomes purposeful and meaningful for you?
3. What new goals would you now add to align with your purpose?

Outcomes Are Not Goals: Appreciative Inquiry of Self

The African saying 'How do you eat an elephant? One mouthful at a time' is entirely relevant to your goals in life. Why?

Because learning is progress.

When you learnt to read, your first job was to learn the sounds each letter made. Then you learnt how to put the sounds together. Then how to recognise the words as whole sounds; the whole word together. After this, you learnt exceptions and constructions (for example, why 'ph' sounds like 'f'). If your goal as a three-year-old were to read a novel like *War and Peace,* this would have been very challenging.

However, at each stage in your journey, you learned and achieved an outcome, even if it wasn't the goal.

Instead of looking at the goal and how far you are away from it, take a few moments to reflect on the outcomes you achieved. As Thomas Edison was reported to have said, 'I found 999 ways not to make a light bulb.'

If you know that each step you take is an opportunity to achieve an outcome – even if it's only a lesson in what not to do – you move forward. If you continue to do this, then it is difficult to get stuck.

Use Appreciative Inquiry (AI)

Appreciative inquiry is asking yourself what has gone well or what could be better, rather than only focusing on what's wrong. It's a really valuable tool when you begin to feel stuck. It was first formed by Dr David Cooperrider and Dr Suresh Srivasta and later became a foundation for positive psychology.

The notion is "strengths do more than perform, they transform."

So, if you've been applying effort and testing out strategies, then give yourself a break and see how far you've come and what you're perhaps doing well. If you reflect, you may also notice what works (do more of that!) and what doesn't (do less or drop it!).

Unstuck Exercise #15: Appreciative Inquiry

Consider where you feel stuck:
1. What was your goal?
    - Describe it in a clear and specific way.
    - How far have you progressed toward achieving it?
2. What are your outcomes?
    - What specifically have you learnt or achieved to date?
    - What has gone well or have you done well up to now? What can you give yourself credit for during this process?

It's true. You can't always get what you want. But if you set high-quality goals and appreciate the range of outcomes you produce through your efforts to achieve them, you move a long way towards being more satisfied. And ultimately, becoming unstuck.

Chapter 4

Compared to What?

Am I Normal?

When people get stuck, they often ask themselves – and those working to help them – 'Am I normal?'

Consider Jin. She reported that she was very unhappy with her life. Jin saw herself as an outcast, weird, different from others. She just wanted to be 'normal'.

What is normal *really*?

Unstuck Exercise #16: The norm test

Write down what the following terms mean to you:
- Normal
- Happy
- In control

Now go and ask two other people to write down what these terms mean to them.

What do you notice when you compare these three lists?

The likelihood is that all three had different ways to describe these terms. Lists like these often produce vague answers, and we already know that non-specificity is a significant issue in goal-setting.

People often say, 'I just want to be happy.' Or they'll confide to me, 'Phil, I don't think I'm normal'. They're implying that they want to be 'normal' and this notion sets them up for failure. Why? They have a belief about what 'normal' is, and it's often completely flawed.

Unstuck Exercise #17: What is 'normal' anyway?

- Write a list of all the specific things you believe makes someone 'normal'. How do they act? What do they think or feel? What results do they achieve?
- Next, to this list, rate yourself on each specific item out of ten.
- Go through the list and out of ten, rate each item regarding how valuable it is to you.

What did you notice?

Common responses to this exercise are:

- 'I don't really know what normal is.'
- 'I can't identify specific things.'
- 'I just have a vague sense of what normal is…and I'm not it.'
- 'None of the things that normal people do are either valuable or exciting. In fact, it looks boring.'
- 'When I look at the list, I do more normal things than I realised.'

Here lies the first problem. We choose to compare ourselves to imaginary states, like 'being normal' yet we have nothing more than a vague definition about what it means. We exaggerate the imaginary state regarding how positive it is, run ourselves down and emphasise what we're lacking in comparison. It's a recipe for unhappiness.

Take it one step further. Think of all of the entrepreneurs who want to be like Tony Robbins or Sir Richard Branson. What they want is often based on what they see from the outside; that is their celebrity status, wealth and perceived power.

But what do they really know about that person? What do they know about their history, their medical problems, their personal tragedies? What about the sacrifices that they had to make, the effort they had to put in, perhaps even the impact of being 'like that' has on relationships and people in their lives?

The idea that we can make broad judgements about someone from a single characteristic is known as the 'halo effect' heuristic first introduced by Nobel prize-winning psychologist, Daniel Kahneman. It is how we make first, and often lasting judgements of others based on a single characteristic that draws our attention. This impression gives us a sense of the person (positive or negative) that we then use that as a basis for evaluating everything about them.

Think about all the things we don't know about people we aspire to be like. People often put on a 'face' to the world, and we only get to see specific elements of them. They project what they want, or sometimes an image their PR manager wants them to portray.

This cultivated 'face' is a mythical thing shrouded in this halo effect. Yet because deep down we know our fears, nasty habits, failures and the like, when we compare ourselves to these mythical types, we're bound to come away disappointed. If we want to set goals to be like them, it would be useful to set our goals on more specific, realistic attributes than just the vague positivity shining from their halo.

Kevin isn't Normal. Why Should You Be?

Let me share with you a story about Kevin. He was 22 years of age and came to see me because of an addiction to porn. Here was a guy that would spend over four hours a day watching adult movies. He felt terrible about himself but couldn't stop.

When we explored further, Kevin disclosed that he was fascinated by how 'big' the actors were. When he compared the size of his penis to what he saw in the movies, it made him feel very small. Somewhere along the line, Kevin believed that the size of his penis was important in defining who he was. The process of watching pornography became a constant way of punishing himself and reminding him of how worthless he was. That he was not 'normal'.

To help Kevin, we applied some simple math. But, more on this in a minute. First, let's go through the following exercise to help determine how you view yourself?

Unstuck Exercise #18: What's *your* thing?

Look in to a mirror for 30 seconds. Imagine there's another person looking back at you. Take a few moments to ask yourself:
- What are they looking at?
- What are they noticing?
- What are they thinking or saying about what they're focusing on?

Listen to the words and tone you use when answering these questions. Listen to how you describe what 'they' are seeing. Write it all down.

Next, look in the mirror again for another 30 seconds. Ask yourself the following:
- If that other person could see your deepest, darkest secret, what would it be?
- What would happen if they knew?

Again, listen to the words, tone and adjectives you use when answering. Write it down.

What did you learn from doing this exercise?

We are all likely to have one (or several) features we don't like about ourselves. We think other people focus on them or judge us poorly. It makes us somehow less than normal. It might be a number of things or one big thing. It can become a point of comparison we make to ourselves and others.

For Kevin, it was his penis. For you, it is whatever you've identified above. But the truth is, you are so much more than that. Which is why it was useful to teach Kevin some math about normal distribution.

The 'Normal' Distribution

In math, there's a concept of normal distribution'. The simplest way to describe it is to think about the number of times an event happens from a range of possibilities. For example, if you were to roll a pair of dice 100 times, out of these 100 rolls, how many times do you think the number two would come up? Or the number three? Or the number seven?

There is a whole game in the casino based on this, called Craps. Think about how it works.

In 100 rolls of the dice, the chance of rolling 1 + 1 = 2 is so much smaller than rolling a four (1 + 3, 2 + 2, 3 + 1), which is again, much smaller than rolling a seven (1 + 6, 2 + 5, 3 + 4, 4 + 3, 5 + 2, 6 + 1). If we drew a graph, with the sum of the dice roll on the bottom, and how many times it happened in 100 rolls being the height of each column, it would look like this:

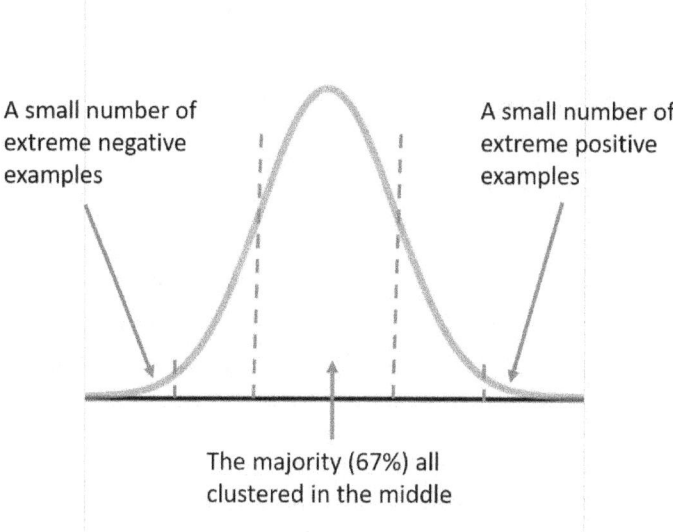

This is known as a normal distribution curve. This means that for normal populations, there will be a range of possible outcomes on any measure. There will be rare events at either end of the spectrum, but the majority of events are stacked in the middle.

Now, back to Kevin — if we were to take 100 men selected at random and measure the size of their penis, what do you think we would find?

There will be those on the small size, those on the larger size, while the majority (about two thirds) would be in the middle. This data describes what we see in a population but does not describe all the other attributes of anyone at any point of the curve.

Hiring for an adult film

Think about the movies that Kevin is fixated on. If you were hiring a male to star for your adult film production, what physical characteristics would you hire for? Where on the distribution scale would you select your 'star performers'? Do you think you would select your performers from the middle range because they are the same as everyone else? Or would you select them from the extreme cases, because they 'stand out'?

If you were to plot all the adult movie stars against the general population, where do you think they would sit? They're most likely going to be at the extreme upper end of the spectrum. This sub-group of males that exist at the far end of the normal distribution and are *not representative of the normal population*.

For someone not involved in the adult film industry, comparing themselves against the porn star subgroup is unrealistic, due to the extreme nature of these people versus everyone else. Unfortunately for Kevin, his only frame of reference for penis comparison was this skewed population. And because he continued to make comparisons as a result, several things happened:

1. He made the error of believing that porn stars represent the normal population. In doing so, he felt his penis size was exceptionally small.
2. He believed that having a large penis was somehow appreciated by women. He fell victim to a false societal message that places male value around penis length and reinforced this belief in himself.
3. He felt a need to belong to this group of men in order to feel 'normal' – which resulted in negative painful evaluation, leading to shame and self-punishment.

But it's not just Kevin. Think about all the magazines that are full of fashion shoots or women models. Think about all the 'get rich quick' schemes that circulate. Think about the fitness industry. Most examples represent the extreme population rather than the typical. The images and stories are easily interpreted as 'normal', but they're false representations of 'normal'.

Consider how these movies and other 'false normals' could impact Kevin's views on how women should look, what sort of sexual acts are 'normal' and how men should behave towards women. What would Kevin expect regarding sexual encounters? If Kevin is using porn as his reference – it's unreasonable and extreme. It's easy to see how the easy access to pornography is harming a generation of young people who have no other reference for healthy sexual behaviour.

The process of how we judge ourselves and the examples and populations represented to us impact how we evaluate ourselves and others. Other examples include: Being a good mother. Being a successful student. Going bald. What normal breasts look like. The type of car you should drive. Being a business owner. The list is endless – and it also includes your particular 'thing'. When you start hearing your own narrative phrases, such as, 'I'm not good enough' or 'I'm a fraud 'it's likely that you're making singular, false comparisons to extreme populations. The truth is, this happens everywhere – and almost happens entirely unconsciously.

Unstuck Exercise #19: Extreme examples and your mind

Pay attention to the examples of people you're presented with. Ask yourself where on the spectrum do they sit? Do they come from a normal population, or from an extreme, highly-selected sub-population?

- Look at the images presented on TV and in advertising.
- Listen to the stories you're told by people.
- Notice the behaviours of people around you.

How are these examples **not** representative of the 'normal distribution' but instead at the extreme and idealised end of the spectrum?

Do this exercise for the next week as you go about life and start to become aware of how the 'aspirational' examples are unrepresentative of the normal population.

What did you learn from doing this exercise?

What you may notice that you're bombarded with extremes. They get our attention. The more extreme we're presented with, the more we can create unconscious beliefs that these examples are somehow 'normal'. The examples then need to become even more extreme to grab more of our attention.

Going back to Kevin, we spent time discussing the reality of the distribution curve. I let him in on a little secret: that he is really the sum of a million different distribution curves, most of which he never pays attention to.

To demonstrate, we drew a series of normal distribution curves. The first one was penis size, where we spoke about the adult film industries' hiring practices. We then shifted to the other curves. For example, I noted that Kevin was reasonably tall, so on a height curve, we determined he would be above the median. He had no glasses, so on an eyesight curve, we determined his eyesight to be better than average.

Kevin could place himself on all types of curves: for example, kindness, honesty, intelligence, time spent sleeping or number of hours driving a car.

The truth is, we exist on so many curves at the same time. Mostly these curves will be the same as everyone else, however, there might be a few curves you push into the 'exceptional' spectrum, or above or below standard.

Now, what if you no longer focused on that 'thing' and instead saw it through the lens of reality? What if you were able to appreciate that the rare specimens you compare yourself to are most likely selected for their ability to be rare?

The reality is *there is no normal*. Not you, or the rare specimens. Each of us is a complex array of traits, preferences, physical characteristics and experiences. There is no such thing as normal, only 'normal distribution'.

In fact, imagine if everyone was 'normal'. No one would be different, interesting or exciting.

Unstuck Exercise #20: About you

Return to your 'things' – those aspects that you judge yourself harshly on. Ask yourself the following:

- How do you determine what to compare yourself to?
- How do you determine if your comparison is an extreme aspirational example or a realistic comparator?

- Relative to a 'normal distribution' where would you sit? That is, about this characteristic, are there people further up or down the curve than you?
- List 10 other features that you possess, including features you may like about yourself.

What did you learn from this exercise?

You Can Never Be 'Normal' – So Perhaps You Can Stop Trying to Be

You can change what you experience and your expectations, but you can't change the fact that you exist in many different dimensions and scales. To use only one scale, or one associated with what you don't like about yourself is always going to lead to dissatisfaction.

Why Your Halo Is Strangling You?

As we mentioned earlier, when we see someone famous on TV which may be popular, funny, rich and nice, we often make wide-ranging judgements about that person. So, when something in that person's life changes – for example, they may get divorced, arrested for domestic violence or enter rehab – it comes as a shock to us because of the 'halo' we had given them is now broken. We learn that they're human just like us.

Think of how reality TV producers use this effect to create 'goodies' and 'baddies' in reality shows. It is far easier to have specific, even extreme, labels for each contestant rather than to try and explain each person's complex array of traits, behaviours and physical attributes. When people leave reality shows and see how they were portrayed, many are absolutely shocked. But these images serve the show well because they create simple stereotypes of people which takes less effort for the viewers to deal with.

The halo effect heuristic is incredibly strong and automatic.

Think of Suzy. Suzy picks up the magazines in the waiting room at the doctors. Each one shows her pictures and tells her stories of how women 'should be': smart, sexy, size 12, coping with life, happy and well-adjusted. Suzy takes what she reads and extrapolates it to how fabulous every woman is, or should be. But not only that, she now compares herself against this standard. Suzy uses the halo effect when thinking of others but never herself. How do you think this impacts Suzy and her self-image and esteem?

But there's one thing people like Kevin and Suzy forget to do. That is to stop and check in on the meanings behind the characteristics we define as good or bad.

Unstuck Exercise #21: What does this mean?

For the next hour, take the time to notice things that you notice. Ask yourself:
- What characteristic am I noticing about what I am observing?
- Does this imply that I think it is a 'good' thing or a 'bad' thing?
- What does this characteristic mean?
- How might I have given that meaning to that characteristic?
- If it were to mean something else, what would that be?

What did you learn from this experience?

Unstuck Exercise #22: You and others

Think of five to 10 people that you have strong feelings about. These feelings can be positive or negative. Ask yourself the following:
- What characteristic, preference or behaviour do you focus on when you think about them?
- What label do you apply to them?
- How do you use the halo effect to extrapolate your belief about them to your whole experience with them?
- How have they demonstrated that they do not fit this label or halo?

Now do this exercise on yourself. Think about yourself for a moment. Ask yourself the following:
- What characteristic, preference or behaviour do you focus on when you think about yourself?
- What label do you apply to yourself because of this?
- How do you use the halo effect to extrapolate your belief about yourself to your whole experience?

- How have you demonstrated that you do not fit this label or halo? What did you learn from this experience?

Unstuck Exercise #23: Know yourself

This is a slightly longer exercise. I encourage you to find a quiet place to sit or lie down, where you can work through the ideas presented in this exercise. Start by getting comfortable. Take a few deep breaths and let the thoughts settle into the background. Create some space inside of yourself.

Part 1:

Take a moment and imagine that there was no one else on the planet but you. You are therefore entirely 'normal' and the reference point for all characteristics on being human. You are the tallest, smartest, hairiest, skinniest, most helpful person… etc., in the world. For a moment, imagine that. Imagine the joy and peace of not needing to compare yourself to anyone. Next, imagine that no one was there to see you, and you could just be yourself. All of the labels – especially the 'shoulds' and 'musts' – just drop away.

What if there were no groups that you had to belong to? Your identities, labels and reference groups would become meaningless. You wouldn't have to *try* to be anything, or anybody, to anyone else. There would be no comparisons, entry-level or pass mark. Allow yourself to close your eyes and deeply experience what this would be like as if it were true.

Part 2:

Now invite the world back in. But let's do it a little at a time. Start by inviting back, those people who are important to you. Those who make you feel good or encourage you in the right ways. These people are your support crew. It is now only you and your support crew in the world. Notice how that feels. Allow yourself to close your eyes and deeply experience what this may be like as if it were true.

Part 3:

Now think about the groups you want to belong to. One at a time, ask yourself *why* you want to belong to these groups. Check your motivation. Does it serve your purpose? Does it empower you to be better? Is it fun and rewarding? Check your skills. Is it an appropriate group for you to belong to? Check your 'why'. Why do you want to belong to the group? Is it for you? Or is to please others or what they might think of you?

Now jettison those groups that don't truly serve you. Get rid of the groups that are not suited to you or your skills. Forget the groups you want to belong for the sake of impressing others. Allow yourself to close your eyes and deeply experience what this may be like as if it were true. Notice how it feels to belong where you do; in those groups that inspire you.

Part 4:

Next, imagine the rest of the world existing behind a glass wall where it doesn't impact your support crew or your key support groups. You can proceed in your life without any negative influences washing in, as they are behind the wall. What do you notice?

Part 5:

Now, gradually let the world flow in. Notice that you have control over *what* influences you and *how* it influences you. Feelings of negativity or need simply wash in and wash out as you keep your focus on what's important to you. As you allow the world back in, noticing how self-absorbed it is, you continue to be yourself; your support crew and key people supporting you as you move forward. The rest can now drop back as white noise. Notice how you feel. Allow yourself to close your eyes and deeply experience what this may be like as if it were true.

What do you notice from having this experience?

General Versus Specific

I cannot cure world hunger, but I can feed some people in my neighbourhood. You may have heard the saying 'think global, act local' – there certainly is some truth in this. Our problems take on global dimensions, yet they cannot be solved at a global level. Instead, we must create *specific* solutions to generalised problems. If everyone fed someone (specific action) it would solve world hunger (global problem).

When someone says that they want to be happy, this is a generalised, non-specific description of a state the person wants to experience. It appears OK to want to be 'happy' doesn't it? The reality is, you can't be. Happiness as a permanent, generalised state is unrealistic. Think of it this way. If you want to *always* be happy, do you want to feel happy when your favourite pet dies?

Wanting to exist in a permanent state of happiness is unrealistic. With no variation in how you process your experiences, life lacks the colour, complexity and wide range of emotions available to you.

Setting yourself a goal of 'always being happy' is a recipe for disaster.

Life is variable, and there's countless opportunities to feel a broad range of feelings. If you only learn to be unhappy or depressed, or anxious about your life experiences, then you'll likely end up stuck.

Unstuck Exercise #24: Are you happy?

Take some time to answer the happiness questions below:
- What specifically do you want to be happy with?
- When specifically, do you want to feel happy?
- How specifically will you know when you are happy?
- What specifically do you want to experience when you are happy?

What did you notice completing this exercise?

Consider depression. When Janice talked about her life, she reported, 'For the last few years I have always been depressed.' When we explored this statement further, Janice didn't report only negative events but also her holiday to Bali, her sister's recent marriage and her brother's beautiful new son. When Janice spoke about these things, she smiled and became animated and positive. Although Janice felt she had 'always been depressed' over the last few years, this broad statement had some powerful and major exceptions. There were many times when she was in fact, happy. Even joyous!

This is what happens with sweeping globalisations. They set us up to ignore specifics. It was easy for Janice to overlook those positive times because they didn't fit her broad generalisation. Janice reported that she wanted to be relieved of depression. I suggested that perhaps there were already times when it was relieved. Janice began to see the gaps in her depression.

This realisation can be a challenge to people when it doesn't compute with the 'story' they've been telling themselves. In fact, it is in these *exceptions* that helped Janice break out of her depression.

What if she spent more time doing things that made her feel different to her depressed feelings? What do you think would happen?

When we set non-specific, globalised goals, we often do ourselves a disservice. Let's get specific instead. Are you ready?

Unstuck Exercise #25: Get specific

What's wrong with the statements below? What questions would you ask in order to drill down into the specifics?

- I want to be rich
- I am always sad
- I'm stupid
- It's always been like that.

Some potential questions you could ask:

- What specifically do you mean by 'rich'? When would you want to achieve this by? What specifically would that mean for you?
- When are you *not* sad? What does 'sad' mean to you? Have you done anything interesting lately? If so, how did that make you feel?
- In what specific areas do you feel uninformed?
- What are you good at? How would you know how intelligent you are compared to others? Which type of intelligence are you talking about in particular?
- How might someone else feel about what you say? When was it not like the way you say?

These are only a few of the questions you could ask to challenge the fixed, global frame of statements. This is a critical, self-reflective skill. Setting your goals in specific language can assist in turning them into valued outcomes.

We'll explore how to do this in the next chapter.

Chapter 5

Setting Goals That Work Long Term

We continually make decisions about what we want and how we want to be. As we evolve and change through life, so do our goals. Whilst setting goals seems a logical thing to do; it's rarely done logically. Often goals are created unconsciously, or by superficial drivers that lack deeper meaning, this can lead to invaluable outcomes.

For some people, setting goals and defining outcomes is challenging – and often painful. Goals can often spark anxiety and uncertainty as they set targets for the future and can act as powerful reminders of previous regrets and shame. They can even remind people of how dissatisfied and stuck they feel.

Consider the following situations, where goal setting could be a tough and potentially painful experience.

- Nikki describes herself as a highly anxious person. She worries about many things. She ruminates and catastrophises anything she is planning. For her, creating goals means more things to worry about. For Nikki, the physical and emotional toll of looking into the future is massive. She is a perfectionist and a harsh self-critic. Any goal she sets is typically unreasonable and unattainable. Her true goal – if she were to admit it– is to find relief from her anxiety – which often means to avoid any plans or significant goal-setting.
- Bryan often feels severely depressed. His life is infused with a sense of helplessness and hopelessness – so much so that he believes it is not worth setting goals or trying to achieve anything. Sometimes Bryan sets himself the goal of getting out of bed before noon; however, because this goal lacks meaning, whether he gets out of bed or not makes no difference to him.

- Tracey is a prior sexual abuse victim. As a result, she has learnt to protect herself by diminishing herself at every opportunity and believes she is worthless. To achieve or 'win' anything for Tracey, would bring attention to her and make her feel she were putting herself at risk of being injured again; a risk she can't stand the thought of. For Tracey, it is better to do nothing and not risk being seen. Her real goal is to survive and feel safe. However, as she's never experienced these feelings or believes they're possible, she only allows herself to 'exist'.

Each person is heavily invested in NOT setting goals and what they really want remains unspoken, even unconscious.

Whilst we can have a belief that setting goals, and even the pressure to set 'big' goals are important, it's equally important to understand that goal-setting is challenging for some. It can be useful to notice the feelings you have toward goal-setting. If setting big goals seems too much for you right now, perhaps experiment with small goals, and perhaps get a sense as to why goal setting may be an issue for you.

The idea of experimenting is incredibly important. Allowing yourself to 'experiment' means that you can have a go at your goal, without the pressure that comes with setting it as a 'must do'. You can simply test it out and see what emerges.

Unstuck Exercise #26: Experimentation

Take a moment now and allow yourself to settle into a comfortable position. As you focus your attention on the following words, simply allow the world around you to fade into the background.

Imagine that you had no need to set or achieve goals. That you could simply exist in a place of comfort, safety and ease. For a few moments, as much as possible, simply sit with this idea. Imagine, even in the smallest way, what it might be like for you.

UNSTUCK

Imagine now that you could explore your world in new ways. There may be some things that are interesting for you, and you want to spend more time discovering them in richer detail. There may be some things that you want to avoid, so you can comfortably, and with ease, move yourself a safe distance away.

As you explore this world, you may discover things that which initially look good, may turn out later to be boring or not so good. There are other things which may seem bland or unpleasant. However, as you explore these, you find they delight you with a positive sense of surprise. Isn't it nice to simply experiment and be curious? To find what is interesting or valuable for you in what you discover?

Can you remember what happened when you learnt to walk? Probably not, but if you have seen a baby learn to walk, there are some very interesting behaviours that you may not have paid attention to fully before. As a baby becomes a toddler, they first make many attempts to pull themselves to a standing position. They have to experiment with pushing up or pulling up. They have to test where their weight should be and how their legs have to be placed. They fall down onto their backsides many times. After standing, the baby has to learn how to take their first step. They have to experiment which leg to move first, if the leg has to be straight or bent and what to do with the arms. The baby doesn't know, just as you didn't know – but you experimented with many different ideas before you found one that worked. How you learnt to walk may have been slightly different to every other baby on the planet – and that's OK. Through the process of experimentation, you learnt and went in small increments towards a goal.

What if the goals you have as an adult are the same? What if you don't have to do it like everyone else? What if you are allowed to experiment and learn in small increments? What if you could surprise yourself by finding new ways to experiment? As you allow yourself to experiment, you allow yourself not to know. You allow yourself the joy of discovery and the pleasure of learning. You create different ways to interpret and explore, with the possibility of joy and surprise. You also allow yourself the ability to learn that it may not have been what you wanted; that it's time to end the experiment with what you have successfully achieved and move on to something else.

I invite you to experiment at the edges of your experience. I invite you to be OK with running small tests and being OK that some will work, and some will not. They're simply experiments.

Take some time now to settle with your experience. Allow yourself to reflect on what you learnt, noticed or found valuable.

Unstuck Exercise #27: The experiment questions

Think of a goal that you have.
- What can you experiment with that is different from what you're doing now?
- How would someone else experiment if they were where you are right now?
- What have you experimented with and done elsewhere in your life that you could consider applying to your goal?

What did you learn from this process?

If you allow yourself to experiment, it takes the pressure off. Experimenting allows you a space to try something different and be curious about the results. It is the nature of science to start with an idea (a hypothesis), and then work out ways to test it. Sometimes the tests show great new advances, while sometimes they show nothing new at all. Both are successful experiments – and often it is the small tests and extensions that allow science to advance.

A useful way to experiment is the 'act as if' idea. If you achieved the target of your goal, how would you be different? How would things be different? What if you acted 'as if' you had already achieved the goal? How would you act and feel? Acting 'as if' can be a useful tool – if the goal is reasonable and possible for you.

Unstuck Exercise #28: Do the 'as if' experiment

Think of a goal that you want to achieve, but feel a bit stuck achieving it. Take a moment and allow yourself to experiment with the 'as if' frame:
- How would you be feeling as if you achieved the goal?
- What would you specifically be doing?
- What would it look like, sound like or feel like as you are getting your outcome?

Take a moment and imagine that it had already happened. Experiment with those thoughts, actions and feelings. What did you notice?

'Go Big or Go Home'

Goals don't have to be big to be valuable.

Whilst the self-help seminars may want you to set 'big scary goals' – my wish is that your goals are *realistic* and *valuable* to you. If that means the goal is massive, then good for you. If the goal is small but valuable to you, then that's great too. In the end, it's *your* goal. It's got to be valuable to *you*.

You can have a range of goals in play at any one time. They can also be extremely varied.

There will be some goals you keep deeply hidden, perhaps even from yourself. For example, whilst you're busy setting goals you may harbour a deep (perhaps even unconscious) goal to 'feel safe more often' or 'to find happiness in little moments throughout the day'. It might be 'to stop worrying', or simply 'to get through until next pay day'.

Allowing yourself to get beyond the stories and appreciate the deeper goals can be a truly valuable and essential step in moving ahead.

When you are wanting to achieve something, but notice that you seem to act against your own best interests: take note. Become aware. There's probably a deeper goal in play that is getting in your way. Later in the book, we will look at how to uncover these drivers and what to do about them. You can make them work for you rather than against you.

The 12-Step Goal-Setting Process

On New Year's Eve, people make resolutions for things they'll do the following year. By February, most people don't even remember what they intended to do. The difference between a resolution and well-formed goal is in the process of its creation. If there's a goal you want to achieve, then it's worth testing and strengthening it through the following 12-step process. This helps people plan great goals and set to achieve them.

The 12 steps are:
- ✓ *Is your goal purposeful?*
- ✓ *Is your goal framed for success?*
- ✓ *Do you know the reality of your goal?*
- ✓ *Are you aware of the motivating factors of your goal?*
- ✓ *Is the outcome of your goal clear and specific?*
- ✓ *Have you got the skills to achieve your goal?*
- ✓ *Have you explored the payoffs of the goal?*
- ✓ *Have you aligned your resources with your goals?*
- ✓ *Have you got the right team around you?*
- ✓ *Have you identified the challenges to your goal's outcome?*
- ✓ *Have you created milestones or steps to break the journey down?*
- ✓ *Have you identified ways to celebrate and/reward yourself for achieving your goal?*

Let's take a look at each step and see how it can enhances your ability to achieve goals.

The 12 steps to Achievable Goals

1. *Is your goal purposeful?*

We have already spoken about purpose and impact. Any goal that you want to achieve must be congruent with who you are – and that means fitting into your purpose and delivering meaningful impact.

For a reminder, head back to Exercise #12, 13 and 14.

2. ***Is your goal framed for success?***
Would you find it easier to 'stop smoking' or to 'start being a fresh air breather'? Would you find it easier to 'stop being fat' or to 'start being fitter and healthier'? 'Get rid of my depression' or 'find some joy and happiness in my life'?

Framing your goals in positive terms helps you achieve them.

Our brains are hardwired to overlook the negative. For example, when you tell a child 'don't jump in the puddle', they must first imagine jumping in the puddle and then work out how not to do it. But because they've already imagined jumping in the puddle, this is often as far as their thinking goes. They get stuck on the 'don't' – the *not* to do – which means they're more likely going to do the thing they've been told not to do.

When you apply this to your goal, if your target is to 'stop smoking', you are reinforcing the 'smoking' neurologically. You bring up all of your associations about smoking, what it gives you and even imagine your next cigarette. Often, goals relating to giving up or stopping can be tinged with emotions of loss, pain and deprivation. Associations that create a 'looking forward' point of view can move you into a new and positive state.

Consider if a parent says to a child, 'go around the puddle and keep your feet dry'. The child's brain would process these words differently. It no longer looks at the puddle.

The statement 'I want to stop being depressed' immerses the sufferer in feelings of depression. However, if the goal was reframed to 'I want to find some joy and happiness in my life', the person starts looking for and imagining very different outcomes. The neurology of language is very important. By looking for joy or happiness, we may just find some – but if we only talk about depression, we may screen some positive things out entirely.

Reframe your goal for success by setting them in the positive.

3. ***What is the reality of your goal?***
If you don't know where you're starting from it's difficult to build a path forward. Defining the current reality of your goal is important. Objectivity is

critical. There is no point underplaying or overplaying your reality; it just gets in the way of planning your steps properly.

Some people naturally underplay their circumstance: 'I don't suffer that much' or overplay it — 'I've been depressed my entire life'. Whatever the circumstance, being *honest* with where you're starting from is vital.

Sometimes this is difficult to see from inside your own experience – like we saw earlier with Janice and her inability to recognise any positive moments amongst her depression. Janice was lost by the labels she gave herself. In her case, an outside observer was essential to seeing the reality of where Janice was actually starting from, and in also knowing that she had resources and experiences to build from in order to move her forward.

It allowed Janice to acknowledge that where she was on her journey toward more happiness and joy which was vastly different to where she thought she was. As a result, her goals changed, her language changed, and her focus changed.

Some people also set goals where their reality is much worse than they believe. 'I want to be a millionaire by the time I am 30' is a classic example. If the person with this goal is 18 years old, running a business or already making investment decisions, it's very different to someone 28 years old, doing part-time work and carrying significant debt.

Being realistic about the starting point allows the goal to be 'reality tested' and changed if needed, or structured differently with more suitable steps. For the 18-year-old, changing the investment strategies, finding longer-term earning capacity and decrease in spending could be the answer. For the 28-year-old, that's not realistic, unless he won lotto or robbed a bank—(I'm not advocating the latter by the way.)

When you think about your goal, where are you honestly starting from?

4. ***What are the motivating factors of your goal?***
For a goal to be achieved, there has to be some benefit for you. The goal that you're seeking might be something that stands alone or is part of a bigger

picture. It can often be difficult to separate an individual goal out of such a milieu.

For example, if I were to give up smoking, this could be part of a much bigger health goal or finance goal. Where the waters get murky is if I achieve the big goal first. Let's imagine that I have a financial win and all of a sudden giving up smoking to become more financially stable doesn't apply. I may lose the motivation to give up smoking.

Find your inner motives and remember to frame them in a positive way.

Unstuck Exercise #29 – Why do you want your goal?

Ask yourself:
1. Why exactly do I want to achieve this goal?
2. What do I get out of this achievement?

Adding Leverage

Leverage is why achieving the goal is important to you. In a way, the leverage represents your 'skin in the game' – what you can lose if you don't reach your goal, rather than what you can gain. Humans fear losing significantly more than gaining and this can create powerful motivation toward achievement.

For example, Sean wanted to 'stop gambling'. In our conversation, Sean was strongly motivated and proud of his social connections and relationships. He highly valued being social. For Sean, reframing his gambling as being 'antisocial' created powerful leverage for him to change. His desire for being social provided huge leverage against the 'antisocial' way he now viewed gambling.

Consider Sophie, who wanted to give up her cocaine habit. Apart from the finances and health implications, Sophie had a deep motivation toward being a good mother to her daughter. She wanted to be proud of her mothering and not harm her daughter. Getting Sophie to imagine her daughter finding and snorting her 'stash of blow' and becoming a cocaine addict had an incredibly powerful, almost visceral response for her. Having this image in her mind suddenly made having the cocaine in the house – or even using it at all – a mortifying thought. This leverage created huge motivation for Sophie to stay on track and get clean.

In both examples, the goal was powerfully aligned to something incredibly important to them. Therefore, *not* achieving the goal was incredibly painful or not congruent to how they saw themselves – this is leverage.

How can you create leverage around your goal?

5. *Is the outcome of your goal clear and specific?*

The best goals are framed in *specific* terms. I invite you to refresh with **Unstuck Exercise #9: What do you want?** (page 21) and review the ideas on 'General Versus Specific' in Chapter 4 to help frame your goals in specific language. Because if your goal is vague, it doesn't provide a clear target to aim for. Vague goals are often generalisations – for example, 'rich', 'happy', 'promoted' or 'in a relationship'.

The key to success in framing goals is the combination of *specificity* and *vividness*. Allowing yourself to have a vivid, specific description of your goal fires off processes in the brain where this imagined state seems real and possible. Without even trying, creating goals that are vivid and specific can set the brain toward problem-solving – it tries to find ways to make what you imagined *real*. A vague, generalised goal, on the other hand, remains highly abstract and not of interest to the problem-solving functions of your brain.

Use specific sensory descriptions such as how your goal would look, sound like, smell like or feel when you achieve it. This adds instant clarity and power to your goal.

For more on this, refer to **Unstuck Exercise #28** – The "As If" Experience. Take time to really enhance all your senses to see, hear, feel, taste and experience your goal.

6. *Have you got the skills to achieve your goal?*

Sometimes we can set ourselves goals that, regardless of how motivated we are, are not possible for us to achieve. A critical component of achieving a goal is making sure you have the skills to make it happen.

A job as a juggler in a circus would require me to have the skill of 'juggling' before I would be able to achieve a positive outcome. Identifying and developing skill can be part of your strategy to achieve your goal. Unless you recognise the specific skills required, the goal remains unlikely for you to achieve.

Consider Tammy, who wants to move beyond being 'a smoker' to being 'free of smoking' (note the positive framing). There are a series of skills that Tammy might need for her to be successful with her goal. For example, skills regarding managing cravings, self-negotiation, seeing positive payoffs, noticing habitual patterns of smoking, choosing alternatives, managing pressure, identifying and celebrating small achievements and being able to notice pleasure and value in being smoke-free.

Considering your goal, what specific skills do you need to learn in order to achieve it? Knowing this, how will you go about learning those skills?

7. *Have you explored the payoffs of the goal?*

For any action, there can be both positive and negative payoffs. Mostly the goals have 'ripple effects' regarding the outcomes. Understanding that some of the outcomes are positive and others may be negative helps make realistic assessments about how valuable the goals really are. This can provide motivation and allow a realistic understanding of any 'downsides' that need to be considered or managed.

Consider Mandy. For a long time, she wanted to lose weight, but couldn't. When we reviewed the ripples of losing weight in terms of 'gains and losses,' we uncovered a frame of thinking that was keeping her stuck.

She said, 'People would look at me. People would expect me to stay thin. There would be pressure on me to maintain my weight. Some people might be jealous. I know that deep down some of my friends wouldn't like it if I was successful.' These were her ideas of what would be 'gained' by losing weight. Notice how they all would add to her distress.

When asked what would she lose she replied, 'I would lose the comfort of my favourite foods. I would lose the anonymity of just being a big girl. I could no longer blame everything I couldn't do on being fat.'

It took a while for Mandy to be honest with herself but when she did, she could see why losing weight had such little payoff for her. Working with her to change her thinking and restructure her beliefs around her identity, allowed Mandy to reframe her 'gains and losses' into an overall positive picture; one that she wasn't conflicted about pursuing.

If you have struggled with a goal, think deeply and clearly about the payoffs. By knowing your payoffs, you can tackle each one – reality check it, reframe it, even tame it. When you are clear that the overall payoffs are important, positive and valuable to you, and you understand what will be gained and lost, you can decide if it's a goal you want to set. It might mean that there's skills you need to learn (including seeing yourself or valuing yourself differently) that could help reframe or revalue the payoff.

8. *How have you aligned your resources with your goals?*

We can set goals, but unless we have the resources and infrastructure aligned to our goals it can be difficult for us to achieve them. It might mean adding things to the mix, or removing things to help provide the infrastructure and skills for the goal to be achieved.

If we want to get fit, we might first have to get a good pair of running shoes and a pair of shorts that fit. If I want to pass my exams, I might need to find a quiet study space and the tech to help me revise.

Sometimes it is about removing things to make the goal achievable. Like when people want to lose weight so they remove all the chocolate and biscuits from their house. It requires them to pick a different option and not fall back into old, unhelpful, patterns.

Resources help you achieve your goal. Removing unhelpful things can be just as valuable sometimes.

Unstuck Exercise #30 – What can I add or remove?

Think about your particular goal:
1. What resources do you need to *add* to make your goal possible?
2. Are there any things you can *remove* to make the goal possible?
3. Which habits or patterns may you need to disrupt to achieve your goal?

9. *How have you got the right team around you?*

Apart from changing your resources, there's real value in ensuring that people around you support your change. Often when we want to make changes, there are some people who may not want you to succeed. This can happen because they consciously don't want you to get the outcome, or they may want the things to remain the same. Of course, there's also some subtle, even unconscious reasons why some people don't want others to succeed.

Being clear about who is in your 'support crew' is important. Identifying people that don't want you to succeed is equally important. Removing your reliance on their opinion may also be helpful.

Adding the right kind of people to your support crew is a huge help.

a) Supporters

Your supporters are your cheer squad. They encourage you and celebrate your success. They can help you find your way or get you back on track if you lapse or fall behind. It's important that you select people who *want you to succeed* to act as your supporters. They're great at providing a kick of positivity and motivation when things get a bit tough on your journey.

Selecting supporters who are really hidden saboteurs is common – so try to avoid this if possible. If people can't truly enjoy and celebrate your success, then perhaps they shouldn't be in your cheer squad.

b) Accountability buddies

Accountability buddies are different from supporters. Their job is to hold you accountable to your goal. Instead of being the people you share your successes with and who give you the rush of the positive glow through their support and cheering, accountability buddies are on standby to help if you're about to fall. They're also people you can commit to or report any lapses. Often having to confess your transgressions to someone is enough to keep you on track.

Choosing a suitable accountability buddy (or buddies) is about selecting people whose view matters to you. And whose view of you matters; so you don't want to let them down. People who will be empathetic but not let you off the hook. People you can reach out to quickly when you are tempted to slip, so they can offer you support to stay on track are good buddies to have.

10. *Have you identified the challenges to your goal's outcome?*
Often, we set goals and run into scenarios that trip us up. Taking time to understand what might be some of the 'knowable' challenges helps you avoid them ahead of time.

Consider Ken who wanted to cut down his drinking. As we looked at the knowable challenges, he identified his work Christmas function, his annual golf day with his old schoolmates and New Year's Eve celebrations as specific times he'd get knocked off course. For each of these events, Ken made a plan. This included how many drinks he would have, what replacements he would use and what he would tell people before and during the events. With a clear plan, Ken was able to face each hurdle prepared to deal with it.

Having a plan gave Ken control of his actions, showed him the choices he could make and removed any surprises that could be identified beforehand. Of course, there may be other things that could surprise Ken, but being aware of specific events or habits lessens any potential trouble.

Notice in Ken's case that knowable challenges can be events like the golf day, but there can be other habits and rituals such as 'When I feel stressed, I drink three vodkas.' By knowing the challenge – the event, the habit or the feeling – anyone can make specific plans for how to respond and stay on track.

11. *Are there milestones or steps to break the journey down?*
Sometimes the goals we set are just too big for us to believe that we can achieve it. Breaking the goal down into steps can be a great way to help us achieve goals. Let's look at an example.

In a company, there were two sales teams, both with the same target for the end of the year. Team A's manager put the number '$1,000,000' on the whiteboard and exhorted his team to 'Go and smash it!'. The leader of team B, however, told his team that they each needed only two extra small sales a day to reach the target or 10 per week.

Team A left highly motivated, however, the big target scared them off, and they rapidly saw how with each day that passed the goal seemed harder. They decided individually, and then amongst the group, that the target was too hard – so they gave up. Team B on the other hand, were able to under-achieve and over-achieve on each day, and each week. If they didn't get a sale one day, they could work to make it up the next. They stayed motivated, made the sales target and received the big bonus that Team A missed out on.

By breaking the goal down into manageable steps, a goal that seems impossibly big becomes something possible. As the proverb says, 'Every journey begins with a single step.'

Unstuck Exercise #31: Small steps in the big picture

Consider your goal.

1. How can you break your goal down into smaller targets or chunks?

Perhaps it's giving up something for one day, then two. Perhaps it is completing three sessions each week.

12. *How will you celebrate and/reward yourself for achieving your goal?*
A forgotten part of the goal-setting process is often rewarding yourself for the achievement. Sometimes this is simply acknowledging the outcome, but it can also be with a specific reward. However, when you select your reward, make it congruent with your goal.

For example, with a weight loss goal, it wouldn't be ideal to reward yourself with half a chocolate cake. Or for a goal of not drinking for a month, going out on a bender. Make the reward something valuable and congruent with you. Maybe book a holiday with the money you've saved or buy a nice outfit in your new size.

The process of setting a target and rewarding yourself for achieving it teaches the brain that this is a worthwhile process to engage in. Simply rewarding yourself with more hard work for achieving something important is not going to teach your brain that achieving goals is a 'good' thing for you to do.

Even more importantly, this process of reflection allows you to see all the outcomes and skills you've developed and achieved along the way. Taking stock can allow you to build a new reality base for future goals and allow you to celebrate all of the small (and big) things you've achieved.

Unstuck Exercise #32: Test your success

Consider a goal that you have held for a long (and maybe not even shared with others). It may have been one of the goals you wrote down at the start of this chapter. Take the time to work through the 12 steps listed above.

- What do you notice?
- Where is the biggest point of weakness?
- How can you refine your goal planning to improve your chances of success?

Now that you have set and tested the goal, the final step is:

Start taking action!

Make an effort, experiment and employ strategies. And as you do, outcomes will flow as you move towards your goal.

If all 12 steps have been reviewed and worked through, there's every likelihood that your goal will be achievable.

Get Your Priorities Right

We can have many goals at one time, and without even thinking about it we naturally prioritise. If there are things that we want to achieve, we may be so busy doing other 'stuff' that we really have no room to achieve our goals. As you set a goal, it can be useful to take the time to consider everything on your radar at the time and identify which of your goals are *priorities* and which can be deprioritised.

There is only so much we can do at one time. Sometimes we need to prioritise other things until we can create the space to really go after a specific goal. Don't expect too much of yourself – if you keep adding new goals without appreciating what you're already pursuing; it's easy to get overwhelmed.

Unstuck Exercise #33: Forgotten priorities

List your goals. This is not only about the 'big stuff' but can also be something as simple as 'getting to work on time.'
- Are there any goals that get continuously deprioritised?
- If so, what sort of goal is it?
- Check it through the 12-point system to see where it breaks down.

Unstuck Exercise #34: Passing the checkpoints

Take your goal and run it through the 12-point process. Use the checklist below to ensure your goal is ready for action.

1. *Is your goal purposeful?*
2. *Is your goal framed for success?*
3. *Do you know the reality of your goal?*
4. *Are you aware of the motivating factors of your goal?*
5. *Is the outcome of your goal clear and specific?*
6. *Have you got the skills to achieve your goal?*
7. *Have you explored the payoffs of the goal?*
8. *Have you aligned your resources with your goals?*

9. *Have you set up the right support team?*
10. *Have you identified the challenges to your goal's outcome?*
11. *Have you created milestones or steps to break the journey down?*
12. *Have you identified ways to celebrate and/reward yourself for achieving your goal?*

Chapter 6

The Behaviour That Gets You Stuck and Learning Your Way Out

Even if you have perfectly formed goals, it's still possible to end up stuck.

Consider Tony. He has a goal to complete his engineering degree. He has everything he needs to get it done – the intellect, the study materials, the time. The problem is that whenever Tony sits down to study, he sits at his desk and is distracted by social media feeds. He uses his study time looking at Instagram and sharing memes with friends. At exam time Tony panics and feels rushed and unready. He performs poorly in the exams and puts his long-term goal at risk.

Unstuck Exercise #35: Tony's behaviour

If you were able to modify Tony's behaviour, what would you have him:
- Start doing?
- Stop doing?
- Do more of?
- Do less of?
- Do you think it is possible for Tony to do this?

What did you notice as you did this exercise?

Behaviours that get you stuck are most often *learned*

If you are wondering how you got to be so stuck in your problem, the answer is *because you are human*. Or, more precisely, you are a human acting like any other animal would – from complex mammals to simple sea slugs.

We all use behaviours that are learned and 'conditioned' often without even thinking about how they were chosen for use. When our behaviours work well for us, things are great. When they don't, we often get stuck. Behaviours can serve us beautifully in one context and not in others.

Consider Bill, who wants to save enough money to travel to Europe but keeps going out on the weekends and blowing his pay cheque downing shots in nightclubs. Until he changes this behaviour, he's unlikely to ever reach his goal. Hitting the clubs each week and hoping he will save money to reach his goal is not an effective strategy. It even seems somewhat insane, doesn't it? When Bill decides to stay home on the weekend (change his behaviour) or have only two beers when he goes out with his mates (also a change in behaviour), he notices that his bank balance begins to grow. He is getting a different outcome because his behaviours have changed.

Someone – perhaps Einstein, but no one is really sure – suggested that insanity could be defined as doing the same things over and over and hoping for a different result. Whilst this is not how 'insanity' is viewed clinically, it perhaps describes the way people behave that contributes to getting them stuck.

This cycle of do-fail-do-fail-do becomes frustrating and leads to a sense of helplessness and hopelessness which increases the person's dissatisfaction.

If you can learn how to perform ineffective behaviours and get stuck, you can learn *effective* behaviours to become unstuck.

As previously described, learning is your most natural skill – and, applied properly it can break the 'insanity cycle.'

The Nature of Operant Conditioning

Let's have a look at how we acquire behaviours.

In 1938, psychologist B.F. Skinner took on the task of trying to understand how people learn. He very quickly realised it was going to be difficult to research, people were too complex to study. Each has their individual stories and issues and there wasn't enough consistency to for firm conclusions.

Pigeons and rats, however, could be bred for this purpose and have their exposure to stimuli controlled. They were free from individual biases and therefore conclusions could be more easily obtained. So, B.F. Skinner used pigeons and rats.

At the heart of Skinner's findings were the discovery that animals (including humans) are *conditioned* to respond to reward or punishment, and in doing so, they develop habitual patterns or behaviour based upon this conditioning or training.

The 'reward' process is strongly related to the release of dopamine in specific regions of the brain. This internal buzz within the brain induce cravings and drives external behaviours. Just like Skinner's pigeons, humans learn from exposure to reward and punishment and develop patterns of behaviour to increase reward and decrease punishment. These patterns are codified as habits.

In this way, we are also no different than the sea slug. Here is a creature that has a very small number of neurons in its brain compared to humans. These simple animals act on a gradient – they move toward positive rewards (food) and away from harm (toxins). Talk about keeping life simple. Move toward good, and away from bad. A simple life we could all admire.

Skinner's results showed a similar principle – that animals acted in relation to the reward or punishment they were offered. The schedule of rewards and punishments, or how these were reinforced, made a big difference to what was learned.

This practice has been used in training all sorts of animals, including the work done with dolphins for marine park shows. To start out, a dolphin doesn't know that a trick can earn them a reward. When the dolphin does something that *approximates* the 'trick' they are rewarded. The dolphin starts to associate particular behaviours with rewards (both the fish, and the dopamine hit in the brain). They keep being rewarded as their behaviour gets closer to what the trainer wants. This shapes the animal until the precise trick is learned. The trainer then starts adding a pre-event signal (such as a whistle signal) indicating that the reward will happen if the behaviour occurs. Over time the dolphin will match the trigger (the whistle) as anticipation of the reward. So, when the whistle blows, the dolphin knows it is up for a fish if it does the trick.

Reward and Punishment

We humans have uncanny similarities. The processes of reward and punishment are present in everything we do. If behaviours are valued, then we can get the 'reward.' If the behaviours are *consistently rewarded*, they can become habitual and mundane. Over time these behaviours become habits.

Think about all of the different reward processes: how you learned to behave with your friends; what is rewarded or punished by the group? Sitting a test at school; teaching a child to use their manners; answering the telephone; engaging in risk-taking behaviour; fitting in; driving on the highway; mowing the lawn; doing the ironing. The list goes on forever.

Every moment in our lives has buried within it a learned pattern of behaviour based upon the concept of a reward or punishment. Think about how people continuously check social media in case there is the incredible reward of someone liking their post. We most often see these conditioned responses as 'rules' of behaviour that we must follow – often without any reference as to why or how that rule was learned in the first place. Often these rules are not even consciously applied; they are habits on autopilot.

Consider Dominique. She has an addiction to playing poker machines. When she first played them, she has no experience with them. As she continues to play, she gets rewarded with 'wins' that make her feel good and hit her with dopamine. Dominique is also doing something interesting; she is creating one feeling to overpower another feeling. She gets the 'winners high' which masks the nagging feeling of anxiety she struggles with every day.

The producers of these machines know a lot about psychology and use complex mathematical tables to work out when payouts will occur.

They provide numerous intermittent rewards to keep Dominique excited and the occasional bigger rewards to motivate her ongoing behaviour.

On the flipside, if Dominique decides to stop playing and the 'hit' is removed, it immerses her back into those unwanted feelings she was trying to escape from. This acts like a punishment for stopping. Can you see how poker machines are designed to keep people hooked?

At different points, we have all learned certain behaviours like Sam. When Sam's dad raises his voice, Sam makes himself small and hid. When Sam gets a job and has to debate his point of view in a meeting – his 'opponent' raises his voice. What do you think Sam's conditioned response to that trigger will be?

Unstuck Exercise #36: Behaviours and rewards

Identify three actions that you have taken today. For each action:
- What was the trigger, the behaviour, and the reward or punishment if not performed?
- How did you first learn the behaviour for that trigger? What was the initial reward?
- Did reward or punishment motivate each action?

What did you notice as you did this exercise?

You Are More Complex Than a Sea Slug

Life is full of reward and punishment. It's simple for the sea slug. The problem is that we're not sea slugs – we don't just operate on the immediate, visible or tangible reward or 'toxin' that we are exposed to.

Instead, we are highly complex beings with social and relational needs, including the ability to imagine and fantasise. We operate with many different rewards and triggers existing at the same time and with different levels of importance and timeframes. Humans need to operate within all this complexity to be successful in life.

We also cannot know what people have 'learned' in their lifetimes. That is, what they associate with reward or punishment; what expectations they have; goals they have or even how much their unconscious mind influences their choices. However, thinking about *visible* behaviour patterns can provide a hypothesis (potential basis) for us to *guess* what is going on and why people get stuck.

If we take the idea that humans are 'learning machines' responding to reward and punishment, we can get an indication of how behaviours are created and turned into habits.

The good news is if you have behaviours that aren't working for you, you can learn and adapt them to better ones.

When feelings are the reward

Humans are social, relational, comparative and complex. We can get a sensation of reward from belonging, being trusted, being liked, being better than someone else or achieving something. Conversely, we can feel punished for being left out, having someone do better than us, having bad feelings and not achieving our goals. We can feel good about one thing and bad about something else.

Macy was a lady who came to the clinic to lose weight. She complained of 'always being hungry.' I asked her where she felt this, and she pointed to the spot just below her solar plexus. I asked her about her anxiety – where did she feel this? She pointed to the place directly below her solar plexus.

Macy had anxiety she wanted to get rid of when she wasn't eating she felt her underlying anxiety and felt bad. When she ate, she felt better. Her interpretation was that she was always 'hungry' – but in truth, she was feeling those unpleasant feelings of anxiety.

Helping Macy manage her anxiety and removing the unpleasant feelings, she realised that it wasn't hunger she was responding to. She soon understood that she didn't have to eat to feel good. Macy moved beyond her anxiety and lost over 26kgs through the process.

It is common for people to get stuck because:
- They try to create a feeling as a reward
- They try to remove a feeling to decrease the punishment
- They try to mask a feeling in order to hide or decrease the punishment

Many people find themselves binge eating ice-cream, sugar or chocolate in response to emotionally upsetting events. How can this be operant conditioning? Firstly, the 'special treat' or reward of the ice cream or chocolate is learned to be associated with meanings such as gratification, celebration, reward or comfort, possibly from childhood when these were seen as 'special.' This, plus the physiological rush from the sugar hit can act as a powerful reward. Over time, we don't see the ice cream or chocolate; we simply attach to the meanings it implied, including 'special' or 'deserving' rewards. We all have some imagined, internal rules and meanings to things we view as special, deserved or a treat.

When confronted with unpleasant emotional experiences, we want to behave as a sea slug and move away from it. Often in real life, we can't. Instead of reducing the pain, we attempt to mask it with something else. We find a way to *feel better,* even if the underlying pain is not removed. We find ways, even if they're unhealthy methods, to feel better.

So instead of removing what causes the pain (the emotional issue), we seek out what makes us feel better for a while (reward). This distraction technique might work for a short time; however, it can also condition a new pattern: trigger (emotional upset) – response (shovel sugary foods into our mouths) – reward (feel the sugar rush and a bit better for a while).

There are several problems with this approach. These include:
- Not dealing with the underlying emotional pain and therefore it can keep recurring as it hasn't been removed.
- Whilst in small amounts, the 'reward' may be OK, habitual use may have negative consequences. In this case, the ice-cream reward may lead to health issues, such as obesity and diabetes.
- Requiring more and more of the reward to gain the internal feeling as the effect can lose its potency over time. E.g., To overcome the

emotional pain, the person may have to binge more to receive the same masking result.
- Coping mechanism. The pattern takes on a new meaning and becomes a 'rule' for the person. "The only way I can cope is to binge eat."
- Not acting according to this rule now increases pain and suffering. So, *not* bingeing on ice-cream after an emotional upset now becomes punishing, and *adds* to the pain already felt.

Did the person mean to become an emotional binge eater? Highly unlikely. Are they stuck with a pattern of behaviour that reinforces itself and is harmful to them? Absolutely.

You may find that you're deploying behaviours that just don't work too.

'I feel emotional pain, so I binge on ice-cream' or 'I feel anxious, so I gamble on the poker machines.' It can be useful to reflect on your conditioning and assess the behaviour. Have you created some 'complex equivalences' like eating for comfort?

Unstuck Exercise #37: What are your bad habits?

What are your bad habits? Make a list. For each habit identify:
- What is the trigger?
- What is the reward? What feelings are particularly important to gain or diminish?
- What is the consequence of the behaviour?

What did you notice or learn as you did this exercise?

Did you notice that you have learned responses that may not be helpful to you? Perhaps you've noticed how the 'meaning' you attribute to something may not be valuable?

Where there are habits and patterns of behaviour that get you stuck, it can be useful to review them in this way and see what you're really trying to obtain, and what meaning they hold for you. You can then evaluate them logically and choose different actions to get what you really want.

Conditioning Is Two-Way

What if you can condition yourself out of problems that you conditioned yourself into? If you believe that learning is possible and you're prepared to make the effort, then you're not stuck at all. You're just waiting to learn better responses.

Aspects of Learning

There are three other factors which muddy how we learn: Fuzzy logic, imagination, and Hebbs law.

Fuzzy logic

The idea of fuzzy logic was first proposed by Berkeley professor and mathematician, Lotfi Zadeh, in 1965, in which he believes there are scientific degrees of truth instead of absolutes. For example, rather than just black or white, there is a multitude of shades of grey in-between.

For example, the first time we eat a red berry, we don't know how it will taste. But when we do, we learn that this particular red berry is sweet and delicious. What have we learnt about all berries? Nothing yet.

As we are exposed to the next red berry, our brain is already looking to create a 'rule' about red berries and eating – in particular, the taste and experience. By the time we've had the third tasty, red berry, we're pretty sure that all red berries are sweet and delicious. This fuzzy logic means that similar events are grouped in our thinking and 'black and white' patterns and rules are created.

Fuzzy logic is something we apply unconsciously when we believe we have enough 'evidence' to create a rule. The rule often starts out very general, and over time our experiences shape the rule to become more accurate and nuanced.

However, if we have a rule that 'all red berries are delicious' and encounter a disgusting red berry, the rule needs some tweaking, and a more nuanced rule can be fine-tuned based on this exception.

The second element that sometimes messes with fuzzy logic is **imagination**.

Experiments have shown that mental rehearsal, or imagination, is highly effective. People can get better results from their physical performance by mental rehearsal alone[1]. Clinical studies reveal that 'learning' regions of the brain can't tell the difference between a real or imagined experience.

The use of hypnosis, for example, allows a person to experience different states and imagine new patterns of behaviour as if they were real. People can mentally rehearse new responses to old triggers, so when they face these triggers in real life, they have different options which have already been learned through 'imagined experience.'

Imagination can be good or bad. If we use our imagination to create negative experiences or replay a negative event in different ways –it can also be a powerful basis for learning what gets us stuck. As we repeatedly imagine the negative event, fuzzy logic can start creating 'rules' about a single real event.

Consider someone that's been bitten by a dog. If they ruminate or imagine getting bitten by other dogs, the brain invokes 'fuzzy logic' and rapidly creates a rule that 'all dogs bite.' If, however, they consider other dogs they've encountered that haven't bitten or don't bite, then their 'rule' that 'all dogs bite' is never created. In fact, a more nuanced rule about which dogs may bite (a useful rule to have when you around dogs) can form.

The ability to discriminate what is real from what is imagined is critical to avoid such black and white rules. Anxiety is often associated with catastrophising real or imagined threats. If a person imagines a bad outcome and catastrophises about its possibilities, is it any wonder they become anxious?

How people learn from an event is enhanced by a thinking bias many people make, labelled the 'peak-end rule' by psychologists Daniel Kahneman and Barbara Fredrickson. It' s also referred to as the 'duration neglect,' which means that people often focus on the most intense emotional experience and/or the final experience in judging something, rather than discriminating across the duration of the experience. If my peak experience (and my last experience)

---

[1] From mental power to muscle power-gaining strength by using the mind. *Neuropsychologia.* 2004;42(7):944-56. RanganathanVK, Siemionow V, Liu JZ, Sahgal V, Yue GH.

was the intense moment of being bitten by a dog, then this is what I am most likely to use as the basis for encoding the experience into memory. The dog may have licked my hand 100 times and bitten me once – but the intensity of the bite will be what I remember about it.

The third element is Hebbs law, originally introduced by Canadian psychologist, Donald Hebb in his 1949 book *The Organization of Behavior*. Hebb's law suggests that neurons that fire together strengthen their connections. So, in developing memories, behaviours, and rules, if we repeat the same thing a number of times (even through mental rehearsal) the neurons 'fire together' and strengthen the neural connections between them.

So if we associate an emotion with an event and repeat it, this will strengthen the connection between them. If I think about dogs and get bad feelings about being bitten, then the more often I do this, the greater the association becomes between 'feeling bad' and 'dogs.'

Although we are designed to be 'learning machines,' it is clear from these three elements that sometimes these processes of fuzzy logic, imagination and Hebbs law create over-generalised rules about what we should expect and how we should respond.

Unstuck Exercise #38: General behaviour rules

Think about the general rules for behaviour. For example, how should someone behave when they meet a stranger? What is the general rule for how you should behave when on a date?

- Think of three situations and the 'general rules' that you apply to selecting behaviours
- Think of at least one circumstance for each where the rule does not apply
- List that the problems that happen applying the 'general rule' in that circumstance.
- What is the general rule that you have for how you should behave where you're stuck?

What did you learn from doing this exercise?

Earlier we discussed that 'insanity is doing the same thing over and over and expecting a different outcome.' Let's add to this the idea by understanding that being 'uninformed' is simply not knowing what you need to know in a circumstance. If this is true, then you may be stuck because your behaviours are 'insane' or because they're continuously repeated when not helpful. Think about all the times you tried to solve problems using the same behaviour. For example, if yelling at the kids to tidy their rooms didn't work the last 10 times, why would it work on the eleventh attempt?

Behaviours can be selectively deployed

Our behaviours are often the cause of why we're stuck. The good news is that we all have the power to select behaviours that will help us overcome problems. We also have the ability to shape our responses and condition new ones. Imagine if you could be your own 'behaviour trainer'?

Consider someone you know who does *not* have your problem. Someone who isn't anxious, depressed, addicted, scared, lacking confidence, unlucky… or whatever the reason you feel you're stuck. Imagine if you did what they did, thought as they thought and responded as they did. Would you still be stuck in the problem you have now? The likelihood is that the person who doesn't have your problem *knows something* or *does something* different from what you're doing.

For example, why is it that if you have a fear of flying, other people can get onto a plane and fly all around the world? Or why you see the world as hopeless and scary, yet others see it as exciting and full of possibility? What if it is only a thing that you're doing, a way of looking at the world or a way of responding to your circumstance, that keeps you stuck?

If two similar people approach the same issue, and one person experiments to find a way of dealing with the issue effectively, we should assume that the other person could learn and benefit from using these same behaviours. We can consider that the difference in the behaviours produce a different result.

Consider Stella and Stacey. Both are business owners that face the same challenge of finding new customers. Stella decides to make 20 telephone calls a day; she worked through her list based on the industries she would most likely be successful in. Stacey, however, sits in front of the computer and keeps redesigning her brochure. Nothing stops Stella from doing what Stacey does or vice versa. The result? Stella's business becomes successful, and Stacey's doesn't.

Think about this carefully. They both had the opportunity to select the 'phone calls' option. If Stella and Stacey suddenly switched behaviours, what do you think would occur? If Stella stopped making calls and sat all day redesigning her brochure, whilst Stacey made 20 calls per day? The answer is, they would each start to get what the other did because it's the *behaviour that leads to the outcome.*

This is a common scenario for small businesses. So many small business owners fail because they have everything they need but fail to engage the right behaviours. Notice, it is not them – it is how they're going about it. Also, notice that business owners can learn from each other and experiment with doing something different to help them new outcomes.

Unstuck Exercise #39: Self-evaluation

Consider where you're stuck. Write it down and answer the following questions:
- What specific behaviours (approaches) have you used to overcome it?
- What external factors have you blamed for your behaviours not succeeding?
- Has someone else ever overcome the same issue? If so, what specific approaches or behaviours did they use?
- Write a plan of how and experiment with those behaviours or approaches to your circumstance.

What did you notice as you completed this exercise?

Behavioural approach and the medical model of mental health

If what we considered is true – that it is not you, but the behaviours you deploy that cause you to get stuck, then the traditional 'medical model' of mental health suddenly doesn't look very valuable as a general philosophy.

The medical model assumes that the problem is with YOU and that you're broken in a way that only chemicals added to your system can fix. This is not a position I can stand behind, and here is why:

- You can take medication, but it does not change what you *do*.
- If you believe that medication will change *everything*, you shift responsibility from yourself to an external 'power.'
- No one has ever put a micropipette into your brain and measured a 'lack of neurotransmitter' in your synaptic gaps. However, we know that flooding it to overflow through medication can have an effect. It is not that you are broken, but the flooding of chemical has some effect on your functioning.
- Irving Kirsch, lecturer in medicine at the Harvard Medical School and leading researcher of anti-depressants and placebos has found in clinic trials that antidepressants are no more effective than placebos.
- Medication can take the edge off, but it doesn't change the underlying circumstance or behaviours you choose. What happens when you come off the medication?

The medical model may encourage people to think that any solution to their problem is not in their control. However, I do see a really important place for medication as part of the process of change, but not as a long-term crutch. Sometimes medication can 'flatten out' the worst of what someone is experiencing and allow them space to make changes. It can be a lifesaver for people who are suffering greatly and need to take the edge off their experience. Medication can also become the person's next 'problem': a reliance on a pill to make them OK. As we know, it is not the person, but their behaviour that is the cause of the issue, so while medication can help it will not solve the underlying problem.

What is very important to know about using medication is that you must only come off it under the supervision of your doctor. The medication may need to be progressively reduced, and it is important that your doctor works with you when it is time. By seeing medication in this way, it can take on a powerful supportive role. It can help you shift to a better place where it is YOU that can drive the change. A further caveat that must be mentioned is this:

There are some conditions where long-term medication is important. You MUST talk to your doctor before making any change to your medications or how you take them.

Behaviours rarely act alone

Often, a trigger doesn't just initiate a single behaviour; it initiates a process of behaviours that are chained together and cascade off each other. Because of their complexity, we rarely pay attention to all of the specific behaviours that we use in a 'meta-routine.' These patterns of behaviour are everywhere in our lives, and once the process begins, we often switch off and think about other things. This is great if the sequence is effective in helping us, but if any part of the process is ineffective, then we have a recipe for getting stuck.

Think of the meta-routines you have. Driving a car and you want to change the radio, taking a shower, answering your phone or coming in the door from work.

For each one of these examples, it is likely that:
- The trigger sets off a usual sequence of behaviours
- The first few times, the sequence (and each behaviour in the chain) took effort to perform
- The behaviours became second nature, and you notice that you can think about other things whilst you're doing this process now.
- You don't think about the individual steps that make up the sequence.

Like when a child learns to ride a bike, once the behaviours are learned, they become an unconscious sequence. From getting dressed to driving a car, we rely on these sequences to get things done. Imagine if you had to think about putting on your underpants every day? Which leg goes in which hole, how to balance on one leg to put the other in, how far to pull them up… it would be annoying!

To shower, you need a sequence of individual actions or steps. You may have been triggered to shower for a number of reasons: because it fits into your morning routine (alarm goes off – hit snooze – get out of bed – stumble to shower…) or because you are sweaty from the gym, dirty from being in the garden, or wanting to get clean for a big date. From the trigger, the action steps follow.

Unstuck Exercise #40: Taking a shower

Think about your process of taking a shower.
- Make a list of each of the action steps that you take.
- Take a look at your list. Review it and make it even more specific. For example, 'get undressed' is a series of actions, as you take off various pieces of clothing.
- For each action step, note what initiates or triggers the individual behaviour and when it concludes (that is, how you know when it's complete).

Taking a step back, you can see how each of these sequences required learning – including learning the sequence, the trigger and the conclusion point for each behaviour.

I have seen Michael Yapko set this as an exercise for people; their first attempts usually result in 3 or 4 lines on a piece of paper. When he explained the nature of behavioural processes, often people could break their experience of showering into more than a full page. The value of understanding that tasks are often sequences of behaviours is being able to challenge any of the behaviours in the chain that are no longer useful or helping you; leading to a potentially different outcome.

Unstuck Exercise #41: Your meta-routine

Write down in as much detail as you can about your experience of being stuck, and how you ended up there. For example, 'Every time someone raises their voice I feel X, think Y, worry about Z.'

- Now take a moment to review your usual reaction. How do you normally respond? Think of this regarding your outward behaviours – what you do, what you say, your inward emotions and feelings, and the thoughts you have about yourself and others.
- Write down the meta-routine of your behaviours, including the thoughts and feelings you create and respond to. What initiates each step? When does it conclude?
- Consider what you know about learning. If you could take one step and change the behaviour, what specifically would you change to get a different outcome?
- Now take a few moments and find somewhere to sit or lay quietly. Using what you know about mental rehearsal and learning, imagine yourself going through that meta-routine with the changes you have defined. See, feel and imagine what it would be like doing each of the steps, including the things you would change. Take your time to imagine three different scenarios – perhaps with three different people or three times in the future where you can follow the new pattern. Enjoy the sense of getting a better outcome. Note how it feels and what you get by this change.

Take a few moments and review this process.

Notice two important points:

1. It is a process.
2. It is a process that you run.

At some point, this may have been an effective process or may have been the best that you could do in a certain situation. Now it may simply be a patterned or even unconscious response. If it is something you want to change, then you will have to change something in the process.

The pattern interrupt

What is interesting, however, is when our processes get interrupted and we can no longer rely on the 'meta-process,', and often we have to really think through things to take any action.

I remember when I broke my leg as a kid. Taking a shower suddenly became a whole new challenge I'd never faced before. My routine had been completely interrupted. Even simple steps like, how do I step into the shower? How do I balance on a slippery surface? In which order do I soap my limbs? How do I get undressed before the shower? The routine was now broken by the change in circumstances. As I attempted to use my meta-routine that had worked for years, I kept coming across 'interrupts' that stopped the automatic process and made me have to think about the exact step I was taking.

We often get stuck when an unconscious meta-routine is no longer relevant for the process. Think about this for a minute. What if your 'being stuck' could be undone by modifying one small step in the total process? When we get stuck in our stuff, it is hard to think that there are other ways to operate. We can get frustrated with 'do-gooders' offering their sage advice and trying to 'help' us. We think 'Of course I have tried that!' or 'Don't be stupid, that won't work!'. Often, we go back to our fixed patterns and hope that we will get a different result.

Imagine if you were able to interrupt unhelpful patterns and meta-routines of behaviour, after they had been triggered? Imagine if, you were able to stop and select a new behaviour and progress toward an effective and efficient outcome?

This is the value of a pattern interrupt.

Unstuck Exercise #42: Can you respond with different behaviours?

You can ask yourself some very important (and quite tough) questions about that behaviour process.

Ask yourself the following: How does someone else who does *not* have this problem, or is stuck in the same way as you:

- Respond to the trigger scenario differently?
- Develop initial thoughts and feelings that are different from what you do?
- Respond to these thoughts and feelings with different behaviours?

Take some time to make a list. If you truly don't know what other people do, then I invite you to go and ask them!

What did you learn?

Exercise #43: Pattern interrupt

Consider where you're stuck. If you respond to a trigger in a way that is ineffective or inefficient for you:

- Map the process as accurately as you can.
- When does the process become ineffective or inefficient?
- In which step can you select the trigger for your interrupt action? It might be something like 'When I feel my face go red,' or 'When I feel the frustration,' or 'When I see Charlie doing...'
- If that could be your new trigger, select a different behaviour that is congruent with your desired outcome.
- Rehearse the new behaviour several times, until you have conditioned yourself.

What did you notice as you did this exercise?

In truth, we have used what we now know about behaviours (operant conditioning, Hebb's law, Fuzzy Logic) to help us train a new behavioural pattern. Make sure when you catch yourself doing it; you give yourself a big pat on the back or other congruent reward!

The Three Responses

In the face of a challenge, there are three different paths open to us – one of which can help you get and remain unstuck.

Our response to being stuck can be like an egg, a spring or a bodybuilder's bicep. This is a concept adapted from the ideas of Nassim Nicholas Taleb in his book *Antifragile*.

If we respond as an egg, we are 'fragile' – meaning that whatever pressure the external force places on us, will break us. If we respond as a spring, we simply bend under the pressure, tolerating the external forces until they're gone. When they are gone, we snap back to how we were before. If we respond like a bodybuilder's bicep, the external force is welcomed, and the muscle uses it as a stimulus to change and grow. When it faces the same external stimulus again, it can cope more easily with it. In fact, it can tolerate more and more stimuli because it has learned and adapted.

How we choose to respond is critical. If we choose to be fragile or simply 'tolerate' the circumstances, then we will remain stuck. Conversely, if we can find a way to learn and adapt our behaviours and responses, we can 'grow' from (and through) the experience. And, like a body builder's bicep, we will be able to easily adapt to the next challenge.

Unstuck Exercise #44: Adapting

How do you respond? Ask yourself the following:
- When are you fragile and let circumstances 'break' you? Describe your behaviours in detail.
- When are you tolerant and bend under pressure, but try to remain unchanged? Describe the behaviours in detail.
- When are you adaptive like a muscle, using the circumstance to change how you respond in future? Describe your response and behaviours in detail.

If you can learn new ways of adapting to circumstances and grow your capability, then facing such circumstances should become less and less difficult. In fact, each time you learn and adapt you are also for all future experiences.

Tolerance is not enough. If we act like a spring, we are essentially acting 'insanely'; using the same response over and over without any learning or adaptation. We may get through (and sometimes if that's the best that we can do, then it's a great first response), but we miss the opportunity to use the situation for reflection, learning, and adaptation the next time.

What if being fragile was a choice? If you simply 'give in' to the stimulus, make no attempt to tolerate or learn from it, this can also be described as the 'victim' approach.

We know bad things happen to people. We know that sometimes things get overwhelming or we feel, through learned helplessness, that all we can do is give up. This speaks to the fragility or excessive 'load' from what is happening. Even in those moments, where fragility seems like the best and even only option, have you considered that perhaps there's another way?

Looking for even the tiniest learning, adaptation or sense of control at the moment may not seem like much, but it's an internally driven response. Even doing this at a micro level that almost no one could tell is *giving you agency*; you are in fact taking control and responding differently. It may not be easy, and it may not always end any differently, but simply choosing to respond differently – seeking to be more 'muscle' and less 'egg' – can introduce an entirely different approach. It can remove the sense of helplessness you feel and open the door on the first tiny experiment to getting unstuck.

Unstuck Exercise #45: Giving up

Think of a time where you simply 'gave up'. Where you allowed yourself to choose the victim stance.

- What was the situation? What was the trigger?
- Take some time to write down at least three other things you could have done instead of giving up. Regardless of how small they are, make sure they are things that you choose and control.
- Take a few moments to role-play the situation again in your mind, allowing each of these three things to be used as ways forward. Let the story unfold and allow yourself to see and experience what happens next.

What did you notice?

Once you're committed to being 'anti-fragile' and new attitude of 'How can I do this?' might start to emerge.

Learning and The Expert Myth

How many times do you hear of powerful, transformative speakers who 'change lives' from the stage? They fly into town, act like rock stars, share a little love and wisdom… and have a special offer for the first 50 people to rush to the back of the room. These guys and girls might be supremely well-intentioned, and exceptionally skilled, but most people go home and *do not change*. Get that? MOST people do not change. In fact, most people end up worse off. They go to the seminar, get wound up and highly motivated, go home and do nothing different. Then when the credit card bill comes in (or the course they bought), they get their first disappointment. Then when they reflect on the event later (if they even do), they see that they have a page of notes but no change at all. They often feel that it is their fault, rather than the process they were exposed to.

I know many people that are self-help seminar junkies. They go from faux-high to faux-high as the celebrity 'guru' pumps up the rock track and the unhelpful rhetoric. It has the same impact as when some well-meaning person says, 'You need to…'

Have you ever found yourself in this situation? If so, then here's a question for you: Why didn't you 'change'? The answer isn't because you didn't invest in their 'platinum program.' These sessions fail because they fail to address the specific skills that need to be learned. They succeed at their key goal – to sell something – but do not succeed in giving people valuable tools for behavioural change. By understanding what really drives a behavioural outcome, you can create a framework in which your own change becomes possible.

Because wanting change and being able to change are often two completely different things.

The Behavioural Outcome Formula

For any behaviour to be demonstrated, three things need to be present: motivation, skills, and infrastructure.

If it were a math formula, it would look like: Outcome = $M + S + i$.

Let me give you an example. Say you came over to my house and asked, 'Phil, can you please show me some juggling?' I could be the world's best juggler – able to juggle two chainsaws and a cat in one hand. However, if I replied, 'I can't really be bothered,' then no matter what you did, you would not see the desired behaviour. My lack of *motivation* stops the behaviour occurring. Or, I could be really motivated to juggle for you and have three shiny new balls ready to go. However, if I have never juggled before, then the balls would just spill on the floor. Regardless of my motivation and having the infrastructure, I lack the *skill*, and you will not see the behavioural outcome. In the third case, I could really want to juggle, be a great and highly skilled juggler, but have no juggling balls. In this case, the lack of *infrastructure* guarantees that you will not see the behavioural outcome. So being able to demonstrate a behaviour relates to the motivation, the skill, and the infrastructure all being present.

Stop for a moment and consider this in terms of problems and issues that you have in your life. If you want to 'behave differently,' or get a different outcome from a circumstance, then it may be any one of these three behavioural drivers that are missing.

As a student of Dr. Yapko, I am such a fan of teaching and learning skill development and practical solutions (such as infrastructure selection), because I believe that *most people are already motivated when they seek my help for their problem*. If you were not motivated, you probably would not be reading this now. However, people are often quick to blame 'motivation' as the reason they can't shift their problem. There are times when motivation plays a part, but I find that it's most often HOW they use and apply that motivation, rather than the complete lack of motivation to change.

So, if we go back to the self-help seminar example, there is a lot of work done on motivating the audience. The generalities shared from stage, such as the rags to riches story, offer no real guide to the *skills* needed to change to a new behaviour. There is often little discussion of specific skills that can be employed, or whether the infrastructure is present. One of the biggest problems is they set up comparative expectations and encourage massive goals without ensuring they are possible.

Motivation is still an important component, but it rarely works on its own. One place where motivation does play a massive part is when people end up in a state of 'learned helplessness.' This occurs when a person has been in their problem for so long that nothing seems to work. It is easier, and often less challenging to their identity, to simply give up and stay as they are, rather than attempt to change, often with the expectation that they will fail again. Finding motivation, in this case, is critical *before* the skills and infrastructure become relevant.

So, as can been seen, all three elements need to be present – and appropriate – for the specific behaviour that we want. Let's have a look at these in a little more detail.

Motivation

Motivation is the pressure or urgency to get something done. There are several ways we can look at motivation, including:

- The direction of motivation (are you moving towards or away from something?).
- Implicit or explicit motivation (is it an act of love, or an act for a tangible reward?).
- Competing motivations and consistency questions.

Here is why I believe affirmations are a waste of time. Imagine standing in front of the mirror each morning saying, 'You are powerful!' when you actually feel weak and powerless or 'You are a success!' when inside you feel like a failure. It is not only a waste of time; it can be harmful to keep berating yourself to be something you clearly aren't. If you do this, please stop.

There are two types of motivation:

Fear-based motivation encourages us to move away from what we fear.

Opportunity-based motivation is where we move towards things that give us opportunity or pleasure.

It might remind you of the reward or punishment conditioning at the beginning of this chapter.

Have you heard the proverb 'Give a man a fish, and you feed him for a day. Teach him to fish, and he will eat for a lifetime.'? As true as this is, there is a very important element missing. The hungry man will not listen to your fishing lesson as he is too busy staring at your fish. This example describes fear-based motivation (wanting the fish to avoid hunger) and opportunity-based motivation (learning the skill of fishing). The missing element in this concept is that to be effective; we need to operate in the space of the current mindset. The hungry fisherman will be looking at removing the fear of hunger before he is open to learning how to fish.

Too often, motivation is all about 'sunshine and possibility,' when all the person wants is relief from what is causing them distress. Neither motivation type is right or wrong; they just serve different purposes.

Unstuck Exercise #46: Fear versus opportunity

Think of five things you did today.
- Were they driven by fear or opportunity?
- Did you do things in your day because you feared the consequence of not doing something, or because of the opportunity it would create?

What did you notice and learn?

Fear-based motivation is not necessarily a bad thing – it gets things done. If you were being attacked by a Grizzly bear, you would want fear-based motivation to kick in and get you out of there. We live complex lives where a mix of both motivational types can exist together. However, when our motivation is overly dominated by one of these types (although it most often fear-based motivation that dominates), it can lead us into problems.

Consider all of the 'rules' that we establish in our lives. All of the 'shoulds' and 'musts' and 'nevers.' Sometimes these rules are based on physical safety, such as you should check both ways before you cross the road. But many are based on social expectation and relational constructs. For example, 'You should never talk to strangers,' 'People from that culture are all criminals', or 'You must do what the priest says.' Without too much effort, you should be able to see where each of these 'social rules' have value – and where they unnecessarily limit or harm.

When we are driven by our fear motivation to follow such rules – many of which we never challenge or examine throughout our life– we create smaller and smaller worlds for ourselves, we lock ourselves in and get stuck. When we explore the conditional field, it's an opportunity to review the rules and find a way to break free.

Extrinsic Versus Intrinsic Motivations

Intrinsic motivation is the drive you feel to do something because you love it or it has meaning for you. Extrinsic motivation, on the other hand, is where you do things because you receive an external reward (or the removal of an external punishment) for doing it.

Unstuck Exercise #47. What did you do today?
- What did you love doing?
- What did you do today because it was driven by external reward?

Imagine a little old lady, Aunty Millie. She loves knitting jumpers, and it gives her great pleasure to give them away to everyone she knows. Her nephew sees this and thinks Aunty Millie is an entrepreneur, so he sets her up in a shop where she can knit her jumpers and sell them for a profit. How do you think Aunty Millie now feels about her knitting? In most cases, Aunty Millie will no longer see her knitting as a labour of love, but rather a burden or chore. By adding extrinsic motivation (the profit she makes), it belittles the intrinsic motivation, and the task is no longer as enjoyable. *It commoditises meaning.*

In many problem states, we commoditise what we love by setting benchmarks and rewards around them. We look for external reward (often in the form of validation from others) in what we do, rather than simply doing things because we love it for its own personal reward. If we seek external validation for everything that we do, then we are seeking extrinsic motivation for things that often should be left as internally valued.

Over time, as we seek approval or validation for what we love doing, it becomes a chore or a task – as we now do it to meet an external benchmark or to receive external validation. If you love painting, but for some reason feel it has to be 'good enough' (some specifying questions: Who for? Decided by whom? Against what standard?), it is easy to stop loving it. Very quickly, seeking external validation (or comparison) adds extrinsic motivation and can turn meaningful, joyous things into hard work. Meaning that they eventually become things to avoid as you fear that you are not 'good enough' at it.

Consider Vincent van Gogh. People thought his paintings were terrible. If he was driven by external validation and stopped painting when people rubbished his work, imagine what the world would have missed out on? Imagine artists like Prince, who were determined to create against their own standard because of the love of what they created, instead of simply bowing to societal pressure and deciding that their work wasn't 'good enough.' Sometimes we have to let go of what others think and do what we love – simply because we love it. There are so many things in this world that many people are better at than I am, but I do them anyway… because I love to. It brings me happiness and joy. Sometimes someone might pass a positive or negative comment about what I do – but that is their opinion and their business.

Dance like no one is watching. Sing like no one is listening. (My kids suggest that is the best time for me to do both of these things!)

Unstuck Exercise #48: For the love of it

- What do you love to do, or would do simply for the pleasure of doing it?
- What things do you stop yourself from doing because it might not be 'good enough' as judged by you or someone else?

Most people are stuck not because of lack of motivation but more so because they haven't got the skills or infrastructure at their disposal to achieve the outcome that they want.

Skills

Once we move beyond the idea that 'you're not motivated' to change, we start moving into the most common reason why people are stuck – that is, they are not applying valuable skills to their problem. Returning to the learning frame, people have either not learnt a high-quality skill (pattern or group of behaviours) to apply to the situation at hand or are applying behaviours they have learnt in the wrong way.

For example, Fred 'learns' as a child that a great response for managing his anxiety is to stay at home. However, when Fred wants to do things, such as go to university, start dating or get a job, using this 'skill' (stay at home to manage a feeling of anxiety) is no longer valuable. Think for a moment about what skills Fred needs in order to achieve any of his goals. Fred needs both 'performance' skills (physical actions that he will have to take) and 'cognitive' skills (how he thinks and processes information). As such, Fred will need to develop the following skills:

- How to determine when he is 'safe' or 'in danger.'
- How to respond differently to a 'feeling' that he has.
- How to work out when being at home and not being at home helps him achieve his goals.

If we consider that most people are stuck because they haven't learnt specific behavioural skills, or they're not applying them appropriately in their problem area, it does two important things:

- It provides a simple framework in which a person can identify overcoming their problem as a 'learning task.'
- It takes the pressure off the person by letting them see that they are not broken, faulty or a failure. When they change their behaviour (not change themselves – note the important distinction), their circumstances change, and their problem often resolves with a lot less effort.

As we saw earlier, as we use skills in meta-routines (like showering), they usually work fine for us until something changes (like when I broke my leg). In Fred's case, the response he chooses to 'keep himself feeling safe' might still work. However, it has a massive impact on him achieving anything else. Without developing and deploying new skills or behaviours, regardless of how motivated Fred is, nothing will change.

The Skills You Use to Keep Your Problem

Perhaps you don't think that you're very skilled? The reality is, you are highly skilled. If you have an issue or problem, then you are incredibly skilled at doing things that keep – and even amplify – the problem. In the face of every other alternative, you may use all of your 'problem skills' expertly to keep and reinforce your problem. That's right. You are skillfully acting to maintain your problem. Consider the following case.

Janette presented with a serious gambling problem. So much so, she had re-mortgaged her house, taken all the money from her family business employee pension payments and drained the company's tax liabilities accounts. It was a big problem. Her addiction had been running for at least 20 years. She was afraid of being found out, and there was a real possibility that she could be sent to jail. Janette was *very* motivated to stop.

To keep her problem, Janette had to be incredibly skillful. She had to be skillful at siphoning off cash without being detected. She had to be skillful at finding the time and opportunity to gamble. She had to be incredibly skillful at not being honest with herself. On deeper investigation, we identified that Janette needed the following skills in order to keep her problem:

- She had to stay entirely in the present whilst she was gambling (and not pay attention to consequences in the future or how much she had lost in the past).
- She had to stay incredibly focused on the process she was engaged in, rather than seeing it in the context of her life.

- She had to use gambling as a way of dealing with feelings of anxiety and discomfort, rather than using other potential options.
- She had to say 'yes' to opportunities to gamble and 'no' to any other actions or behaviours that presented themselves.
- She had to believe that she was somehow immune to the laws of probability.

…and many more.

For Janette, being able to relax the skills that made her gambling problem rigid and powerful and exchanging them for high-quality skills or behaviours, made the whole problem collapse. By helping Janette learn these new skills and how to apply them, she was able to 'bust' her addiction. By getting her to identify the triggers, and the sequence of behaviours that made her incredibly skilled at keeping her problem, she was able to modify these to get a powerful, positive shift.

At her six-week and 12-week follow up, Janette reported that she had closed all of her gambling accounts and had not gambled since. She had owned up to her family and was taking great action to manage her feelings and pay back the amounts she had wasted. Simply through understanding the skills which entrenched the problem and considering other skills to support a solution, Janette's problem collapsed.

What if your problem is based on powerful skills that you use to sustain it? What if you could learn new skills or apply known skills in different ways so that the problem is no longer possible?

Unstuck Exercise #49: Skills keeping you stuck

Consider where you are stuck:
- What skills or behaviours do you use which maintain or supports the problem?
- What skills or behaviours do you have to overlook or forget to remain stuck?
- What do you say to yourself, or what specific actions do you take, that support you being stuck?

The great news is that regardless of how stuck you are if you take responsibility and thoughtfully learn different skills and behaviours, imagine what could be possible?

What did you notice or learn from this exercise?

Infrastructure

The third element of the behavioural formula is infrastructure. Infrastructure is having the tools (including the time, resources and opportunity) to carry out the behaviour. For example, if I want to take up bike riding, but I don't have a bike, I won't get the outcome that I want.

Consider Mavis, an elderly woman that presented with sleep disturbances. She was afraid of the increase in crime and worried about what could happen to her. By asking a few simple questions about her bedtime routine, the following information emerged. When going to bed, Mavis left the back door open for her elderly dog so she could go outside to the toilet at night. Regardless of any other work we did to lessen her fear to deal with morbid terror; we first had to take care of the *infrastructure issue*. If Mavis continued to keep the back door unlocked and open then feeling insecure in her home wasn't going to change.

Mavis installed a doggie-door and trained the old dog to use it. The back door was now dead-bolted at night. She reported much less anxiety about being attacked in her home and was sleeping better.

Infrastructure is often overlooked as people look for deeper, more 'psychological' reasons for problems. Start with the simple. For example, if you want to lose weight, do you have the time, space and equipment to exercise? Do you know how? Do you only have healthy food in the fridge and the cupboard? If you want to start a career as a dentist, do you have the qualifications, the office space, and the dental chair?

Unstuck Exercise #50: Anything to add or remove?

Consider where you're stuck. What infrastructure would you need to better support achieving your goals? What would you need to add or remove to achieve better outcomes?

Now, going back to the formula: If you were to look at the whole behavioural formula, can you now identify why you're not getting the behavioural outcomes you want?

Is your issue based on motivation, skills or infrastructure?

Start with the simple. Try not to describe deep, psychological reasons for what's happening to you right now. Start practical, not Freudian!

Unstuck Exercise #51: The formula to define change

Consider where you're stuck:

- What is your motivation for change? What would motivate you to keep the problem?
- What skills would you need to add or change, so that the problem becomes impossible?
- Check the infrastructure around your problem. Is it appropriate for where you want to get to?

What did you learn from this exercise?

The Importance of Learning Your Way Out of a Problem

Everything we have covered up until now has been to make this point. The best way out of your problem is to learn your way out. As new behaviours are learned to different triggers, and future behaviours are 'shaped' by rewards and punishments, we can continue to learn new ways to deploy behaviours that change the outcomes that we get. Imagine if you could learn new ways of acting that would make the thing you are 'stuck' on no longer a 'roadblock (maybe just a speed-bump)?

Think about this: We often get stuck simply because there is something that we haven't yet learnt (and need to learn) in order to override our problems. It is this capability to learn which is often the unspoken path to getting unstuck. Consider a child that learns to ride a bike. Maybe this was you as a child.

Consider the time before the child learnt how to ride a bike. They were stuck. Perhaps they even berated themselves for being no good, too stupid or uncoordinated to ride a bike, or perhaps even thought that they wouldn't be able to learn.

When you're on *that* side of learning, what's in front can look difficult, sometimes impossible. Because having never achieved the outcome, it can feel a long way from accomplishment, However, going through the process of attempting to ride—something begins to happen. At some point, the experience of 'riding a bike' occurs. It might occur as Dad pushes, or rolling down a hill. But as the experience of riding a bike happens more and more, soon, something clicks – and without thinking, you can simply jump onto the bike and ride off. That kid that couldn't ride is now *on the other side of the learning*.

No longer that child feels like 'that kid that couldn't ride the bike.' They simply see themselves as a bike-riding kid.

What if this was also true with your problem, or wherever you're stuck? Right now, you may be the kid who is stuck. You might beat yourself up, give yourself a label or have beliefs that things cannot change. However, what if it's something you *haven't yet learned* that's keeping you stuck? What if, when you learn what you need, you could simply 'ride away' from being stuck?

'Not me,' you say, or 'maybe someone else.' Or 'I don't deserve it.' Regardless of what you tell yourself, you have the capacity to learn.

Unstuck Exercise #52: Lifetime lessons

You have spent your whole lifetime learning. Take the time to answer the following:
- Think of three things in your life that used to be a frustration or a problem but aren't anymore.
- List five behaviours or actions you learned at some time in your life.

- List three things you learned from someone else and applied in your own life.

What did you experience as you did this exercise?

Modelling Behaviour From Others

The concept of modelling behaviour[2] from others can be very useful. I don't mean that you should get up onto the catwalk and strut your stuff, I mean using other people as models of behaviour that you could experiment with and even adopt.

If someone else has an effective set of behaviours that achieves a positive result in the current context, how can these be decoded or adopted for your benefit? If someone else with the same resources can do it, why can't you?

If you are open to learning from others, the possibilities to try new ways of behaving become endless. Some things are not possible – for example, if you wanted to fly without assistance from a mountain top, I would suggest that this wouldn't lead to a good outcome. However, if you were to consider what resources or behaviours would be required, you might decide to hire a hang glider and take lessons. Or, strap on one of those crazy wing suits, use a parachute or base jump. The point is that by knowing how other people have 'done it,' we're able to evaluate which skills and resources are required to get the same result.

On this basis, how do other people go through life without anxiety? How do people get over depression? How do people bust addictions? If we take the skills and resources of others and *adapt* our behaviour to model theirs, we might get the outcomes we want.

The three key elements to modelling are:
1. Having the courage to experiment
2. Knowing that you can adapt
3. Being able to identify the appropriate models

---

2 Bandura, A. (1962). *Social Learning through Imitation*. University of Nebraska Press: Lincoln, NE.

Playing the investigative reporter

A great way to move forward is to find someone who reacts differently (who isn't stuck like you) and ask them some questions. Often observing someone may not be enough, you may have to dig a little deeper. Become an investigative reporter and try to understand what they respond to, how they select their behaviours and what's important to them about what they're doing. For example, if you're afraid of public speaking but have a colleague who excels at it, a question might be, 'How do you know that you're prepared enough?', and 'What do you do to feel calm and confident when you first go on stage'? Sometimes they don't know (because they are operating from an unconscious process and haven't given it any thought), however asking, watching and figuring it out can allow you to learn from people who are brilliant in areas where you're not. And let's not forget, there's probably lots of areas where you are brilliant, and they're not. Learn from them. Which brings us to back to the idea of uninformed behaviours.

You get to choose which learning you employ.

Yes, you get to choose your response to your circumstances.

Consider the things you've learned throughout your life. From being toilet trained to reading, to learning how to eat without spreading your dinner all over your face. You have learnt how to respond to others. Life is full of things you have learnt. As we saw earlier, when we look at the way we organise behaviours into meta-routines, we often believe that we do not choose the action, but it happens automatically or unconsciously. Equally, the exercises above may have also shown you the value in being informed of your behaviours – especially those that don't serve you. Yes, even by changing small steps, big changes can occur.

Chapter 7

What Drives Your Problem?

Once you have well-designed goals and have identified and modified the behaviours that you use, there's a 'special class' of behaviours we can now explore that may be the key to breaking free, especially if you've been stuck for a long time.

When people get stuck on issues relating to events from their past, it's worth asking if the problems are truly based on content or process. Let me explain the difference.

- **Content**: if the *specifics of the circumstance* is the thing that causes you the problem.
- **Process:** if the *way you refer to the content* is the thing that creates the problem.

To put this into context, is it the way your dad treated you when you were seven or is it the way that you continuously reference it from the past and bring it into the present, that's the problem?

The first is content; the second is process. Another example: was it that you were laughed at during your first day at school, or is it that every time you go to present in public you focus on this and the feelings resurface? Again, the first is content the second is process. Triggers in your current experience can lead to a set of behaviours that 'bring up' and relate to events that happened in the past.

Now, unless you have a time machine, it is IMPOSSIBLE to change the content of what's already happened. Let me say that again...

It is impossible to change the content of your past experience, but it is possible to change your processes around it.

When you change the process, it changes your relationship to the content. It even changes the meaning.

Consider Post-Traumatic Stress Disorder (PTSD), the content (what the person experienced) has ended (often a long time ago), but the way they *reference* this content and the meaning they give it continues for extended periods of time – for some, the rest of their life.

If the person does not have the skills to effectively and appropriately deal with the content, then they develop patterns, meanings, and processes that entrench and amplify the content to the point that can be debilitating.

For example, consider Cassie. As a child, she suffered horrendous sexual abuse. This ended by the time she was 11 years old, but now at 50, the content is still having a massive impact on her life. Cassie is a wonderful, caring and highly intelligent person who suffered something awful. However, something that ended nearly 40 years ago still deeply impacts how she experiences life and her expectations and beliefs about the future.

As much as we would love to have a time machine to go back and 'fix' the horrific content and stop the awful things that Cassie experienced— we can't. Nothing can stop the content. As terrible as it is, we simply cannot change this. However, if we consider it from a process perspective, we can immediately see potential points where changes could be made to assist with Cassie's recovery and repair. Cassie came to see me after being particularly 'triggered' by some confronting things that a work colleague said in a training session. It rendered her almost immobile – flashbacks, sweats, tremors, and feelings of being stuck on the spot and unable to escape. She wanted to be physically sick.

As we investigated her circumstance, there were some things that became clear and often are common in PTSD situations. Such as:

- She would see things in her current environment and immediately try to equate them to aspects of her past content. A look, a word, a face, a smell – anything. This acted as a 'trigger' for a cascade of behaviours accessing and referencing the past.
- Any detection of anything similar to her past trauma would initiate a full defensive reaction – regardless of the appropriateness of this response for the circumstance. Once it started, it ran full-steam ahead.

- She would reference the event as a 'reason' for every problem she had – she would always find a plausible connection to her past for being stuck in her present.
- She would be hyper-vigilant in an attempt to keep herself safe to anything that could remotely remind her of the event.

On top of this Cassie also:
- Believed she had some responsibility for the acts committed against her, even though she did not know what these responsibilities were.
- Felt massive shame – both to the content and how it affected her.

Imagine living life like that? PTSD sufferers have not only experienced terrible content (trauma, war, violence or abuse), but their *process* means that they carry it forward and keep being severely affected by it throughout their lives. There is no doubt that people with PTSD experience a high level of suffering that people who've never experienced it could hardly imagine.

Why me?

Why is it that two people can go through the same horrible experience and one will get PTSD and other will not? Think of two soldiers in a same platoon. They are exposed to the same horrific content, one gets severe PTSD, and the other doesn't. When people are exposed to the same circumstance, it reveals that it has to be more than 'what happened' – it's the process they use for understanding the circumstance and the ongoing triggers and processes for re-experiencing it.

What if this were also true for the other experiences? How can two people experience the same family situation and one becomes anxious or depressed or addicted, whilst the other does not? If the content is the same (or fundamentally similar), then the first place we should look is in the process of how they understood the circumstance. How did they build their processes and triggers?

Consider it from the other side. Imagine a person living a normal, happy life. All of a sudden, they adopt the triggers and processes of a PTSD person.

Consider how difficult it would be for them. People who suffer from PTSD have generally developed incredible coping strategies just to get through each day. They try to fit in to the 'real' world whilst attempting to manage the suffering that arises.

Let me ask you the original question again: *Are your problems based on the content or the process?*

The stories we tell

Often, people who have suffered extreme circumstances in their past have visited them over and over in their minds. Replaying them, often trying to understand them. They ask, 'why me?' This allows them to create a 'story' of the event – one they have told themselves, and often others, many times.

It is very common for people who have been intimate with their problem for a long time to almost have a 'pre-recorded' mental version of their experience. In a way, it keeps them 'safe.' They don't have to explore the content any more deeply than their 'recording.' It is also the story they tell themselves (often over and over) about what happened at that time. The person can enter 'download mode' – and in an almost unattached way, hit 'play' on the mental track, and let the story be told.

There is a massive difference when someone is exploring their story for the first time. In cases where people have not 'allowed' themselves to review a terrible situation or share it with themselves and others, it can often take time for the person to find the language and build the narrative. This requires empathy, generosity, and space to allow yourself (or the person sharing) to be able to find the language and references to capture their experience.

Unstuck Exercise #53: Your content

Think of the content 'stories' that you tell yourself and others:
- What 'stories' have you told yourself and others many times?
- What do you experience when you switch into 'download' mode and repeat the same story?

- How many times do you think you have shared this story with yourself and others?
- Who do you keep sharing the same story with? How many times do they need to hear it to understand it?

What did you notice as you completed this exercise?

Unstuck Exercise #54: Your story

Think of the content stories of your life.
- Make a list of bullet points of what you would tell others willingly about your 'story'
- Make a short list of what you would only tell yourself about your 'story'

What did you notice as you made, and compared, these two lists?

Unstuck Exercise #55: Exploring the untold stories

Think now of the content stories you have never told or explored. There may be issues or events from your past that you haven't shared with anyone. Maybe they're too raw or tough to manage.
- If you were to explore them or share them, what would happen?
- Who could you share your story with for the first time?
- What would happen if you only shared it with yourself?

What did you learn as you did this exercise?

Let's return to Cassie. In our session, she switched into 'download mode,', and her story came out. She had shared the story with herself many times and with numerous friends and therapists along her journey. If you were listening to Cassie, how much of her 'story' would you hold as being true?

The problems with memory recall

As Cassie rehashed her recollections, we can trust that she *perceives* that they're real. However, they may or may not reflect what actually happened.

This is not personal about Cassie, but rather the way in which humans create and access memories.

A lot has been investigated and learned regarding how much we can trust memory recall, especially the way memory and imagination are interwoven.

I'm sometimes asked to help people recall memories. They want to 'remember what happened' at a certain time in the past. Knowing what I know about memory and imagination, I simply refuse. Because if you don't remember something, it's not that it's always repressed or somehow hidden. It's not possible to magically 'find' a memory in your brain. Sometimes imagination can create a 'version' of what may have happened and encode it as a 'true memory.' It's important to be aware of.

Helping people try and access memories they 'can't remember' is also like asking them to 'imagine' what happened, this fuzzy area can lead to creating false memories.

This was a significant issue in psychotherapy when 'helpful' therapists worked to reclaim lost memories, usually of sexual abuse. The therapist was determined to believe that such memories were 'repressed' if they weren't fully remembered. They would inadvertently create 'imagined memories' that got many people into all sorts of trouble.[3]

If Cassie has been telling her story over and over, do you think it's possible that it may've been open to modification over time? Each time you recall and reconsolidate a memory, it is open to being modified.[4] So, a large number of recalls and retellings can mean that the 'truth' of the memory may change.

How you recall a memory is also dependant on context. Memories can also

---

3 Loftus, E L. &Yapko, M.D. "Psychotherapy and the Recovery of Repressed Memories." In T. Ney (Ed.), True and False Allegations of Child Sexual Abuse. New York: Brunner/Mazel, 1995; and Yapko, M.D. "Hypnosis and the Repressed Memory Controversy." In G. Burrows & R. Stanley (Eds.), Contemporary International Hypnosis. Sussex, England: John Wiley & Sons, Ltd., 1995.)
4 Tronson NC, Taylor JR. Molecular mechanisms of memory reconsolidation. Nat Rev Neurosci. 2007 Apr;8(4):262-75

be influenced by suggestions – both direct and indirect.[5] It's not the 'truth' of the memory that is the issue but the fact that the memory is continuously recalled and incorporated into the current experience when it shouldn't be. Regardless, the 'story' and the memories still contain the pain and the emotional punch.

But here's a thought: If the memory is open to change, wouldn't it be valuable to perhaps change some aspects of the story? Reduce some of the pain and suffering?

Stories are not lessons

Events that happen can be valuable if we're able to 'decode' them and draw lessons from them.

In Cassie's case, she had developed such a generalised series of triggers and behavioural processes that they were initiated in all sorts of environments– when she watched TV, when a work colleague said something, when someone had a 'tone' or a 'posture.' Even when she smelled certain foods.

Helping Cassie identify that it was not the event in her past that was her problem now, but rather the *processes* she had established thereafter.

After gently interrupting Cassie's well-worn 'download' and asking her specific questions about her behaviour and triggers, Cassie was able to see that these learned patterns could be shaped, interrupted, and updated into new and more valuable ways.

Cassie's previous processes:

- The triggers that set off her behavioural responses were not specific. She had no process for understanding if they were signals of danger or not.
- She did not have a useful strategy of what to focus on in a situation and instead 'hunted for threats'.
- She could not determine at any moment if she was safe or not. She felt in danger all the time.

---

5 Chan J.C.K. LaPaglia, J.A. Impairing existing declarative memory in humans by disrupting reconsolidation, PNAS June 4, 2013 110 (23) 9309-9313

- She did not know what thought or feeling was valuable to her. If it was intense, she used it as a trigger.
- She did not have a process for working out what to expect from people. She felt that every person was 'bad' and she could only predict negative outcomes.
- She did not have a clear strategy for determining the motives of others; her fundamental belief was that 'everyone is out to get me.'
- She did not have a valuable method of ascribing *meaning* to what happened to her in the past. He belief was that she was responsible for the events that had happened.
- She lacked a process for determining what she was in control of. She believed she was in control of 'nothing', including her own behavioural responses.

Imagine going through life trying to live with this set of processes. Imagine doing day-to-day activities – going to the shops, going to work, going out to meet friends – whilst having these processes. How would you cope? Cassie's effort to cope and get through each day was stoic, though incredibly draining.

What if your problem – regardless of what it is – only remains because of the processes you're using?

The Problem with Content and the Power of Process

Here is a little truth: **Your present and future are not built on the past.**

I once went to a seminar with a 'rock-star' coach who called a woman from the crowd and asked her onto the stage. The coach looked the woman up and down as she sat on a stool in front of more than 100 people. The coach raised her hand to her temple as if deep in thought and then proclaimed, 'Hmm, I see the way you're dressed, the way you smile… It was your father, wasn't it? It was what happened when you were about seven?'

I call trash! I call this malpractice. Why? Because…

- If this woman had a healthy relationship with her father, then the

coach has now possibly destroyed that.
- 'Cold-reading' tricks are for speaking to the dead and for cheap magicians.
- The coach had no idea why this woman dressed the way she did or the reason she smiles.
- The woman now looks for 'hidden' problems in her past. If she has no memories, she can make them up with imagination.
- The coach is reinforcing unchangeable content as the 'reason' for some unspecified problem.

I wanted to vomit. Rather than adding anything of value, this 'coach' was creating problems and helping the lady manufacture things 'in her past.' This is not helpful, regardless of how impressive the 'supercoach' intended to appear to the crowd.

The outcomes you get are based only on the *efforts and strategies* you use NOW. They are based on the circumstances you find yourself in rather than the content of your past.

If you want to improve your life, it happens *in the present* and in *how you approach the future*. At this point, people often tell me, ', but it was such a big thing.' And they're right – some of the things that happen are huge and terrible, but through their processes, they are continuing to make it a big thing. The truth is, bad things can happen to the very best people. It is not what happens to you but how you *choose to respond* that determines your outcome.

For example, think of the different ways that people respond to an injury. Some people choose to take an amputation or serious injury as something that 'happened' and still enter the Paralympics or climb Mount Everest. Other people look at it and see it as a reason to give up. Some stuff isn't easy. Often what is easy is not valuable, and what is valuable is not easy. The secret is in the *process of making the choice*.

I remember my father had a serious fall. The hospital stuck all sorts of pins and wires in his wrist and told him he had little chance of getting meaningful use of his hand in future. Think about how you would respond.

Would you accept that and just give up, or would you challenge it and try to get the hand working again? At this point, the answer is less important than how you decide – putting yourself through unnecessary pain for no gain seems silly. Letting a hand, that could get better, simply wither away seems like an equally bad choice. The quality of HOW you make the decision determines the value of the choice.

In Dad's case, he knew that when things healed there would be no structural reason he couldn't get some movement back in his hand. Everything was still there; it was just 'messy' at the moment. So, he chose to make an effort to improve his strength and range of motion. Small, painful improvements every day. It was not easy, but it sure was valuable. Eventually, he was able to regain about 80 per cent use of his hand and wrist. I am incredibly proud of the effort and persistence he showed to get the best outcome he could; one which surprised his doctors who obviously thought he 'couldn't do it.'

Bad stuff happens to people. It is the choice of how you respond that determines the possible outcomes open to you.

Give Up or Keep Going?

So many people have used a terrible experience to re-define who they are, both positively and negatively. Often it is the 'setback' and resilience to pursue the goal which leads to success. However, it is also true that the 'setback' can be the trigger for giving up.

Sometimes, giving up is the smartest and most valuable course of action. Think of football players who go on for a season too many and end up playing poorly, getting chronic injuries and damaging their legacy. Think of mountain climbers with frostbite on both feet, who can hardly walk and face having their feet amputated (or die) if they don't turn back. Giving up is sometimes the best strategy by a mile.

The problem is not 'giving up' or 'persevering' but in not having a *valuable process for deciding* when giving up is valuable.

Unstuck Exercise #56: Give up or keep going?

Consider a challenge you're currently facing. How will you determine when it is more valuable to give up than to keep going?

Most people don't even take time to carefully evaluate this important question. Perhaps you are using a habitual, even unconscious process that is both non-specific and 'intuitive.' Maybe it is based on a feeling or on what someone else thinks. Sometimes people simply reach a cut-off point, e.g., 'When I run out of money.' Or perhaps it is based on fear, habit or personal value, e.g., they say to themselves "I'm not worthy," or "Why would I bother when I am useless," etc.

And here lies the problem. Unless you're discriminating in your choice, you can be open to creating problems and less valuable outcomes than you may want. We will explore this in more detail later.

What About Cassie?

Are you wondering what happened to Cassie? To help her get unstuck from her unhelpful response pattern to her past, we looked at the way she created meaning around the event and reframed that. We worked to stop the event being a source of ongoing suffering and instead became a remembered experience without the emotional loading. We were able to work on new behavioural processes, interrupting her generalised stories, programs, and triggers and adopting new, more valuable behaviours. We spent quite some time helping her define better processes and beliefs around her behaviours, particularly around responsibility and control and building up Cassie's belief in her ability to better respond and act.

I can report that several years later, Cassie has moved on with her life and is now a powerful advocate for others who have been through similar experiences. She has used her past and found new capabilities and strength. She loves to support other sufferers and help them move on with their lives. She's making a real difference. Cassie is now able to reflect on the events of the past in a new and valuable way, including having a positive view of what she wants to do in the future.

To do this, Cassie decided to build a series of skills in self-awareness and self-management. Learning these skills, including new behavioural processes, set her free. Though we didn't change the past – Cassie was put back in control of how she interpreted the event and what she wanted to do as she looked toward her future.

As Cassie kept moving forward and progressed, when things 'came up' she was able to make conscious choices on how to respond.

Common Issues That Create Problems

Let's take the following two statements in order to understand your thinking process and strategies.
1. Your present and future is not built on your past.
2. How you respond to the current circumstance through the choices you make determines the quality of your present and future.

Knowing what you know now, think about the ways you repetitively act to triggers in your life and how you make decisions that create your experience.

Getting unstuck is not all about 'revolution' but more about being self-aware and flexible. It's about learning to identify and modify the reflex behaviours that don't serve you. It's the evolution of learning that accessing painful memories from the past is not a valuable way to create a quality experience in the present.

If you can now see how there's opportunity to change your behavioural patterns– then there's a path to move forward.

If we recognise that changing behaviour can change our outcome, then it's time to dive below the 'waterline' and into our 'conditional field.' You won't be disappointed.

Curious? Are you ready? Let's go!

Chapter 8

Diving Below the Waterline: Into the Conditional Field

'Now the unconscious mind is a vast storehouse of memories, your learnings. It has to be a storehouse because you cannot keep consciously in mind all the things you know. Your unconscious mind acts as a storehouse. Considering all the learning you have acquired in a lifetime; you use the vast majority of them automatically in order to function.'

– Milton H. Erickson

So far, all that we've discussed in this book has been above the 'waterline.' By looking at goals, outcomes, and behaviours – we've focused on things that are visible and observable to ourselves and others. Now our journey goes a little deeper. We have to dive beneath the waterline and enter the world of the invisible. As we dive into the conditional field, we enter the territory of all of the 'invisible' things that shape, control and limit our behaviours.

It can sometimes seem easier to make changes in things we see. It's also easier to note when these things have changed. However, sometimes the work that needs be done is at a deeper level.

We can think about our experience like this iceberg.

Overhead is the 'star' we're aiming for—our goals and the outcomes they create.

Below sits the mass of the iceberg, with only a small tip being visible above water. The 'visible' aspect are the behaviours we see. Below the waterline is the larger portion of ourselves, our conditional field and all of the elements it contains.

You Cannot See It

Imagine that you've stopped to watch a tree out of the window. You can't see the base of the tree, but from where you sit you can see the upper branches. As you watch the tree, the upper branches begin to sway, and the leaves shake. Can you guess what's happening? You can't see the wind, but you see how the wind shapes the behaviour of the tree's branches. Sitting at home, it might be a reasonable prediction that the wind is causing the movement. What if it wasn't the wind?

Visiting Africa, you often see big animals like elephants use trees as scratching posts, the upper branches sway, and the leaves shake from the elephant's efforts to gain relief from its itch. Some animals, like giraffes, reach up and browse on the branches – the tugging on one part of the tree affecting the other branches. If you've visited Tokyo during an earthquake, you would see the trees swaying and the leaves shaking.

From where you sit you cannot see *why* the tree is moving. However, based upon what you know, and your experience, you could make close predictions as to what's causing the action. The swaying branches (the behaviour) and the

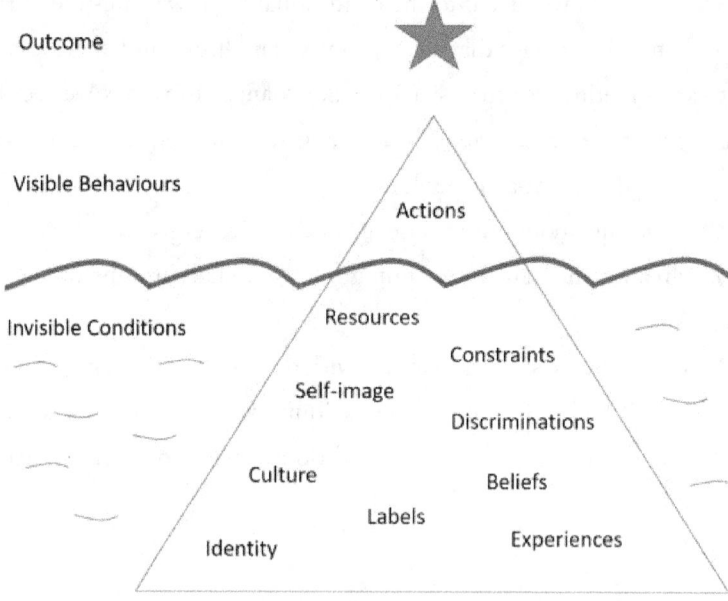

shaking leaves (the outcome) are caused by something we can't see. We can only guess (based on our experience and what we know about the conditions) as to what's creating the conditions we observe.

Our conditional field is much the same. The outcomes and the behaviours can be observed. However, the *conditions* that make these things happen are often not visible. At best, we can guess what's driving or even constraining the behaviours. For example, I can see, feel or hear an outcome. I could set measures and benchmarks that tell me if the goal was achieved. Making a million dollars by the time I'm 30? I can measure that by looking at the balance sheet on my birthday. To feel better about myself? I can measure and rate how I feel before and after what I do to change it.

Behaviours can be described and noted. For example, drinking less than two glasses of wine at dinner is entirely possible to observe and note whether it's achieved or not. Getting up at 6 am to go to the gym – again, this can easily be observed and noted.

In previous chapters, we considered how we learn to respond, often without thinking, to triggers we encounter. These 'habitual response patterns' to our unconscious, suggests that these are held in our conditional field: the vast storehouse, as described by pioneering psychiatrist, Milton Erickson.

This vast storehouse (our conditional field) is built up over a lifetime of learning and shaping. Over time our behaviours are largely applied unconsciously – that is without conscious thought. So it would make sense that sometimes in order to change an outcome, changes have to be made in aspects of the conditional field. The problem is that all of this is invisible, intangible and requires inference to access. To investigate your conditional field and create some self-awareness you have to investigate the intangible. If we cannot see it or measure it directly, what can we do?

Where there is smoke, there is fire.

Just because you see smoke, do you know the colour of the flame? Just because there's heavy traffic, do you know what specific incident or series of events led to it occurring? Going from observable to intangible provides the greatest challenge in self-development, self-awareness, and insight. The lack of observation in what's happening within the conditional field makes it difficult to really know.

Yet, because we can see most of the outcomes and behaviours, it allows us to tune in and decode the behaviour into the various elements within the conditional field. Though the conditional field sits below these behaviours and is intangible and not directly observable, we only can recognise what's within the conditional field by what comes out of it. We cannot see 'hate,' but we can see the behaviours that emerge when 'hate' is experienced. Equally, we cannot observe 'love,' but we can observe the thoughts, feelings, and behaviours of love. We have to infer what colour the flame is by the smoke we see.

Which Model Is Right?

So, how can someone understand their behaviours? Or make sense of the outcomes? If you we were to ask Freud, then he might say it's about 'ego and super-ego.' If we were to ask Jung, he might say 'subconscious archetypes.' If we're to ask an organisational psychologist, they might say 'personality type.' There are countless different models of 'personality' and what drives behaviour. So, on this basis, who would be right? Well, all of them and none of them.

For something as complex and intangible as our conditional field, one way to approach understanding it (and therefore ourselves) is by using 'models.' A model is an approximation that allows us to fit what we observe into known and established patterns and to potentially use this to derive some inference of meaning. Whether it is Freud, Jung, Myers-Briggs or whomever – each proposed a *theory* and a 'model' for our conditional field. These models allow us to define what's important in our conditional field and what may drive our behaviour.

Unstuck Exercise #57: Models of choice

Think carefully about what you believe is the basis of your behaviours and actions.

- Which models or theories do you accept in relation to what drives your behaviours?
- Which models have you considered but rejected?
- Which models have you heard about but not explored?
- Look up on the internet at least 3 other models of personal behaviour and explore them.

What did you learn from doing this exercise?

All models are useful to a point. Each model has strengths and limitations, includes certain information and excludes others. They aren't perfect, but they give a way to approach complexity in an easier form. Whichever model you apply to understanding your conditional field, I hope that you can be open enough to see your 'human complexity' in other ways.

How I describe the conditional field is also just another model of the intangible part of us.

The value of the conditional field?

Can you imagine if you had no rules, conditions or patterns to your behaviour? Imagine that you acted without thought to particular 'triggers' from the world around you? What if each time you approached a situation, you faced it with no reference to experience, or relied on what you had previously learned before.

The difficulty would be immense. Consider the following circumstances:

You attempt to put on clothes.

You attempt to drive a car.

You need to choose something to eat.

Unstuck Exercise #58: Without prior knowledge or learning

For the three examples listed above, ask yourself:
- Without thinking, what process do I use to achieve these outcomes?
- What information do I consider consciously, and what things do I just *know*?
- What errors would I be likely to make if I had no prior learning?

What did you learn by doing this exercise?

Consider the first option – putting on clothes. As yourself these questions:
- Why do I put on clothes?
- Which clothes do I put on?
- Where do I get clothes from?
- How do I know they are safe?
- How do I know they are appropriate?
- How do I select them from a range of clothes?
- In what order do I put them on?
- How do I put each garment on?
- When do I stop putting clothes on?
- When do I take them off?
- What do I do after I take them off?

In reality, you make all of these decisions (and many more!) with little or no conscious thought. You have learned – some time in your life – things about 'wearing clothes' that you simply rely on to help you achieve the outcome you're after.

Our conditional field is the 'vast storehouse' of all of these unconscious processes, knowledge, and beliefs. As they have been learned, codified into habits and stored away to be used as *low effort processes* when common situations arise.

Over your life—all of the beliefs, conditions, rules, and processes you acquired have become your conditional field. From whatever 'genetic' basis you started from, how you learned, adapted and shaped your behaviours is the source of your conditional field.

The beauty of knowing what drives your behaviours is that's it's continuously evolving as you do. **And that means that if you've learned your way into a process, you can learn your way out.**

In short, you are where you are because of what you've learned.

A life of learning

Science has now revealed that you don't only learn by experiencing things, but you also learn by watching. Italian researchers[6] found that the neurons in the brain that fire when we reach and grip food also fire when we see someone else reach and grip food. First studies involved Macaques monkeys, the scientists discovered these 'mirror neurons' in the brain allow a primate to experience something at a neuronal level *just by observing it*. This is also true for humans.

Consider the implications of this when paired with fuzzy logic, Hebbs law, and imagination. When we see something and process it at a neural level—we experience it. Taking fuzzy logic as an example, after observing something, we may indeed create psychological 'rules' about what we've seen as if we've actually experienced it.

Think of everything that you are exposed to from the time you are born, right through until today. Influences from your closest family members all the way through to your exposure to social media, advertising, and entertainment. Without even trying, you can be filling up your conditional field, and constantly reshaping it based upon these exposures and influences.

If you're learning and adapting from these influences, often without actually trying to learn or consciously pay attention to what's influencing you – imagine how you may be stuck by some rule or condition that has evolved in your conditional field but doesn't apply to your current circumstance?

---

6 Rizzolatti, Di Pellegrino, Fadiga, Fogassi, and Gallese

Culture

Culture can be defined as *the unwritten rules that evolve in a group that governs its behaviour.*

It's a *group conditional field*. The group's unconscious culture drives and limits behavioural selections by members of that group. The culture sets the outer boundaries for all the behaviours between what is accepted and what is valued. Think about this for a minute:

- The standards that are set by the group define what's acceptable and unacceptable within that group. Each group develops different behaviours that are considered acceptable or not acceptable. For example, the behaviours that are unacceptable in some Middle Eastern countries are not only acceptable but valued in Western Europe. Or behaviours that are not acceptable in church but are acceptable on a football end-of-season trip.
- Behaviours that are identified and praised are valued. People within the group seek to perform these behaviours because the group values them.
- Behaviours that are *not* identified as valuable or unacceptable are tolerated and form the basis of the culture.
- The culture is unique to that particular group. Changing people in the group changes the culture.

Think about the groups you belong to – or aspire to belong to. The behaviours you use are constrained by the 'unwritten rules' between valued and accepted. In any circumstance, these rules can help direct behaviours that help an individual fit into the group. However, for an individual, the unwritten rules might also constrain behaviours that would give them better outcomes. What makes you popular at the local football club might not work so well at your church group!

As you grow up in a specific family, community or nationality, you unconsciously learn the behaviours that are valued and the behaviours that are deemed unacceptable. As you watch others, you learn the culture of the group. When these behaviours are relevant and effective (particularly for keeping you safe within the groups), then there's no problem. However, acting 'blindly' from these limitations and constraints without understanding *why* you're behaving as you do, can keep you stuck.

I have seen many 'culturally learned' norms and behaviours cause all sorts of issues. These are often referred to as 'cross-cultural clashes' where a person behaves according to their learned cultural context in a completely different context. For example, Americans and their behaviour as tourists in France, German businesspeople working in London, Middle Eastern men in a Russian resort. In each of these contexts, their behaviours may be perfectly acceptable in their country or home, but not in other countries or situations. They haven't adapted their behaviour to suit the new context.

Culture is such a powerful source of behaviours and standards. Reflecting on what you've learned from your culture – what it values and what it shuns – can be instrumental in understanding why you're stuck.

The need to know

People, in general, seem to struggle with uncertainty. They have a need to not only know things but to understand the reasons or logic behind them. Just take a walk with a small child, and you'll frequently hear 'but why?'. It seems this need to understand is innate. In a way, it also makes models (like the conditional field) useful because it helps people anchor their experience and knowledge in a way that can make sense to them. This process, however, means that people often ascribe meanings to things that are simply random, or simplify things in ways that removes the complexity and value from them.

For example, why do people spend so much effort trying to understand dreams? What if they didn't actually have a meaning? Or why someone at the office said something hurtful to you? How do you know that they have the same 'meaning' for what they said as you do?

As you create meaning, especially when you do so with 'certainty' – all of your learned processes can kick in and very soon you can have a lovely set of rules, beliefs, and conditions built around nothing more than a guess. With fuzzy logic, Hebbs law and imagination all working on this 'fact,' what you 'learn' may not represent the truth.

What we believe about ourselves is a critical factor to the behaviours we use. We have beliefs about ourselves, and we also have beliefs about everything else in our lives. These beliefs shape our expectations, behavioural selections and even what we're prepared to accept as valid information or opinion.

Unstuck Exercise #59: Your inner beliefs

Think about your beliefs on the following topics:
- God exists
- My intuition is powerful
- People cannot be trusted
- The world is heading for disaster
- The world evolved, it was not created in seven days.

What did you notice about your thoughts on each topic?

Now take the opposite stance –if you believe there is a God, now put yourself in the shoes of someone who doesn't. Repeat the following questions for each of the topics above.
- How does the world look different from this perspective?
- What behaviours would they take that you would not, from your normal belief position?

What did you notice? What if the beliefs you had were not accurate, valuable or current? Understanding how powerful your beliefs are, makes them a critical player in your conditional field.

Unstuck Exercise #60: Changing beliefs.

Ponder this:
- Did you believe in mythical characters such as Santa, fairies, and monsters when you were young?
- Can you remember when you changed your beliefs around these characters?

- How did you learn this was no longer true?
- What would you now need to know to change your mind about other things you believe in?

What did you learn as you completed this exercise?

The good news is that like all learning, beliefs, and rules developed in this way are open to shaping and change. The things that you once believed with certainty may not be what you believe today. The beliefs, rules, and conditions that you have developed can flex. The meaning you gave things may not be the same meaning now.

Unstuck Exercise #61: Making meaning

You walk into a café, and a man looks over his paper and scowls at you.
- What meaning do you make of this?
- How did you decide that this meaning is accurate?
- How do you know what the man was thinking or doing at the time?

What did you notice as you did this exercise?

Perhaps as you ran through the questions, you may have started with 'certainty' such as 'He doesn't like me.', 'He's old and cantankerous.' As you reviewed the questions that followed, perhaps you noticed that your degree of 'certainty' might not have warranted that level. What if you could notice the event but not ascribe meaning to it?

What do you really know? Over time, you have learnt skills, developed insight (perhaps even wisdom) and accumulated information. Some of this knowledge is hard fact, some of it is subjective and based on opinion, as with the exercise above. We also know that throughout history, knowledge has changed and been updated. Think of the way medicine has evolved from the Dark Ages to now. Think of what people understand about physics today, compared to the past. Knowledge in all its forms is a key part of the conditional field. It feeds and justifies our beliefs and provides certainty. We know what we know – yet what we know may not be true. Being open to *not knowing,* to having your knowledge updated or revised is a critical skill in evolving.

Nature or Nurture?

Do you believe that you're stuck because your situation is genetic? For some things, this will be true. If you have Cystic Fibrosis or other genetic diseases, then there's certainly some issues based on genetics. But what about 'experiential' conditions, such as anxiety, addiction or depression? There has been significant debate in the scientific community regarding the 'Nature versus Nurture' controversy in these situations. Are we 'like this' because it is coded into our genetics, or because we have been conditioned through the way we have been nurtured?

The answer seems to be both, but with an important caveat. Genetics can provide a series of 'increased risk factors,' from which, based upon specific things that have been learned, can lead to a specific experiential outcome. A good analogy is with certain cancers – you can have genetic risk factors hard-coded into every cell. However, many years of smoking increase the chance that these genetic pre-dispositions will express as cancer. A person with these risk factors who doesn't smoke can live to 100. It's not just the risk factors; it's the way these are 'activated' that get an outcome.

It seems to be the same with depression, anxiety, and addiction. There have been 'genetic markers' identified that may potentially *increase the risk* of developing a condition, however, no markers have been found that *guarantee* it. As Lohoff[7] describes in the case of depression:

"Despite all efforts, thus far, no single genetic variation has been identified to increase the risk of depression substantially. Genetic variants are expected to have only small effects on overall disease risk, and multiple genetic factors in conjunction with environmental factors are likely necessary for the development of major depressive disorder."

---

7 Lohoff, F.W. *Overview of the Genetics of Major Depressive Disorder.* Curr Psychiatry Rep. 2010 Dec; 12(6): 539–546.

Michael Yapko's books: *Depression is Contagious: How the Most Common Mood Disorder is Spreading Around the World and How to Stop It* and *Hand Me Down Blues: How to Stop Depression from Spreading in Families* also explore this complex topic.

It seems that research is beginning to identify that the underlying risk factors are only activated when the 'environmental' and 'behavioural' factors come into play.

So, what if these situational factors were not applied, and these risk factors remain dormant? What if something else was creating the issue, rather than some unchangeable genetic trait?

Viewing your circumstance as 'genetic' and 'hard-wired' means it can be difficult to believe that it can be changed. However, by appreciating that the basis of a 'problem' might have some genetic risk factors but is specifically the environment and behavioural elements applied to it that make it 'real' means that things can shift – even if only a small amount. A small amount of movement is sometimes all you need to get unstuck.

People with risk factors may never get the condition linked to those genes. Regardless of the genetic risk factors, behaviours will more reliably predict your outcome. If you have genetic risk factors for a certain condition, it may make things harder, or require different approaches or more effort, but this does not mean the outcome is beyond your reach.

Think about how differently you'd behave if you believed your situation was unchangeable, versus if you believed it was malleable and open to change?

Why is my conditional field not working for me?

Most of the time, our conditional field operates perfectly well. It helps us do things efficiently and valuably. However, there are times when what we draw on for our behaviours may be out of date, poorly defined or inefficient for the purpose at hand.

This occurs for a number of reasons, including:
- We learned a 'general rule' that is not nuanced enough to deal with the current circumstance

- We learned something that's no longer relevant because things have changed since we learned it
- We are applying rules not designed for the task at hand
- We learned the wrong thing from what we were exposed to
- We have changed – including our skills and capabilities – so the limitations and conditions may no longer apply to who we are now
- We have gathered more information, and things we once believed are no longer 'true' – but we still use these facts as part of our decision-making process.

If we keep applying the same rules, conditions, restrictions, and beliefs to solving problems when they don't serve us, we get back to the 'insanity loop' – and rapidly feel stuck. We want to achieve something different, keep deploying behaviours based upon ineffective conditional field elements, and simply keep missing the mark.

Diving below the waterline and examining our conditional field does not mean that we need to know and test every process, belief and decision-making frame before every action. Instead, when we get stuck, it can be useful to review the elements within our conditional field to see if something needs to be modified, updated or removed to help get us unstuck. As we update the operating software to be more relevant, we evolve in who we are and better adapt to our circumstances. This implies healthy growth.

Circumstances

Circumstances are not a part of your internal conditional field. However, your circumstances dictate which behaviours you select. Understanding that circumstances are *beyond your control* is the first critical point in improving your outcome. Believing that you can change the weather is less effective than choosing an outfit that best *responds* to that weather. Circumstances set the conditions for how we operate; our conditional field sets the framework of how we respond.

Consider that at any moment we do not control any number of things. The following is an example:

- The weather
- The future
- What someone else thinks of us
- The number of arms or legs that we have
- The actions of others
- What thoughts or feelings we generate.

In each of these cases, the circumstance provides the conditions in which we can respond. Our conditional field then chooses the response. We can respond culturally, from our beliefs or from our knowledge (or lack thereof). We can respond to satisfy a deep social need, or in line with our self-belief. We can respond as we always have, based around some long-forgotten rules and because of some specific triggers.

As part of getting unstuck, it can be useful to simply be aware that whilst we cannot change circumstances, we are in control of our responses. And our response often leads us to next set of circumstances that we need to respond to. If we respond thoughtfully, and congruent to our purpose and goals, we immediately get a higher quality outcome. If we start to choose better responses, we create better circumstances. Imagine the difference this could create.

Choosing your response, rather than letting it be unconsciously dictated by your conditional field, can rapidly get you unstuck.

Uncovering the Conditional Field

It's all about perspective.

Have you ever travelled in an aeroplane and looked out the window at the landscape below? Sometimes you fly above the clouds, and the ground is obscured. You see the clouds and bask in the sunshine above but have no idea of what lies beneath. If the plane descends through the clouds, you may be able to see the topography of the ground below.

I love flying into cities where you dive down through the clouds and are surprised by what you see. It might be the city of London, the anchored ships off Singapore or the azure waters and red terracotta roof tiles of Sydney. When you fly over the fields of rural Germany, depending upon the season, each field has a different colour due to the crops that grow. As you fly over Switzerland in the winter, the Alps sparkle with snow.

Sometimes we don't look down. We are absorbed in our meal, sleeping or trying to finish that last-minute business presentation. Regardless of what we do, there's something which lies beneath. If at any point we were to look at the landscape – really look – we would see that it is made up of so many different things. The 'big picture' vantage point can give a very different perspective from being immersed within the landscape.

When standing in the middle of a village, you can see the street you're on and the houses to your left and right. From the point of immersion, you have a limited view. However, in the aeroplane you can see that the street may be a dead-end, or that it may connect to a highway. Being able to step back and get an overall wide picture provides critical context.

It is the same with our conditional field. If we're only immersed in what we do, we may find ourselves stuck on a dead-end street. However, if we can get the broad aeroplane view of the conditions, boundaries, rules, and expectations that are present – we can reframe our view and work out different ways to shift from where we're stuck.

Unless you can take some time to step outside your immersed state and gain you'll often miss something that can be changed. Too often we cruise through life without really looking at what lies beneath. There are many reasons for this. Some of the most common include that it requires effort, the outcome is uncertain, or it may be painful to do. In fact, to really develop insight into your conditional field means you must face these three hurdles squarely:

1. Take the time and effort
2. Embrace the spirit of discovery
3. Cultivate courage

The Avoidance Trap

For many, it can be easier to build a 'story' around why they're not getting what they want. The stories often talk about the poor circumstances or the lack of something such as luck, skills or resources. It takes less effort to accept the excuses and lies we tell ourselves, rather than make the effort to look within and investigate our self-imposed rules, boundaries or expectations.

Humans are designed to avoid cognitive effort. Thinking actually takes a huge amount of resources, the brain is 3 per cent of the body's weight yet has 20 per cent of the blood flow and energy consumption. It's far easier for a person to run on autopilot with known patterns of behaviour than spend the cognitive effort examining and revising them. When under stress, there's even less chance of effort or energy toward self-reflection; it's easier to switch into our fight or flight mode to get ourselves out of any perceived danger.

Uncertainty is enormously challenging for many people. Why would I go exploring my 'stuff' if I don't know what I may find? What if I find something that I don't like or want to find? This uncertainty and fear act often persuades people from engaging in true self-reflection.

Consider Vivian. She was so unhappy with her appearance that she would refuse to look in a mirror. Instead of really 'seeing' what was there, she would stick with her story and excuses. It was painful for her to admit the truth about how she looked – relative to how she wanted to see herself, and what she wanted to see. Vivian was scared that if she saw how she looked, she would have to do something about it, and even worse, was scared that she would be unable to do so.

Changing the Intangible

If you own a smartphone, then every so often the maker of the operating system pushes an update to your phone. Sometimes the updates are big changes, like going from a version six to a version seven where many things change. Sometimes there are smaller updates, like 7.01 to 7.02 which are designed to iron out an unexpected bug and to make the system run more effectively and efficiently.

In a way, this is what happens with the conditional field – it runs in the background. Sometimes it needs a 'big update' to stay relevant while other times it only needs a small bug fix to make it efficient and effective.

When you use the programs on your computer, you don't often see the operating system running in the background – however, you certainly notice when there is a bug. This is the same as the conditional field. When things go well, you have no need to make changes. However, when things are not working efficiently and effectively, you certainly know it. It's a sign that your conditional field could do with an 'update' – maybe a big version or maybe just a little bug fix.

Chapter 9

Self-Awareness: Exploring What Lies Beneath

Getting Below the Line

In the previous chapter, we saw how Milton Erickson referred to the unconscious as a 'vast storehouse' of learning and memories. Because we rely on it to automatically supply the conditions and rules for our actions, we rarely take the time to shine a light into this warehouse and see what's inside.

In general, we usually just allow our conditional field to do its thing. However, when our conditional field is the reason we're stuck it can be useful to investigate it more deeply. This means we have to shine the spotlight on some dark corners within this vast storehouse, areas we usually like to keep in the dark. As uncomfortable as this can be, the process can be highly valuable to getting you unstuck.

Consider a situation at the local supermarket, you see someone pick an apple, sniff it, and put it back. What judgements do you make about their behaviour? What motivated this behaviour, and why did they make that decision?

From your external perspective, you really cannot know. All you can do is observe the behaviour and outcomes. You simply cannot know all of what's happening in another person's internal world. This internal, or subjective world is only available to them. What they think, feel, remember and focus on is only available to them. What meaning and associations they make is totally personal. All of the elements that make up a person's conditional field are both private and highly subjective. Sometimes, regardless of how hard a person seeks to understand the 'why' of a behaviour, they may land on a story or assumption, but maybe not always an objective 'truth.'

Versions of Us

As we start the process of becoming more self-aware, it can be useful to understand that there's multiple versions of us.

First, there is the *subjective self* with access to our internal world.

Second, there is the *objective self* which contains all the things that external viewers would notice – like the 'apple sniffer' example.

These versions of *self*-overlap, and sometimes we can be aware of the subjective and objective elements at the same time. However, often there are 'things you do' that others are aware of, but you're not. There are also many things in your conditional field that you're not consciously aware of.

Therefore these 'objective' (what can be seen) and 'subjective' (what I think or know about) views are incomplete versions of ourselves. We all have the capacity to know more about what we do and our conditional field. Self-awareness comes from being open to observe and expand these incomplete versions of ourselves.

The Role of Self-Awareness

As with any discovery process, the first stage is being open to observe. That is, to see something that maybe hasn't been studied, or take time to view things previously overlooked. As we observe these things, we become more aware. As we take time to observe the objective and subjective aspects of ourselves, we gain greater awareness and a more complete version of who we are.

Observation only provides information, but not meaning or insight. The 'data' collected from observation has little value until patterns, meanings and associations are derived and allow the 'first hypotheses' to be drawn. A hypothesis is a 'best guess' as to what's happening. In science, a hypothesis is set for any experiment, and then data is collected to see if the hypothesis might be true or not. This is really important to understand. Once we think we know what something means – or we think there's a pattern or rule that applies – it is useful to take the next step and test if it's reliable.

The insight from this self-observation and testing its 'meanings' may help get you unstuck. However, it is useful to remember that behaviours (and hypotheses) are highly specific. The data you collect about your behaviours in one circumstance won't automatically apply in other circumstances. You would have to test your hypotheses to know if they're true.

Taking time to notice the behaviours and areas you are stuck provides the first level of information. With this awareness, perhaps you can 'test' some hypotheses (potential meanings) until you find a meaning that fits – so you gain some insight. Quality insight allows us to understand what we're seeing. In this case, recognising the behavioural processes and the conditions that lead to getting stuck.

You can be self-aware as in 'I am aware of what I do' but have no self-insight, 'I understand the conditions and rules that shape my behaviour.' You can have self-insight but do nothing with it to improve your specific circumstance. In both cases, you will remain stuck. Doing work in self-awareness leads to the opportunity for deeper self-management and allows you to consciously select what you apply from your conditional field to get the outcome you want.

The path to getting unstuck suggests that simple self-awareness is not enough – rather, it is the first step in the process of reorienting what you choose to do to obtain higher quality outcomes.

No Value in Deep Purge. Process Versus Story.

It is rarely necessary to do a full forensic investigation of your conditional field to get unstuck. Instead, it's about having the courage to explore the specific areas that you're setting the conditions for. In fact, most of what's in your vast storehouse is probably working completely normally and valuably for you, and there's no need to dig around where things are working fine, right? Better let your conditional field do its thing.

When your conditional field is working against your outcomes, then it's worth spending the time and effort to dive deep. To return to the software analogy, if being stuck is just a 'glitch' in your experience, then you're more likely to just need a bug fix (like version 7.01 to version 7.02) rather than a full upgrade.

Even the process of gaining self-awareness is impacted by your conditional field. For example: what you believe about yourself, what you think are your limitations, what your beliefs around your ability to change, what models you use for evaluating your behaviours – all directly impact your self-awareness processes. As much of ourselves are kept 'private', it is only thorough introspection and reflection that we can evaluate and understand the private aspects of self. Our subjective self – in particular, the way we *allow ourselves to see ourselves* – is skewed by our conditional field.

The rules we set about how we see ourselves will skew what we see, what we accept and what we are prepared to believe about ourselves. Particularly where we have developed a subjective view that is quite negative (often as a means to defend ourselves by diminishing how we see ourselves). True self-reflection can be painful and challenging.

How to Observe

Let's return to the 'big picture' metaphor as a way of describing the process of observing our conditional field and drawing insights. Imagine that you're looking out of the window of the aeroplane and below is a village nestled on a hill.

The quality of observation = seeing, interpreting and experiencing.

As you begin the process of developing self-insight, it is useful to review these three levels of observation.

Level 1: Categorising.

At this level, you know that things you see can quickly and efficiently categorised and labelled. This is a low effort strategy that draws on what you've already learned and categorised earlier. You can look out the plane window and say, 'That's a village.' Here, we use our heuristics to access our 'conditional field' and simply recognise what we see as a member of a category that we already know.

Level 2: Seeing.

At the seeing level, you abandon the top-level of categorisation and see what's really there. In a way, you're observing 'this village' more closely. You might notice houses, roads, trees, and people. There's still a certain amount of labelling about what you see and the unique parts that make up this specific village.

Level 3: Experiencing.

At this level, you move beyond the second level labels (house, street) you may experience the elements of the village more perceptually, like recognising the patterns in the fields or the way light reflects off surfaces, but not others. You might recognise colours, shades, shapes, and relationships. It is observing without attribution of categorisation.

As we look out of an aeroplane window and see a village, the three levels of observation come into play. Level 1 takes provides a quick, general 'category' answer. The same answer you would get no matter how many villages you flew over. At the deeper levels, we look at elements specific to the village and perhaps what makes it unique from other villages. Finally, with a lot more effort and a lot less judgement we pay attention to what is being experienced and perceived at that time.

Unstuck Exercise #62: The art of observation

Wherever you are, sit or stand quietly. Observe your surroundings.
- Start with level 1 observations. Categorise what you see.
- Now shift to level 2 observations. Can you notice the elements of what you observe? To what level of granularity can you begin to observe what is in the field in front of you? What things are specific or unique, and what things are common?
- Finally, take some time to observe the experiences, perceptions, tones, shapes, and relationships of what's in the field.

What changed as you shifted your observational level? How would you describe the effort, the engagement, the value, the quality and the learning from the observations?

I would like to introduce you to a fourth level of observation:

Impact

Pay attention to how your level 3 observations *impact* you: your thinking, feelings, what you focus on, what you interact with and how being 'in the field' changes you or your experience.

The act of observation is not done in isolation but in deep connection (even immersion) in what is being observed. For example, observing the process of how I respond with 'anger' may bring up other feelings like shame or fear. I can then allow myself to explore these experiences. That is, I can notice the *impact* it has on me. This allows an even deeper understanding about the experience, by recognising that 'the observer' is never completely isolated from what they're observing when doing self-awareness work.

Self-awareness is often regarded as difficult and painful – not because of what we observe, but the *impact* observation has on us. Approaching self-awareness with the understanding that looking beyond labels and paying attention to impact can bring value makes a massive difference to the outcomes you get.

Consider Jayde. She had a terrible home life and unfortunately had to 'manage' her responsibilities. She had elderly parents, a challenging partner and difficult kids all under the one roof. She constantly exploded with rage and returning home after work made her physically ill.

Teaching Jayde a skill in self-observation made a massive difference. I encouraged Jayde to say to herself 'that's interesting' when she noticed a thought, feeling or reaction was being triggered. As she drove home, she would notice a thought or feeling and simply noticed it. 'That's interesting!' Jayde said. This gave her adequate distance from unwanted thoughts and feelings and encouraged curiosity towards it. Jayde applied the same technique with her interactions in the house – both to what others did and to her responses. Jayde's first comment was how liberating it was not to be immediately impacted by everything. She also noticed how it allowed her to see the elements of each pattern of behaviour. How each thought or feeling contributed to her state of distress. By having observed these things, Jayde was able to decide specifically what to work on and where to intervene, so her responses and reactions changed significantly.

Unstuck Exercise #63: Observing yourself

Take some time to explore your *immersed* observations about where you're stuck and its impact.

- Start by working down the observation levels. For example, if you observe that you 'lash out from anger' (level 1 – Category) can you also notice the elements of anger (level 2 – 'I feel powerless', 'I want control', 'I shut down my thinking and just react', I feel bad after')
- Can you now observe the small feelings and thoughts that happen just *before* and just *after* the event? Can you feel the changes in the body and the thoughts you generate?

For example, someone investigating anger might note 'I feel small and distant. I notice a flush of warmth. I see my vision narrowing. I have a tightness in my chest and throat. I feel myself sneering. I feel strong. My heartbeat rises. There is a moment of power and strength. After I feel exhausted. I begin to think bad things about myself. I worry that no one likes me. (Level 3).

- Take time to progress through these three levels and write down what you have observed.
- Now move to being the 'immersed observer' of your experience. Observe the *impact* whilst you are experience it. What comes up for you? What self-talk is generated? Review what you have written down and as you 're-live' the experience, pay attention to what you experience and what impacts it generates.

For example, 'As I observe these changes, I feel ashamed. I feel like I'm just like my Dad. I feel that I should be better than this. I feel that I can't control it.'

- Write down whatever it is that comes up for you. Note these are only 'hypotheses' and observations about the experience.

What did you learn?

This is a simple and powerful process to understand the behavioural processes of being stuck. It can help you gain insight into what sits behind the processes in the conditional field.

The act of observing changes not only in the observer but also in the subject observed. When we observe something, we often fix a label to it and keep it. That is, I observe at a deep level but automatically shift to 'categorisation' to help me understand and see it in context. This can create issues where things are falsely categorised – for example, imagine having a feeling in your chest and calling it 'anger.' If you have that feeling at other times (or involved in other processes), your immediate and easy recourse is to recognise it as 'anger.' You may wonder why you get angry at something – when in fact you may be having a whole other experience (an allergy response, anxiety, a heart attack). Please be aware that creating labels and categories for things may keep you stuck.

What to Observe

Do you really know yourself? Is it *actually* possible to know yourself?

While these seem like highly philosophical questions (and perhaps they are), they're important for anyone seeking to understand themselves better. It allows a person to work from this point to create a different and hopefully more valuable set of concepts in their conditional field. As we have seen, it is possible to be aware of outcomes and behaviours through external observation. However, it's often difficult to conduct these observations by ourselves.

Part of who we are is known only to ourselves, while there are elements of ourselves that we express outwardly that others can see and describe. There are also parts of ourselves that are unknown to us. This is because we cannot see all that we are; we have a limited ability to understand and interpret all aspects of ourselves. The parts that are not known are often substituted with how we 'imagine' ourselves to be. Because we don't know, we create a 'story' for who we are when we don't have conscious knowledge.

This 'imagined' self is how we would describe ourselves versus who we expect or want to be. This imagined self is a key part of your conditional field and sets up a very strong 'category' belief about who you are. So, while you believe that you are 'worthless,' 'brilliant,' or a 'fraud' (examples of imaginary selves), you're not seeing the full picture, you're simply creating a Category level 'story' about who you might be. This drastically skews what you're prepared to believe or observe about yourself – both objective and subjective. On a whole, we often confirm our bias by observing that which only shows our imagined view. Even though this occurs, the real version of who you are does not actually change.

You are always more than you allow yourself to believe.

This is worth repeating. *You are always more than you allow yourself to believe.*

While your 'imagined' self is entirely subjective – and subject to all the heuristics and biases. The complete self is so much more. Depending upon your view, you may only see the good, the bad or something in-between. You never get to see the whole.

Unstuck Exercise #64: Get to know you

- Describe yourself as completely as you can. How do you see yourself? What do you think is valuable? What is not?
- Ask someone you know and trust and ask them these same questions about you – with the preface that you want honesty, not just platitudes.
- Where there are differences in the internal subjective and external subjective view of yourself?

What do you learn from this exercise?

Triangulate with Feedback to Learn More About Yourself

Most of the time we get stuck because we believe that the 'imagined self' is, in fact, the real self.

The process of liberating ourselves from our own stories is achieved by continually pushing the boundaries of the imagined self to more closely resemble the true objective self.

There will always be things about yourself that you can't know (and these things will also change over time as you learn and grow). However, we can dramatically shift from being stuck through honest self-reflection and gaining quality feedback.

Gaining quality feedback allows you to see what is known by others but not known to yourself. Choose your sources of feedback wisely, as bad feedback can reinforce unhelpful elements in your conditional field, including your self-image, your rules and how you decide to relate to yourself. Remember, it's only ever the person's *subjective perspective* on your 'self' that they can offer you – never the truth. This means that whatever feedback you receive is going to be filtered through several powerful social and cultural lenses by that person. In fact, what you hear in feedback is often a direct reflection of the way the person offering the feedback is filtering the world through their *own* belief systems and things in their conditional field, rather than accurate and specific information about *you*.

When you receive any feedback on yourself, your character, behaviours or elements of your conditional field, it's best *not* to accept the feedback straight away as 'truth.' Instead, sit with it and work out the value of it. Consider it through the lens of 'that's interesting,' determine how much of it could be true in light of what you already know about yourself. If the feedback is observational and specific, then it's worth valuing the feedback and search for more insight into yourself.

Feedback is not opinion

The biggest problem with feedback is when people start giving you 'meaning' for behaviours or applying rules to what you do or did. The worst case is when people start advising you on what you 'should' or 'shouldn't' do. This would be an appropriate time to tell your feedback partner to shut up or go away – as they're no longer being helpful and likely shifting into creating harm.

Feedback from others should focus on what is *objective* and *observable* by them. Quite simply, they cannot know the 'meaning' of your actions, or what drives you. Even Freud could only take a guess at that with his clients (and most of the time it was something about their mother. Hmm…). At best, the person can only guess or *suggest from their own perspective*. They cannot know if what you did was 'good' or 'bad,' as you're operating with your own moral compass, not theirs. They cannot know what part of the complex landscape of your conditional field was involved in driving the choices you made, or why it was important.

Feedback is not advice

Feedback is *not* advice. Statements such as 'you need to,' 'you should,' 'you must' or 'don't' is simply someone (often with great intentions) attempting to apply their conditional field onto your behaviours or situation. *For self-discovery purposes, avoid this at all costs.*

The best way to get quality feedback is to ask for *specific* feedback in a specific way. For example, what specifically did they observe? What did they notice? What was the specific effect on them? You're not looking for explanation or meaning, only seeking to obtain objective data from other sources to process, so you can better understand yourself.

Feedback for Self-Awareness

Knowing the patterns of behaviour (the observable responses) and pairing them with their triggers is a great step toward self-awareness.

The observable response is what is noticed by you internally (such as feelings, thoughts, and emotions) and what can be observed through your actions externally by you or others.

Expanding what we know about ourselves means taking the subjective views of ourself and adding high-quality feedback from others. Then, taking time to sit with that data and come up with a hypothesis for insights into these processes and patterns.

To get unstuck, first fully explore the process.

Unstuck Exercise #65: Gaining self-awareness

Where you're stuck or have a repetitive unhelpful behaviour, investigate and write down the following:
- What outward actions are demonstrated?
- Which thoughts, feelings and emotions do you have?
- What triggers the actions, thoughts or feelings?
- In what order (if any) do you create the inward and outward elements?

Can you write out a progressive list of steps in which the behaviours occur?
- When does it end? What brings it to a conclusion?

What did you learn?

Consider Alan, a fitness trainer. When Alan goes out with his mates, he can't 'help himself' and drinks until he passes out. He complains that he has no self-control to stop at one or two drinks. This repeated behaviour is having huge impacts on his life and how he sees himself—a healthy fitness trainer. He hates himself for doing this.

In working with Alan, we observed the following:

- Alan's outward actions included: aggression, incredible focus on consumption of alcohol, being loud, not listening to advice that he has had enough to drink and drinking to an almost comatose state.
- Alan's thoughts feelings and emotions were reported as: 'Nervous beforehand. Feel thirsty. Feel empowered and strong when I'm drinking. Feel happy. Sweat quite a bit. Think I'm popular and fitting in. Get angry when others try and stop me.'
- The trigger for the event appeared to be the combination of friends and availability of alcohol. Alan doesn't drink at home and can control himself at work functions.

- The behaviour ends when Alan can't get access to any more alcohol, he passes out, or he is alone when his friends have gone.

Unstuck Exercise #66: Decoding the problem state

After looking at Alan's responses, think about the following:
- What do you think might be the process for Alan's problem behaviour? Can you create a stepwise 'map' from the above information on his behaviour?
- If you were Alan, what part of the process would you try and change?
- What rules do you think Alan has?
- Which rules does he not apply to his problem that he applies elsewhere?

Creating maps for where you're stuck can be incredibly valuable. Creating a series of progressive steps from trigger to unwanted outcome allows you to objectively review the process and determine where – and how – it's not working.

Note that Alan's 'problem state' is specific. There are times when he applies valuable rules (work functions, when he is home) that he does not apply to the problem state. It is incredibly important when doing self-awareness work on processes that you stay highly specific.

As you will see later in the book, it's often in the exception that the solution lies. For example, what if Alan could apply his work drinking rules when he was in social situations? What if he could see 'social situations' as being a type of 'work'? [Isn't it true that Alan's friends and the people he meets could either be customers or could refer customers to him?] What would happen to his behaviour?

What To Do About It

Self-awareness is only the first step. Once you're aware of your responses from the internal and external perspective, you can begin the process of *insight*. The big danger here is that insight can lead directly to 'stories' and content. Which is exactly what we want to avoid.

Self-insight relates more to understanding the process in the wider context of which it's deployed. So, what triggers it? In what *specific* circumstances does it work, and in which does it not? What are the common factors you feel, see, think, hear or experience that may *predict* the behaviour?

Insight is about creating understanding, not stories, of what's going on. By creating a hypothesis, you can find a way to predict the outcome based on history. Once you have insight, you may then be able to identify any rules, limitations or drivers based on your belief systems or conditional field that may be impacting your choices.

Once you gain insight, you're now in a position to implement self-management – that is, deliberately changing the steps in the process, and your response to those triggers. Remember what we know – behaviours are open to adaptation and shaping. As we experiment with new ways and are rewarded with better outcomes, we can encode new beliefs, patterns, rules, and conditions – especially more nuanced ones.

Sometimes we don't know how to change. We haven't yet learnt. This is when seeking a teacher or a coach to help you move forward can be really valuable. What if you were to set change as a goal and approach it through the 12 steps outlined earlier in the book?

Unstuck Exercise #67: Deepening your insight

Take some time to answer the questions below. For each question, challenge yourself. Don't stop at the first superficial answer. Allow yourself to go deeper. Have the courage to push yourself into your 'darkest corners' so you gain the most out of this exercise.

Explore the following questions:
- How specifically do I judge myself and my value?
- What measures do I use to judge myself and others?
- What is my purpose? What is it important to me to be seen as?
- What standards do I always hold myself to? When do I let these slip?
- What are the 'should' and 'must' statements that drive my behaviour? What rules apply to how I live?

If you can, take time with this exercise. I would suggest doing this exercise over an extended period, perhaps a week. At the end of each day, note down in a journal what you've discovered from that day. How did your rules, judgements and frames of reference show up? How were they helpful or not? When were you uncomfortable?

What Makes Us Tick

Our vast storehouse (our conditional field) contains so many rules, beliefs and processes that it's often difficult to single out one driver or condition for one problematic behaviour or response. Instead, many things can influence our behaviours and responses – some are going to be more readily discovered than others. The more you stay out of 'story' and 'imagined self' —the easier it becomes.

Where Did It Come From?

The least valuable question you can ask is 'Where did it come from?'

This question takes you out of your process and into your story. Knowing that you apply certain values and rules to a circumstance allows you to examine these and decide if they're appropriate. However, deciding that 'I do this because I learned it from my Dad', or 'It was because I was bullied at school' may offer you comfort, or even an excuse, but it does not do anything to change it.

Regardless of where a pattern of behaviour, condition or rule started, unless you identify where it's NOW unhelpful – and then do something different NOW – you may remain stuck.

If you notice yourself disappearing into your story then it's time to stop, take a breath and simply be aware of what you're doing.

Chapter 10

Identity – Who Are You?

How we define ourselves – our identity – is a critical part of how we interpret our experience; how we set rules, conditions and expectations about what is possible. The question 'Who am I?' is often the basis of so much suffering and causes people to underappreciate themselvesand their experiences.

Who we think we are – and *who we think we should be* – sets up powerful boundaries and limitations in our lives.

Last chapter we looked at the versions of our 'self' – the subjective self (the parts of us that only we could know), the objective self (those parts that any external observer can know), and the actual self – which is both of these and so much more.

Yet, we can discover some parts of ourselves that we don't yet know through the process of self-awareness.

From Self to Identity

We can define *identity* as: how we describe and value our self.

This is strongly shaped by the things we *identify with*. This means that whilst the 'self' is the 'thing,' our identity is the evaluation of the 'self' in its contexts, especially by the groups we associate with, want to associate with and how we reference ourselves in relation to these groups.

How we define ourselves within groups creates a structure for how we value ourselves and create an 'identity picture' of who we are.

Factors such as:
- Are you in or out of a group?
- Are you a leader or on the fringe?
- Are you trusted and liked by other members?

How you describe your identity will alter the behaviours you believe are acceptable and valued by the group. It may be these self-imposed boundaries and limitations on your behaviour that work against your ability to achieve a goal – and therefore a key reason to why you're stuck.

Unstuck Exercise #68: Identity

Consider the following list of identities that people may take:
- Banker
- Politician
- Housewife
- Motorcycle gang member
- Priest
- Homeless person

For each person, ask yourself the following:
- How would they typically behave?
- What would you expect them to want?
- What would you expect them to never do?
- What would you expect that they would value?

What did you notice?

For most people, the way that they define their identity creates limits, rules, expectations, and conditions on many aspects of their experience. Notice that for different professions or circumstances, it is easy to describe boundaries and conditions to their behaviours? What if you are *inaccurately* doing this to yourself, creating limitations or conditions that don't serve you, and getting yourself stuck?

Unstuck Exercise #69: Defining yourself

Take a moment to clear your thoughts and ask yourself the following questions:
- Who do you want to be that you're not currently?
- How would you want others to describe you?

- Which group would you like to be identified as a 'typical' example of?

What did you notice as you completed this exercise?

In this exercise, your responses will describe the 'gap' between how you currently see yourself and who you potentially want to be.

Unstuck Exercise #70: Mind the Gap

Review the previous exercise. In particular, approach the review from the standpoint of 'impact.'

- What impact did your discoveries have on you?
- What did you notice regarding the thoughts and feelings it generated?
- What else did it bring up for you?

What did you notice about your 'desired identity' versus your current perceived identity from this process?

If your identity picture is positive, accurate and flexible, then the rules regarding how you feel, think and respond are all likely to be healthy. However, if you hold onto an identity picture that is limiting – you may be keeping yourself unnecessarily stuck. That is, imposing rules and limitations on what you do, what you believe that you're capable of and what you expect for yourself.

The likelihood is, that who you think you are; who you think you're not; who you want to be and who you don't, could be sitting squarely at the heart of much of the distress in your life.

Sometimes, when we allow these identity pictures to set limitations on our behaviours – or drive expectations of how we should behave – we get stuck. We may not even be aware that we are referencing these old, outdated constructs, or referencing pictures that aren't valuable anymore. They unconsciously set the rules around who we think we are and how we should behave.

Consider Robert. At one point in his life he was a 'student,' then a 'party boy,' then an 'athlete.' More recently, he is a 'business man.' In Robert's life, his vision and understanding of 'who he is' had to change many times. For Robert, understanding that we are always growing into – and out of –

versions of our self, and allowing our self-image to evolve was critical for him to change. Robert came to recognise that some of his old identities were outdated. He was no longer a 'party boy' and his behaviour at social functions needed to change dramatically to be congruent with 'senior executive and father.' Acting unconsciously from the old identities and behaviours that were valued and accepted – was now getting Robert into trouble. His current behaviours were simply unacceptable to his new circumstances, in had led to complaints at work and had the potential to end his career.

You may notice that you may sometimes act your best in one circumstance and at other times act in ways that's not appropriate for what you want to achieve now. Even with an idea of how you *want* to act, unhelpful patterns slip in, and sometimes it leads to regret (like Robert).

Through Robert understanding that he was fixed into old and outdated identity pictures, he could see how the behaviours he chose weren't appropriate (and later regretted). By updating his 'identity picture' for who he is now – and letting go of the older versions of himself, he was able to adapt his behaviour to the new context and become a valued and successful member within his workplace.

Valuing yourself and seeking more

Did you know that you're special? Start from the position that the chance of you *actually* being here is tiny. So much has gone *right* over millions of years for you to be here. The chances of you being you and being able to be self-aware and self-competent is at such long odds you couldn't bet on it. Even amongst the human race, you are special. If you can read this book and had a meal yesterday, you're one of only a few per cent of people in this group on the entire planet.

There are so many reasons for you to acknowledge that you are special or even 'lucky' amongst all the humans on Earth. You would think that once we understood this, we would be free from suffering and could relax and be happy, right? It appears not. But then, you wouldn't be human. We are geared to be social animals always seeking 'upward mobility,', and it is rare for people to be happy with their 'lot.' Instead, due to the ways we think and learn, we always strive for more. Your identity picture has a massive part to play in all of this.

Consider Martha. She wants to feel good about her life. Then she pulls up at the traffic lights, and the person next to her has a better car than she does. Before this, she thought her car was OK, but now she gets a little tickle of jealousy and an 'I'm not good enough to deserve a car like that' story starts. At work, she likes to do a good job and feels really good about completing the report for her boss. When she gets home, she settles in to watch some reality TV show, she sees a celebrity and wishes she looked 'as pretty as them.' And why can't she be famous and admired like that? She takes a look on social media and sees all the holidays and great things other people are doing, that she's not. It makes her feel upset, disappointed and even a little angry. For Martha, the 'gap' between *who we think we are*, and *who we want to be*, opens up and starts driving her thoughts, feelings, and behaviours.

Perhaps these are similar to the ones you noticed in the previous exercise?

Learning our identity

Your identity picture evolves and changes throughout your life.

Unstuck Exercise #71: Through the ages

Consider when you were seven years old.
- Which groups were important to you?
- Who did you want to be with?
- What have you grown out of?

Consider the same questions above, but you're fourteen. Think of how different the answers are. What about at age twenty-one? Or your current age?

Can you see how your identity reflects who you are and who you want to be, relative to your social situation at that point in time? Think how someone who is twenty-one would get on in life if they employed the identity pictures they had as a seven-year-old?

As we learn and grow, we shift between groups we think are important to us. As we take on new definitions (even labels) about who we think we are, and who we want to be 'a gap' opens up. Without consciously learning and adapting our 'identity picture' for who we are now, we rely on old, unconscious views of ourselves that keep us stuck.

Let's frame some things we've learnt so far throughout this book and see how they fit into forming our identity.

- When we first join a group that we feel is important to us, we get that rewarding hit of dopamine. Our brain can't tell the difference regarding the source of reward or punishment.
- The novelty effect comes into play – as we stay in the group, the reward diminishes, and we have to either change our place in the group or change groups to get the 'reward.'
- If we fear dropping out of the group, we receive a punishment signal (removal of reward), so will fight to stay in groups even if they're not in our best interests. Belonging is rewarded.
- We can use imagination to believe things about being in groups and punish ourselves for not being what we imagined.
- As situations change, so the groups that we hold as important also change. Important groups are more rewarding to be a part of.
- Sometimes how we behave in a group relates to how we see ourselves within the group. If we believe we need to act a certain way to belong, we will receive a reward for behaving that way (regardless of its appropriateness).

Let's go back and have a look at Martha:
- She imagines that she *should* have a car like that – and doesn't. This comparison causes a punishment.
- Martha has a view of herself as being a competent employee; she works hard to maintain this by completing the report for her boss and feeling good about it when she achieves it.

- Martha watches TV and thinks being a celebrity would be great. When she reviews her current identity, this causes distress.
- Martha's friends are all posting great stuff on social media, but she's just on the couch in her slippers. She wants all the good things that she sees in the pictures and stories, but when she examines her own existence, she can't see them.

All the comparisons Martha is making is on the basis of comparison: who she thinks she is versus who she thinks she should be or wants to be. The problem is that both of these states are essentially *imaginary*. Until she stops comparing these different identity states, she will continue to find the 'gap' and feel distress. She won't even fully know why she is feeling that way. Martha will remain stuck and not even know why.

Unstuck Exercise #72: The ideal you

Take the time to think about the following.

If the world were perfect:
- How would you describe yourself?
- What groups would you belong to?
- How would you be seen by others in those groups?

Now review your answers to the above questions:
- Take a moment and rate yourself out of ten for what you believe to be true.
- Consider what you've learnt about goal setting. Would you evaluate becoming these 'ideal' states as realistic, practical and valuable goals?

What did you learn?

Why do we do this to ourselves?

As you explore these questions, you may feel tension between how you see yourself and how you want to be seen. This internal 'pressure' has survival advantages in social animals as it drives social rules, culture, and hierarchy. Individuals in a troupe evaluate themselves against the group, and a pressure to 'conform' to the group norm is created so that the behaviours of all members is moderated for the benefit of the whole. In this context, the conditions on behaviour by the culture are readily seen. In any troupe, there are behaviours that are valued, and those that are shunned.

Things became even more complex for humans when they created societies. Gone is the simplicity of being only in or out of *one* group – rather, we are faced with many groups. These groups encourage individuals to have a range of identities and don't encourage us to understand ourselves outside these groups.

Consider Dougall. He was a very successful marketing director reporting to a supportive board in a large company. He was also a parent, a husband, a football team coach and a sibling to a troubled younger brother. Look at all the different 'versions' and identities Dougall had to manage to try and be 'successful' within each group. On top of this, Dougall carries a view of himself as a 'fraud' and 'not good enough,' so he never feels like he successfully belongs to any group. There was always a huge tension between how he wanted to be seen and how he perceived himself within each group. He felt great when he was made to feel a part of a group, but was always in fear of being left out. Dougall presented with social anxieties, anger management problems and sleep issues that stemmed from this gap of wanting to belong, but not feeling like he did.

Bringing the identity picture in line with our greater 'self'

If we were able to take a step back and allow ourselves to see our *self* and to reduce the social pressure around establishing our identities, imagine how much distress and suffering would be removed.

Understanding what drives our story and its impact on the behaviours we choose is important. So, too, is understanding how our identity story shapes our thinking and causes conflict between what we want versus what we aim for. When we understand these powerful elements, we are better placed to feel better and judge ourselves and our actions more appropriately.

When you become congruent, often the thoughts and feelings of being stuck no longer exist.

Why does being social matter so much?

Humans are highly social animals and belonging to a group is hardwired into us for survival. We seek to belong, and social contact is critical to our development and well-being. Think of all the 'tribes' that you belong to, or seek to belong to. Think of how your identities create a series of tribes that help you work out where you 'belong' in the world.

The psychology of groups is incredibly powerful, exerting significant behavioural pressures of individuals within groups, and groups as a whole. Pioneering work by social psychologists Henri Tajfel and John Turner in the 1970s and the 1980s became fundamental to believing that at our core humans are social creatures and a sense of belonging has significant impacts and implications.[8]

Our need to belong, and our drive for upward mobility, encourages people to establish 'reference groups' that we see ourselves relative to. These groups, and our ability to be recognised as part of these groups has a huge impact on how people judge their intrinsic value. Their identity and self-worth is often a direct link of how they perceive themselves relative to their chosen reference groups.

For example, I see so many small business people that have the reference group 'successful entrepreneur'. They often don't feel that they've made it, but work so hard to belong to this group. I see new mums who want to belong in the 'capable parent' reference group (even though, like almost every parent, there are moments of overwhelm and challenge!). I see people who want to be in a reference group that could be termed 'happy' and others who want to be

---

[8] Tajfel, H., & Turner, J. C. (1979). "An integrative theory of intergroup conflict". In W. G. Austin & S. Worchel. The social psychology of intergroup relations. Monterey, CA: Brooks/Cole. pp. 33–47.

Tajfel, H., & Turner, J. C. (1986). "The social identity theory of intergroup behaviour". In S. Worchel & W. G. Austin. Psychology of Intergroup Relations. Chicago, IL: Nelson-Hall. pp. 7–24.

Turner, John; Oakes, Penny (1986). "The significance of the social identity concept for social psychology with reference to individualism, interactionism and social influence". *British Journal of Social Psychology.* 25 (3): 237–252.

'normal.' There are people who want to be 'loved' or 'famous' – as if these are defined groups that one can buy an entry ticket for.

In fact, there are competing 'imaginations' at play. The first is the imaginary boundaries that the person places on the reference group. How specifically do they decide when they have 'made it'? How do they know that this belief is true, or even reasonable? Imagine the small business owner wanting to be a 'successful entrepreneur.' How specifically do they achieve this? The truth is that they're likely to be setting their boundary conditions (what it means to be a part of the group) on imaginary rules or milestones they create, or comparatively to people they think fit the bill. Imagine how hard it would be for me to be a 'successful entrepreneur' if my role model for having made it was Sir Richard Branson? Think of all of the things he has achieved – If I set that as my benchmark, how difficult will it be for me to make it? Equally, if the mother of the crying infant has her reference point as the mythical 'perfect' mother seen in the magazines. Imagine the challenge for her to 'make it.'

The other 'imaginary element' in play is that the person might not truly value themselves. Think about Dougall, who considers himself a 'fraud' or 'not good enough.' Regardless of how well he performs, he's always undervaluing his own efforts. In the end, the combination of mythical entry criteria and inappropriate ability to judge himself creates a massive 'gap' driven by imaginary identities.

Is that the right group for you?

Unstuck Exercise #73: Testing the group.

Think of some things you aspire to be.

    For each, imagine there's a group of people who represent this aspiration.
- Who is an example of someone who is 'in' the group, or a leader of that group?
- Which specific behaviours do you need to demonstrate to be part of the group?
- What value to you is there being part of this group?

- What specific things do you need to achieve to 'join the club'?
- What cost or trade-offs will this have for you?
- How do you decide if that group is valuable and relevant for you?

What did you notice?

Perhaps you identified that:
- The group you want to belong to is difficult to define – you have no specific metrics or ideas about how you would belong.
- The group really has no value to you.
- The cost of getting there is higher than you're prepared to pay.
- You really don't have the capability to reach the boundary of joining the group.

If any of these are true, perhaps it is time to think about different 'target groups' to aim for, even just in the way that you describe them to yourself.

Learning to belong

As social animals, we have been working all our lives to feel like we belong. Just like you learnt your identity, you also learnt how to belong. Depending on where you did or didn't fit in – you may have developed specific habits and behaviours of how you attempted to fit in. You will have also developed some baseline expectations of yourself in groups; these may have led to unconscious evaluations and judgements about your ability to truly belong.

These behaviours, evaluations, and expectations you have all form part of your conditional field. Without conscious thought, you will access these constructs as you approach social circumstances. If these constructs are outdated or poorly formed, you may feel stuck. Remember Dougall – he had a deep sense that he was a 'fraud' and didn't belong. Maybe he learned this because he thought he was 'lucky' to be accepted into a group, or maybe he hasn't got a valuable way of deciding how to trust himself and others. This can have a dramatic effect on how Dougall feels about himself or the actions that he's prepared to take to generate the feeling of belonging.

It takes two to tango

Consider that any social situation contains two or more people. Humans have such powerful imaginations that they can even be alone and have to manage how they feel and how they act through 'imaginary' social frames.

Imagine two people attempting to socialise like Dougall. Both driven to belong but believing they don't deserve to. Now consider a room full of people, each with their self-beliefs, identity pictures, imagined reference groups and learned behaviours of how they should belong. Imagine how complex it becomes when we attempt to get people to connect deeply and work together?

Consider coming together in such a group, with so many different levels of dynamics in play. Once we have worked out if we are 'in' or 'out' of the group, we then work hard to define if we are 'up' or 'down' in the hierarchy of the group. The higher up the pecking order, the safer we feel and the and more control we feel over the group. The bottom of the pecking order and we're easily excluded, and our position in the group remains tenuous at best. There's also massive uncertainty at the bottom of the order because our position in the group is completely out of our control. As we form groups, there's a lot of pressure to work out our 'place' within the group. Some people feel a compelling need to be at the centre of everything, while others need to belong (even on the fringes), but not be in the lead. With every person having their own identity picture and social needs, is it any wonder that getting teams to overcome their personal stuff and work together can be a challenge?

Relational Dynamics – people, relating in groups

Imagine you were standing on the San Diego docks during the height of the Cold War. From here, US submarines departed with large crews for three-month rotations to cruise off the coast of Russia. They aimed to cruise in silent, cramped conditions, with their finger poised on the 'big red button.' If the signal came, they would have to fire nuclear missiles at Russia – and knowingly 'destroy the world.' All the time, they were being hunted by the Russians, so they had to be silent and stealthy in their actions. If you thought this was a stressful work environment, you would be right!

A strange thing happened. When the crews arrived back, some of them would be in fist fights and open conflict on the docks. Others would plan to catch up at Bob's for a barbecue and beer and see each other as friends and trusted colleagues outside of the sub. Under the stress of the Cold War, how could the Navy recruit or develop teams that were less like the first group, and more like the second? The problem for the Navy was to work out how to create crews that would work well together before they were sent. It's obvious to understand that even under strong discipline and stressful environments, harmonious teams work better in every way. What makes one team gel and the other self-destruct?

Helping people get along and thrive as a team has been extensively researched. During the Korean War in 1952, Will Shutz was recalled into the U.S. Navy and undertook research on understanding and predicting how any given group of people would work together. This resulted in his first book, *FIRO: A Three-Dimensional Theory of Interpersonal Behavior*. From this research, it's possible to take away a few simple commonalities that would have made a huge difference to the process of that submarine team selection.

The crux of Shutz's research suggests that the team function comes down to individuals within the group getting what they want and need from the group they're in, and furthermore that it's aligned with their imagined and perceived identities. Simply put, people have unique needs and wants from relationships and social circumstances. People who have these needs and wants met then function at a higher level within the group, those who do not have their needs met are likely to act in unconscious defensive ways in an attempt to get their needs met, often at the expense of team performance.

The three drivers of social behaviour that everyone seeks are **inclusion, control, and openness.**

Have you heard of the group development idea that teams go through 'forming,' 'storming' and 'norming' stages, before they become 'performing'?[9] These can be reflected on to this simplistic model of social drivers.

Inclusion: People first seek to find their place relative to the amount of inclusion (in or out) of a group.

Control: Next, they work out who is competent and in control of what's in the group. E.g., up or down the ranking.

Openness: Finally, they have to decide how much they can share with others – or, how open they can be with members of the group (trusted/distrusted).

Once all of these social drivers are sorted, people can begin operating without the need to 'act out' to get their social needs met, the team can move into 'performing.' When clarity of the social drivers is gained, and the person feels that they're getting what they need relative to their own identity within the group, they move into their 'comfort zone' and are able to bring forth their best.

Everyone has a preference for where they want to be in the group, depending on how they see themselves and their place within the group. Some people need to be the most significant, some need to show off their competence and some need to share lots of information and build trust before they're comfortable. Conversely, there are others that feel they don't really belong, or that standing out or taking control would be very scary. These people often hide at the edges of the group and feel happiest there.

Unstuck Exercise #74: Group behaviours

Consider some groups you're involved with. Think about the following:
- Which people in those groups act or behave in ways to draw attention to themselves (for good or bad reasons)?
- Which people in those groups seek to exert control over the group?

---

9 Tuckman, Bruce W (1965). *"Developmental sequence in small groups"*. *Psychological Bulletin. 63 (6): 384–399.* doi:10.1037/h0022100. PMID 14314073.

- Which people go out of their way to demonstrate how competent they are?
- Which people in those groups share a lot of information? Which people share little or nothing?
- How do you behave in these groups?

What did you notice as you completed this exercise? How do you reflect on the different ways people feel driven to behave to ensure that they can satisfy their need to belong?

Unstuck Exercise #75: What are your hidden identity drivers?

Consider the following three circumstances. In doing so, respond honestly to what you would feel or how you would act. Imagine for each situation that it's a 'normal' day when you're feeling pretty good and stress-free. Pay attention to the thoughts and feelings you have to each scenario and use this as information to help answer the question.

Notice how your answers are also context dependent – for example, how you act at a sporting club is often different to how you act in the office or workplace.

Remember, there are no right or wrong answers – only what is true for you.

Scenario 1 – Inclusion:

Imagine you're at work and there's a group getting together in the coffee room or kitchen. It is a social get together. As you sit at your desk, notice how you feel.

Do you:
A) Feel an urge to join the group – perhaps feeling left out or are asking yourself why you're not invited?
B) Feel ambivalent and not fussed one way or another?
C) Feel relieved that you don't have to engage with the group and happy to not be invited?

Scenario 2 – Control:

There's a decision that needs to be made. There are a couple of clear choices with consequences for each that will affect the entire group you're with.

Do you:

A) Feel compelled to make the decision, arguing for your view and imposing yourself strongly on the process?

B) Feel you can take it or leave it. You will add something if you think it's valuable but not driven to be involved in the decision making.

C) Want to avoid having your opinion asked and are more than happy for others to make the decision. In fact, you feel uncomfortable if you were asked to make the decision for the group.

Scenario 3 – Openness:

You have to work closely with a colleague. As you approach them on a Monday morning, are you the type of person who:

A) Wants to discuss all the personal details of their weekend, what has happened in the soap operas or at the football? Do you want to talk about everything that's going on in their lives?

B) Happy to cover off a bit of small talk, but don't get overly engaged with them?

C) Wants to talk about tasks – being 'business only' in your conversation and feel uncomfortable discussing things from outside of work?

SCORING

Look at the answers you have marked. Each answer can be classified as the following:

A = High for that characteristic
B = Medium for that characteristic
C = Low for that characteristic

Remember, there's no right or wrong, only your preference. This is critical because a preference implies that you can operate in other ways – it's just that you prefer to act in certain ways in certain situations.

What did you notice as you completed this exercise?

Unstuck Exercise #76: Reflection on social drivers

Take some time and space to clear your thoughts.

Consider now the 'social drivers' you perhaps discovered in the previous exercise. Think about how you behave in social situations.

Pay attention to each one:

- **Inclusion and significance.** Where do you notice your desire to be more or less significant in a group? What behaviours do you notice?
- **Competence and control.** Where do you notice that your desire for more or less competence or control in a group drives your behaviour? What behaviours do you notice?
- **Openness and trust.** Where do you notice your need for more or less openness or trust? What behaviours do you notice?

Now imagine that you were conscious of the needs that drive the behaviours. What if you could take a moment to sit with what you've learned or noticed, and decide if those behaviours are valuable, or derived from outdated identity pictures stored in your conditional field?

Unconscious preferences drive behaviour

Our preferences – if unconscious – act as drivers of behaviour. If we feel that we're not getting our needs met, we can act out in all sorts of ways to get our needs met and feel comfortable that our identity is 'correct.' If we're aware of our needs and wants, and can recognise the feelings they create that drive behaviour – we can intervene and choose higher quality, goal-orientated actions instead.

Michael, Thomas, Peter, and Mohammad

Consider Thomas and Peter. Peter was a hotshot employee brought in from another department to work under Thomas. However, within a couple of months, Thomas was moaning that Peter was not really working out. Peter was also feeling that things were not working. Peter came to see me about this problem. We reviewed Peter's interactions with Thomas. We examined Peter's potential preferences for how much he included Tom, how much control he gave Tom over his work and how open he was with Tom with information that he shared.

Redesigning the framework of the relationship was as simple as making small choices to interact differently. First, Peter realised that he was not including Thomas (who had a seriously high inclusion need). Peter changed this behaviour and started to invite Thomas to lots of meetings, copied him in on irrelevant emails and invited him to team get-togethers, where he previously thought Thomas had no time for these things. Peter also made sure that Thomas felt more control and did this by running things past him and simply asking 'Is this OK to go?' As a result, Thomas felt back in control of what was going on in the department.

Peter had previously assumed that all of this would burden Thomas and he was simply getting on with his job. Next, Peter identified that when he would ask about personal topics (for example, Thomas's weekend or his daughter's ballet), it made Thomas uncomfortable. So, he reverted to talking about 'business only,', and Thomas was a lot more comfortable.

The outcome? Seven days after Peter changed his approach, Thomas reported to the leadership team the significant 'turn-around' in Peter and that he should be considered for a substantial promotion that was on offer.

Consider Michael. Michael has a messy backstory, but at the heart, he is a man that was bullied and ignored as a kid. As a result, he desired to be significant. More than that, he is driven to be seen as significant regardless of its value or impact on others. Michael started this by hitting the gym (and, I suspect, some steroids) to become 'big,' got tattoos and a big motorbike. He felt he could be significant by throwing his weight around and use his tough guy image. Michael was driven to get a high-powered job and revelled in telling everyone how much money he earned.

When Michael felt uncomfortable or thinks people aren't paying enough attention to him, he switches to a different set of behaviours. He becomes loud, rude and insulting. He tells off-colour jokes, uses inappropriate language and becomes physically threatening so that he becomes 'significant.' Later, Michael will often say he is 'just having a joke' or makes up an excuse for what he's done, but it's a pattern he repeats with monotonous regularity. It has cost Michael friends and invitations. People can't tolerate his sexist, racist and demeaning jokes, poor language or threatening physical actions.

In essence, Michael is seeking to be significant – the 'urge' flipping him into behavioural patterns to get the feeling (and the dopamine reward) of being significant, noticed and important. Though he gets the 'hit' he's craving; it comes at a massive cost to his relationships and opportunities. What if Michael could be aware of this urge – this need to feel significant – and to sit with it and choose better behaviours to achieve it?

After some time working together, Michael came to realise that he's not his history – rather he has choices for the actions he takes. He learnt that his need to be significant can be expressed in so many other ways. Through experimenting with new behaviours in different contexts, Michael came to recognise his defensive behaviours, and learnt how to manage them. Michael is now seen as a gentle giant – a guy you can trust and a great guy to have at a party.

Consider Mohammed. Raised in a strict Muslim family in Indonesia, he attended school and university in the US and completing a PhD in marketing. I observed Mohammed while in a meeting, it appeared he felt the need to demonstrate his competence by spending the first 15 minutes of a 30 minute 'pitch' explaining the ins and outs of marketing. It was clear that he was fulfilling his need to demonstrate competence and show 'control' through being the expert. However, Mohammed completely missed the signals from the room. He had annoyed the board members who also thought they were 'experts' in marketing. They felt their time was being wasted and thought they were being 'lectured to' by a junior. Needless to say, Mohammed's pitch was shot down. After working with Mohammed on what happened, we identified that by unknowingly trying to feed his own need, he had driven the board members into a defensive state. We also discussed why he felt the need to demonstrate competence. Following our sessions, and with new skills in learning how to read the room, Mohammed pitched his idea at the next board meeting – it was approved.

Unstuck Exercise #77: Your drives

Go back to the previous exercise and note where you have high or low values for any of the three basic relational drivers.

- What do you notice when your needs or wants are not met? Describe your feelings and thoughts.
- What behaviours seem to always happen (that perhaps you regret or don't like afterwards) that could be linked to these drivers?
- For each, take some time to think of three other ways you could feel more significant, in control or trusted. Experiment doing these things consciously the next time you're in a small group.

Defensive Mindsets

When we select a behaviour (either consciously or unconsciously), we can do so to further our aims, or to defend our current identity picture. If we operate with an open approach to achieving our goals, we're likely to experiment and learn with new behaviours as we attempt to reach it. However, when we operate to serve our outdated identity picture, we often use known and historic behaviours that we associate (unconsciously) with what we know fits that identity. The most common time people act to defend their identity is when they feel under stress – either because they're not getting what they 'need' or because they unconsciously revert to old patterns of behaviour.

Have you ever chastised yourself after you've reacted? Have you experienced getting angry, avoiding a circumstance or overthinking a situation and said, 'Damn, I always react like that!' And no matter how many times you tell yourself to behave differently—you find yourself repeating the old behaviour? Guess what? Your defensive behaviours were triggered, and you reacted to serve your identity picture. We all do it – but the big questions are how we can be aware of the situations that trigger us? How we can act differently and intervene with a more valuable strategy?

Also, being aware of other's identity needs is an important step in building social skills. If you're not aware of what people's social needs are, you can trigger them to act defensively to protect their identity view, and your relationship with them can get stuck.

Often, the social drivers change to serve the defense of our identity. For example, my need for control might massively increase when I'm stressed. Or, I might have a lower inclusion need as I believe I need to 'do it all myself.' Or, I might decrease the amount of information I share as I go into a less trusting state.

Exercise # 78: Changing states

Go back to the exercise regarding your social drivers.
- Answer the questions again from the standpoint of imagining yourself when you're highly stressed, under pressure and not feeling at your best.
- Write down what scores you get for 'Inclusion,' 'Control' and 'Openness' (high, medium and low). Take a moment and compare this to the way you rated your preferences in this exercise. Has anything changed?

What did you learn from doing this exercise?

When you are aware of the ways you behave to defend your identity picture, it gives you the opportunity to intervene. It allows you to recognise that you're no longer acting to serve your goals, and instead you're acting unconsciously to serve the identity picture.

Unstuck Exercise #79: What's your state?

Review your social preferences in your 'goal oriented' state and your 'identity defensive' state. What are the major differences?

How do these show up in the ways that you...
- Behave toward yourself?
- Behave with others?
- In specific things you do to get your needs met?

What did you learn from this exercise?

Reflection leading to learning and adaption of behaviour

Within our conditional field exists both the view of the 'self' and the 'identity' we've developed over time. As you can see from the examples presented here, these have the ability to unconsciously drive behaviour. Whilst we might feel that we're getting what we need from a social situation, the beliefs aren't valuable or relevant to achieving our outcomes. This is most likely to happen when the view we have of our self is old and outdated.

Consider Michael again, who had developed a view of himself completely outdated for the circumstances he finds himself in. As he came to terms with how he changed over time, he was able to update and redefine his view live a happier, healthier life. We're always learning and evolving, and our behaviours adapt as our circumstances change. If our view of self does not keep up, is it any wonder that we sometimes act in non-valuable ways, and get ourselves stuck?

Consider Dennis. He noticed that part of his self-view was that he 'didn't like confrontation.' This set him up to be avoid any conflict at work or home. Though he wanted to be seen as a successful and capable business leader, the view tucked away in his conditional field, was getting him stuck. Any time there was an issue to be dealt with, he found a way to avoid it. This unnecessarily escalated many issues in the workplace, causing him to be viewed as an ineffectual leader. Working with Dennis, we investigated what he understood by the term 'confrontation.' To do this, I asked the questions 'What specifically do you mean by confrontation?' and 'How do you know that confrontation cannot also be valuable?'. These questions challenged the automatic, unconscious beliefs he had consigned to his conditional field where for whatever reason, 'confrontation' had to be avoided at all costs as it was dangerous to him.

To move forward, we reframed the concept of confrontation as 'negotiation' and explored how he had developed so many more skills and capabilities to be able to cope with, manage and get value from 'confrontation' in his life.

Dennis had negotiated so many things with himself, including when and how to successfully avoid confrontation. As we explored these skills, it became clear that the 'rules' around confrontation that he derived from his self-image were no longer relevant. Dennis had a whole set of skills he could artfully use to negotiate with people no matter how 'confronting' they attempted to be.

Unstuck Exercise #80: No judgement

What beliefs do you hold about yourself that conflict with the identities you want to assume?

It can be useful to look for the places in your life that create tension or distress. Take the time to think of situations that feel stressful, create negative thoughts or feelings or that you want to avoid. Note these down. For each situation, ask yourself the following:

- How can you positively describe your skills and capabilities in this area? What are you good at and how can these skills be used?
- Where is your self-view not valid anymore? What examples can you provide that demonstrate the old self is no longer true?
- If there was no judgement of self, what would stop you getting what you wanted?

What did you notice?

Let's go back to Dennis. In his case, he wanted to be a successful business leader but felt his fear of confrontation meant that he could never do it well. He noticed that he was good at negotiation and had lots of examples where he had negotiated very successfully – even under pressure and in hostile circumstances. By reframing confrontation as negotiation, identifying his strengths and examples of success, Dennis was able to shift his self-view relative to his identity goal state. With some specific goal setting, he was then able to approach work with a new sense of self – including a new appreciation for his strengths and a plan to move forward. His old self-view was no longer valid and would not hold him back anymore.

Who Am I?

Instead of asking the existential question "Who am I?" perhaps start by considering that who you are *right now* is actually the sum of *what* you do and *how* you do it.

People with low self-esteem are often continuously 'pinging' those around them, looking to see that they belong. Their capability to make decisions for themselves and about themselves often comes second to getting their social needs met from others. In particular, they act in ways to confirm who they want others to think they are, rather than acting consciously for their own goals and benefits. This self-identity gap unconsciously drives behaviour and can lead to actions that simply get the person stuck. As I stated before, and it bears repeating:

You are either acting toward your goals or to defend your identity picture.

One is a path forward in your life; the other will keep you stuck.

Your Critical Voice

One way to help unravel the self-identity gap is to listen to your critical voice: the voice in your head that is an absolute expert on passing judgement about you.

Unstuck Exercise #81: Whose voice is it?

Take the time to reflect on the following.

- What does the voice in your head say to you, about you?
- When does your critical voice get the loudest?
- When is it quiet?

Your critical voice is a key to understanding much about your self-definition and your identity. Sometimes it speaks in your own voice or uses the voice of someone from your past. For some people, it is a constant, nagging challenge about who they want to be, versus who this voice thinks they should be.

In truth, the critical voice is just a behaviour that you've developed. It only works because of the tension created between who you want to be *now*, and a past view that you believe you are. When you spend some time on the exercise above, it allows insight into some strong belief patterns about your identity. Take time to listen with curiosity. What if, instead of trying to suppress the critical voice, or simply listening and believing it, you were able to say to yourself 'That's interesting'?

Based upon this, you can now sit with the critical voice knowing the following:

- That it represents a version of your identity from the past, rather than who you are today.
- That you get to listen to it and then choose your response (such as, follow what it says, ignore it or integrate it into information before you take action).
- That you can update the critical voice to have more realistic and valuable insights. By taking action and proving to yourself that you are different to what the critical voice suggests, you start to change the voice.

The critical voice is only one way you get to see your self-description. If you're prepared to be honest with yourself (which can be challenging and scary for people), you might find that in different circumstances, you actually have strong identity views of yourself. For example, how do you see yourself at work, in a relationship, as a parent, as a sports person or as a friend?

Unstuck Exercise #82: The definition of you

Reflect on all the different roles you play in society: boss, worker, father, husband, friend.

For each role:
- List all the 'descriptions' you have about yourself in that circumstance or role.
- How many of these are:
  a. Out of date?
  b. Not effective in the current context (created in a different context)?
  c. Rigid in your belief?

What did you learn from this exercise?

If we go back to the idea expressed earlier in the chapter, defining yourself at seven years old and later at fourteen. Notice how differently you define yourself now compared to either of those two points in time. If you could change your identity and your self-definition throughout your life, who said that you couldn't do it by choice, right now? If you can re-define yourself, then perhaps the problems become malleable and open to adaption into newer, more valuable behaviours, thoughts, and patterns.

Your identity lags behind your context and your behaviour. As you approach a new context, you do so with an identity picture already formed. As you apply yourself to the circumstance – and perhaps learn new behaviours – you may also gain a modified insight about yourself or your identity. Only then will it change. Therefore, you can be certain that your identity is never truly current. Often it can be absolutely healthy and fit-for-purpose. However, by simply appreciating that it's always lagging your current experience means that it can be useful to consciously review your identity picture when you're stuck, as it may not be serving you well.

It can be scary to give up what you know and deeply believe about yourself. There's a measure of security and safety in holding onto your stuff – it is YOUR stuff after all, and often the comfort of the discomfort that you know seems much safer than the anything thing else. It can be difficult to get yourself unstuck by redefining yourself. But this is where I invite you to experiment. An experiment is really a low-risk trial. You're not 'committing' to the outcome, you're simply running a small test to see what happens.

Unstuck Exercise #83: Upgrade yourself

Return to the list of positive and negative self-descriptions. Ask yourself the following:
- Which ones are no longer relevant and need updating?
- For the ones you want to update, think of a description of yourself that's not a big stretch from where you are now, but represents a positive shift.
- What would you be doing (specifically) if you were to 'earn' that description?
- Experiment now with doing that. What happens? Does your experience improve? Is this updated self-description more relevant to who you are now and where you're now going?
- What would happen if you were to adopt it as an 'upgrade' on the old self-view?

What did you learn?

Becoming Authentic

Authenticity is nothing more than working to have a realistic identity picture of ourselves and be comfortable in expressing that through our actions and behaviours. Being authentic means closing the gap between our outdated self-assessments and our objective, conscious and real self-assessments. A key component of authenticity comes from self-awareness and insight – to realise when the descriptions we're using are not valuable.

Consider Davey, who has been to many self-help workshops and wants to be authentic. He acts completely from his old identity picture and drives everyone he works with crazy. After he acts in ways that he doesn't like, he then flies into tears and suggests that he 'acts the way he does' because he's more authentic than everyone else. When I called Davey out on his behaviour and suggested that he wasn't being authentic but defending his identity picture and then using the 'poor me' play – Davey got it. He realised that being authentic meant updating his identity picture rather than finding novel ways to defend it.

Being authentic is not an excuse, it's more a declaration to the self that it is OK to be on a learning journey, to see where the identity picture may need updating. To be willing to be open with yourself and others about your actions.

When we are authentic, we have not become 'transcendent' to some perfect way of being. No one is perfect – we all have feelings, thoughts, urges, and desires. We are all perfectly imperfect – and imperfectly perfect. That is the human condition. However, our aim is not to be transcendent; our aim is to simply be more authentic.

What if authenticity was simply an alignment with the self and identity? What if authenticity was being aware of yourself and having a clear view of your groups and identities and being comfortable with the 'gaps' as you work to overcome them?

Authenticity starts with self-awareness.

Authenticity comes from appreciating that *who you truly are in the world is always in front of the identity picture you carry of yourself.* As you work towards your goals – even towards changing who you are now, to become more of who you want to become – then your identity picture needs to come along on the journey of change too.

Chapter 11

Sticky Labels

As part of their identity picture, people often create 'category level' labels for their experiences and processes. These labels are shorthand ways of explaining complex phenomena in a simple word or phrase.

Earlier we explored the idea that we can observe at different levels: from 'Category' labels to more nuanced descriptions. We also explored the nature of identity and its powerful impact on our behaviours.

In this chapter, we'll bring these two elements together and see how the way we choose to describe our experience and connect this to our identity can make a huge difference staying stuck or moving forward.

Labels are occasionally helpful, but mostly they form part of our identity and serve to provide fixed views of ourselves. When we create labels and stick them firmly to our identity picture, they can be hard to remove.

The Care Instructions on The Label

Go to your cupboard and select an item of clothing. Look at the label and read what it says. You may notice:

- What it's made from.
- How to care for the item, such as washing or cleaning instructions.
- It may have very clear guidelines of how not to treat the piece of clothing (such as 'do not dry clean')

These things don't change across the lifetime of the item.

Unlike a shirt, people don't come with a label saying what they are or with care instructions about the best way to deal with them. People also evolve and are very different across their lifetimes. What they do and how they do it will adapt and change throughout their life.

Recall the last time you bathed or had a shower. When you were drying yourself, did you notice a little tag attached somewhere? Maybe under your arm, along your flank or the back of your neck? No? That's because you are not an article of clothing with only one way of being cared for.

Having a label is great if you're a shirt, but it's useless for humans. Why? Well, you're a highly complex individual – made up of many different characteristics, habits, values, and behaviours. You were born without a label and care instructions because it isn't needed. The question you should ask yourself is: If you came into this world without a label, why do you work so hard to attach labels to yourself regarding your problems?

Think of some of the common labels we attach to ourselves:
- I'm depressed
- I'm an anxious person
- I am not good enough
- I'm not likeable, and people don't like me
- I'm a fraud
- There is something wrong with me

Do any of these labels sound or feel familiar for you?

The way you develop labels and then attach them to your identity is a key factor in how you unconsciously create beliefs about your limits and possibilities. As your experiences change, your identity evolves, yet the labels we create often stick to our identity like an anchor keeping you stuck. An opportunity to review your labels might be what sets you free.

Unstuck Exercise #84: What's on your label?

Take a few moments to think about the labels you give yourself.

Make a list of all the labels you have. The more honest you are, the more helpful it will be.

What Is a Label and Why Do We Use Them?

Labels put a name to a complex array of human traits and experiences in a way to make 'meaning' out of them. We use labels to make complex phenomena simple. It reduces the ambiguity and gives the comfort of understanding.

A label is an entirely personal construct. Two different people can have the same 'label' to describe similar things, but sitting underneath this description are a wide range of different experiences.

When two people report being 'severely depressed' (the label) the nature, reasons, severity, and processes of their depression can be completely different.

Whilst a label can give you the comfort of 'knowing,' it can reduce the complexity and specificity to a single piece of jargon—a label.

Consider Daisy. She had been suffering from a range of experiences for some time. She went to her GP, who saw her for 6 minutes. In that time, her GP gave her the diagnosis of 'depression' and prescribed something to help her with it.

At first, getting the label was a relief for Daisy. Now all of her 'suffering' made sense. She could now ascribe all of the things that she experienced in this way and bundle them up as 'depression.' Over time, this label took on more and more meaning and became associated with who she was – she stuck the label on her identity. Soon she would think about her whole experience through the label – 'Oh, I can't do that, I'm depressed,' or she would screen out her experiences – 'No, I didn't enjoy myself, how could I, I'm depressed?'

Daisy's label impacted her identity picture and became fixed and rigid. She wanted to be 'free' of her depression, but it now seemed like removing part of her.

Labels not only tell you what things and people are, they tell you what you're not. If you label yourself 'depressed,' what does that mean that you're *not*? What does that mean that you *can't* be? Think of how Daisy decided she couldn't have been happy because she was depressed. If she wants to be happy, what sort of bind does this put Daisy in?

Like a shirt, a good label comes with appropriate care instructions. In medicine, constellations of symptoms are diagnosed (you have a cold, an infection, or appendicitis) – in other words, given a label. A diagnosis is really useful when there is a 'category level' solution for the problem. If you have an infection, then a proven treatment would be antibiotics. If you have a virus, then bed rest, fluids and fever management would be recommended as antibiotics are proven to be ineffective. The right label can lead to the right treatment. However, if you have Ebola virus, it might require a different treatment to a common cold virus. Sometimes the label does not provide enough information to really understand and deal with it effectively.

Unstuck Exercise #85: Who gave you the label?

One of the big issues in 'accepting' being labelled (diagnosed) is who we let label us. Consider the labels you listed in the earlier exercise. Go down the list and write down who gave you each label. When you have completed that, ask yourself the following:

- Was the person who gave you the label 'qualified' to do so?
- What the person's motivation in giving you that label?
- Is that label useful and appropriate? Is it even still relevant?
- When has the label been reviewed or changed?

What did you learn?

Labels are valuable when they provide understanding and simplify things into categories. Labels are not useful when we attach them to our identities, use them as excuses, or forget that there's a complex array of personal experiences that make up that label. Labels are useful when they provide a path to treatment, and the person's experience mirrors what has been proven to be effectively treated or managed in similar cases. A label is unhelpful when it consigns a person to a rigid, unchangeable view of their experience with no path out.

Consider the labels you have adopted. What if, just as you have adapted to so many different circumstances in the past, you were open to adapting again?

What if you could change the label to something more specific? Or change the contents of the label (the experiences you bundle up inside it) or change the meaning of the label, so that it represents something different?

Unstuck Exercise #86: Adapting the label

Consider a label you adopted at some time in the past:
- In what ways is the world different now from then?
- In what ways have your personal circumstances changed?
- What else could you call your experiences, that you currently include in that label?
- What experiences could you now see as not belonging to that label?
- What else could that label now mean to you?

What did you notice as you did this exercise?

Perhaps you started to see that the label is more flexible than you thought.

Labels Are Simplifications and Globalisations

When Daisy walked into my office and said, 'I'm depressed,' she was overlooking so much more about herself. She is not 'depressed' – she is Daisy. Daisy has such a rich range of experiences, learning, and skills that she has to overlook to see herself only as 'depressed.' It's sometimes surprising to clients' when I say something along the lines of 'No you're not, you're Daisy, and that is so much more than just depressed.'

Your label globalises your specific and unique experiences. It acts as a powerful filter to exclude non-conforming facts from your life story. People will say, 'I have been depressed for 10 years,', and you have to wonder, have they been depressed for every single moment of it? When you dig into their story, you find that there have been happy times, angry times, motivated times and all sorts of experiences that are not 'depression.' However, having the label dictates the filter. Often even when you locate an exception to the label, such as, 'Oh, yeah. That holiday was wonderful', the person still wants their story to confirm the label. It's only when they break the label from their story, and their story from reality, that they can see they've been creating unhelpful ways to process their experience. And now, they can choose something different.

The Four Stages of Experience

Regardless of the label, there are four levels of experience. Each one has greater and greater levels of filtering, bias and self-reinforced storytelling associated with it. Let's take a look.

Level 1. Experience

At this level, you recognise there's a range of experiences, each one individual and specific. The one you focus on now can be labelled according to the specific, individual and context-dependent nature of what's happening. For example, 'I experienced an urge to gamble,' or 'I experienced some fear when I saw that spider.' We all have experiences— both positive and negative. This is simply identifying 'what happened.'

Level 2. Suffering

At this level, we start to globalise the experience. For example, 'I suffer a fear of spiders.' In this frame, it is almost something 'external' to you that has happened to you or that you have 'caught' (like a virus). Think about this statement: 'I crave chocolate.' Notice the 'urge' to eat chocolate has now become something greater – a craving. In a way, we start a process of ignoring the immediacy and uniqueness of the experience and turn it into a globalised, abstract thing (for example, suffer or cravings). Like a virus or an infection, we are open to taking our 'medicine' and getting rid of it. It is no longer just an experience, but something more.

Level 3. Possession

The experience now becomes objectified. It becomes a tangible thing you have. For example, 'I have a spider phobia' or 'I have anxiety.' Just like owning a bicycle, you now possess it, and it possesses you. It becomes a 'thing' in its own right. So, when the doctor says, 'You have depression,' it's as if you now possess this 'thing' that you have to carry around with you like a tattoo. Imagine if the doctor instead, said, 'You're experiencing some sadness, low mood, and reduced motivation right now.' How different is that regarding describing your experience?

Level 4. Identification

At this level, we create a label and attach it to our identity. For example, 'I'm an ice addict,' 'I'm bipolar' or 'I'm depressed.' The problem is, we then reduce ourselves to the label and it becomes either a part of our identity, or our whole identity, and we become only a part. We know that our identity has the ability to shape and constrain our behaviours. Think of how you might change your behaviour when you shift from 'occasionally feeling sadness,' to operating from 'I'm depressed.'

Trading down

If labels are globalised, non-specific shorthand descriptions of our experience, what if we could 'trade down'? What if we could shift from experiencing our issue at Level 4 to see it at Level 1? Consider the following examples of how labels can be traded down:

I'm depressed – I have depression – I suffer from sadness – I'm experiencing some unpleasant emotions and feelings right now.

I'm anxious – I have anxiety – I suffer from worries – I am experiencing some fear in relation to some things in my life.

I'm an addict – I have an addiction – I suffer from cravings – I am experiencing an urge to act in ways I don't like.

I'm not good enough – I have times where I'm not good enough – I suffer from feelings of not being good enough – I experience moments when I believe that I don't measure up to a standard I have set on a specific topic.

I'm a fraud – I have a fear that people will find me out – I suffer from feelings that I am a pretender – I sometimes experience a feeling that others overvalue my inputs, more than I value them myself.

In each case, be aware of the change that occurs: specificity is added, perhaps even context. The experience is described for what it is, rather than simply categorised. Even more important, it harks back to one of the first ideas in the book: It shifts the issue from being a part of you to simply how you are going about it.

Unstuck Exercise #87: Trading down

Perform the trading down exercise on your issue. Regardless of whether your issue is a 'Level 4' or 'Level 3' write down what you say to label your circumstance.

- Start by writing down the 'label' for where you're stuck.
- As you shift down levels, what do you notice thoughts, feelings, projections or beliefs?
- Does your issue lessens? If so, how has it changed?
- Does your issue seems less permanent or fixed? If so, what do you notice about its permanence?
- Can you perhaps create space to explore the exceptions – or even space to see alternate possibilities? What happens when you do?

What did you learn from doing this exercise?

Doing the above exercise is powerful from a neurological point of view. The posterior cingulate cortex (PCC) region of the brain strongly fires when we self-reference, that is, think or talk about ourselves. When people meditate, this area quietens down. By shifting down from identity to experience, we are encouraging this part of the brain to settle and become less active, because we're no longer focusing on ourselves, but instead, focusing on the experience. We are encouraging the deep emotional connections to shut up and the pre-frontal cortex (the logical thinking part of the brain) to wake up and get involved. We are shifting from 'subject' to 'object' and thereby creating space and decreasing the 'pressure' on ourselves. We are encouraging thinking and problem-solving associated with pre-frontal cortex activity. At Level 1, we may find a solution for our experiential problem. At Level 4, we are stuck only thinking about ourselves.

The Power of Language

Part of shifting down is also about changing the language, in particular, shifting from global language to specific language. The language we use can either cement an issue or open the space for possibility. As we describe an experience in terms of specificity and context, it suggests there may be other specifics or contexts that we could explore. When we remain in global frames of language (always/never/must etc) there's no possibility of an alternative, and we're providing certainty that there's no other option.

Unstuck Exercise #88: Mind your language

Catch yourself. Every time that you catch yourself applying an unhelpful label in your thoughts or in your language—STOP!

- When this happens, use the trading down Unstuck Exercise #83.
- Pay attention to global modifiers (always/never/must/I am) and consider how you can replace them with context-specific experience descriptions.
- Feel what happens when you apply this alternate language.

What did you learn from doing this exercise?

You may become aware of how powerful your language is in framing your experience. Consider what happened when Nelson Mandela stopped being a 'terrorist' and started being a 'freedom fighter.' What happens when you stop being 'bipolar' and start having a range of experiences that are 'challenging to regulate'?

In the previous chapter, we investigated how the critical voice is a powerful tool employed by your outdated identity. The language used by your critical voice is also worth paying attention to, as it will give a clear indication of what 'labels' are stuck to your identity, and what things are just experiences.

Unstuck Exercise #89: Decoding the critical voice

Listen to your internal voice. When it shifts into a critical, labelling or destructive mode, listen to the language it (you) speaks.

- If you need to, write it down.
- Now take the time to change the language. Shift down from labels to descriptions of experience. Replace these terms in your own narrative and repeat them to yourself.

What do you notice?

Opening a door of possibility

It's simply amazing the way people's experiences change based on the labels given. There are many stories of people that have carried an incorrect medical diagnosis around for years, and across many practitioners until someone decided to look at the individual, rather than the label. Then, with a simple but personally appropriate treatment, they were able to overcome their problem. There have been cases reported where a person was diagnosed as a 'hypochondriac' – and every subsequent doctor that treated them saw only in this frame. When the patient finally found a doctor that looked at the individual, the 'real diagnosis' was found.

The way we approach getting unstuck can be highly dependent on the label we're given. If someone is given the label of 'hypochondriac' consider the way others will approach them and view them. How do people respond when they're diagnosed with 'depression' or 'anxiety,' and how does it change the way they approach their 'cures' or attempts to get unstuck?

What if we took the labels we're given as mere 'suggestions' rather than fixed definitions? What if we used them as a useful base but remain flexible enough to see the individual behind or in front of the label? When we truly believe that the individual is bigger than their label we invite the possibility that they have more experiences, more resources, and more skills than we allow ourselves to see. We can recognise these individual elements may be either contributing to their problem or be used as powerful resources to move beyond their label and problem.

Working backwards

Sometimes, our behaviours are a great way of seeing when our labels are getting in the way. When you notice behaviours that get you stuck – or you have the feeling of your defensive 'pre-programmed behaviours' it can be useful to work backwards from your story to your labels.

Unstuck Exercise #90: Working backwards from behaviours

Take a moment and find a place to relax, perhaps sit or lie somewhere quiet.

Imagine observing yourself at a time when you were stressed. Notice the unconscious behaviours that came into play, and how it feels when that happens.

From your safe distance of comfort, pay attention to the story you are telling yourself about why you're acting like you are. Pay attention to labels you find emerging in your story.

Take a moment, and from this safe distance, notice the labels and consider what you have learned. Can you see yourself beyond these labels? Or trade them down to changeable descriptions of past experiences?

What did you notice, experience and learn as you ran this process?

As you go through the process of identifying the labels you attach to yourself, and the ones others have stuck there, and you've accepted, you can begin to find ways to shift to a more updated view of yourself.

By peeling these labels off your identity and updating what needs to be updated, you can start to move forward.

You are more than your problem. You are more than your label.

Whilst a label can be useful for understanding a range of symptoms, it ignores the incredible additional values, skills, and experiences you have that aren't associated with that label. Your unique 'care instructions' can be based on what works with people who share the same label as you; but remember — you are unique and it's often your individual motivations, skills, and experiences that rapidly get you unstuck

Chapter 12

Deciding How to Decide

We have seen how our identity and the labels we apply, impact our behaviours and the outcomes we get. The link between the conditional field—what we do and what we get is based on the *decisions that we make*. This link – how we decide to decide – is often the overlooked key to getting unstuck and moving forward with your life.

We make decisions all the time – about big important things as well as tiny, mundane things. Some choices we sweat over, and perhaps put a lot of time into, and others we make almost unconsciously.

- Consider Andy, who got good grades in school and received offers to attend 3 different universities. How should he decide which one to attend?
- What about Roger, who wants to go out with his mates on a Friday night but has an assignment to finish. How should he decide what to do?
- And Samantha, she sees a handsome man across the bar and might like to get to know him better. She may give him her phone number. How should she decide?
- Consider Ashley. She is in the shower. How should she decide when it is time to get out?

Unstuck Exercise #91: How do you decide?

Look at the four cases listed above.

For each, take time to reflect on *how* you would make the decision each person has to make. Write it down.

How easy or hard was it to make the decision?

What did you learn from doing this exercise?

Note that the exercise asked how would you make the decision – not what decision would you make. This is a critical distinction in getting unstuck, as you will soon see.

Unstuck Exercise #92: Flipping the decision

Return to the four cases and the decision that you would have made. What would you need to know to flip the decision that you made to another choice?

What did you notice from this exercise?

Note that this exercise starts to identify what are the most important pieces of information in the decision-making process, for you (but maybe not for someone else).

The makings of a great decision:

To make a great decision, there are a few things needed:
- A high-quality question.
- An understanding of the options that are possible.
- Knowledge of the criteria used for selecting between options.
- A way to rank the criteria to deal with conflicting options.
- Information to prove when the criteria is met.
- A way of testing the reality of the choice.
- Commitment to the choice and taking action.

Does this seem excessive? For many decisions in your life, you don't take any time with the process of making a decision. You simply allow your learned patterns from your conditional field to make the decision for you. When you're eating a square of chocolate, you're able to easily decide you should put it into your mouth and not into your ear. So many actions are driven by decisions that are taken within 'sub-routines.' Over your life, as you've learned processes, the decision points on when to start, stop, or how to act are already built into these routines.

As I have said many times, when your unconscious processes are working for you, that's great. When they're not, and you're stuck, it's time to have a look and see how they can be adapted to work better.

Decision Making as a Critical Skill

The quality of your decisions will dramatically impact the quality of your experience.

Decision making is a key skill; one that we think we have mastered as we live our lives. However, unless we are making high-quality decisions for the circumstance we're in, we're likely to remain stuck.

Problems with decision making

If we return to the list of how we make a decision, we can see all the ways it can go wrong. For example, what if we are asking poor questions – either the wrong question for the situation, a poorly framed question, or simply not asking any question at all? What if we are not aware of the options? What if we had terrible criteria or no way to decide between the importance of the criteria? What if our sources of information were poor? What if we can't test the decision in reality? What if we don't take action?

Making decisions has many touchpoints where things can go wrong – but also many places where only a small change might get us moving again.

Fast track to poor decisions

There are reliable ways to make poor decisions. I'm sure that you can look at the list and see how errors in the decision-making process can cause issues. An even bigger problem is when people decide not to decide – and even allow the decision to be made by others on their behalf. There are times when this may be a valuable strategy (for example, you want your doctor to make a decision about a diagnosis because they're expert), but most often the strategy of avoidance or 'mindless delegation' brings a low-quality result.

Deciding not to decide – or to delegate the decision – is a decision in itself. Simply allowing this to happen without understanding this as a choice you're making is a fast track to poor outcomes.

To avoid making important decisions poorly, it's useful to remember that you get to choose your response to the circumstance you're in. That choice requires a decision. Imagine the difference if you choose your responses via high-quality decision making, rather than just 'rolling the dice'?

Over time you may have developed great decision-making processes that are simply not relevant anymore, or that work elsewhere in your life. Blindly applying decision processes to the wrong questions or in the wrong context is a sure-fire way to get stuck. One of the most common ways for this to occur is through unconscious process initiation. Sometimes we make high-quality decisions that then initiate an unconscious 'programmed sequence' of actions. The problem that gets us stuck may lie in the subtle decisions buried inside this automated process.

Consider Amanda. She wants to discuss a pay increase with her boss. She's been doing excellent work, and on all criteria, she deserves it. She builds up the courage to initiate the conversation. Until now, her decision making has been high quality. When Amanda meets her boss, she feels uncomfortable. She responds by making herself small. She chooses not to stand her ground, because she has been doing that most of her life. Her boss says no and Amanda accepts it, rather than negotiating. In this case, Amanda started with a great process, but once she hit a 'trigger scenario' it led to a cascade of actions – and decisions – which were poor for the context and circumstance. All of the decisions within her process were poor – and as we will see were likely unconscious and driven by her conditional field elements such as her identity picture and beliefs.

Whilst we can take time to understand the importance of a decision, the implementation of a process that's outdated date or out of context will surely stop us achieving our outcome. If we understand that after each decision (and action) there emerges another decision (and action) in a sequence, it can be useful to think about this chain of events where we are getting ourselves stuck. The series of circumstances reinforces that:

Decision making is done best when it is both *specific* and *in context*.

You can leave it to chance, or you can use logical processes to help make the highest quality decisions for the specific circumstances you're in. As we explore the process of decision making, I will highlight some areas that are quick routes to making poor quality decisions and what you can do about them.

Exploring questions

If you ask the wrong question, you're guaranteed to get the wrong answer. We have previously explored the idea that you're either operating towards your goals or in defence of your identity picture. Consider when what you want conflicts with your identity picture, your labels and all of the other 'stuff' in your conditional field. Without realising it, your first decision point will change everything – do you act toward your goal, or defend your identity picture?

It may seem like a silly question – of course, you *want* to act towards your goal. However, when we allow this question to be answered without conscious effort, the likelihood is our identity picture will drive the decision, and you're already heading down the wrong path.

In the chapter on identity, we saw how the unconscious social drivers of Michael, Mohammed, Thomas and Peter directed their behaviours. In each case, the first decision they had to make was left to their unconscious. Without thinking it through and seeing what the 'first question' really was, they unconsciously followed the old path.

Unstuck Exercise #93: The first question:

Consider where you're stuck. Take a moment to test if you've answered the first question:

Am I acting towards my goals or to protect my identity picture?

How much effort did you put into deciding to act as you have, or was it unconscious?

What did you learn from this exercise?

Once you're past the first question, the way you frame your question becomes critical.

Consider what we explored in the 12 steps to Goal Setting, much of that learning also applies here. Allowing yourself to ask a well-framed question, with positive attributes that's both relevant and in context, will provide a great starting point for making high-quality decisions.

Once you think you have a well-framed question for decision making, look back and ask yourself if it's really serving your goal or just defending your identity. We can be great at fooling ourselves into believing that we're doing serves us when in fact it's really protecting the old identity picture. Pay attention to when you find yourself justifying a poor option. Perhaps, then it might be valuable to update your identity picture or even trade down your labels?

Exploring options

Once you have a high-quality question framed toward your goal – it's important to have a sense of what your options are. Sometimes we can feel stuck because we look at the options and don't like any. What if there were:

- Additional options you hadn't thought of yet?
- Options identified that could be reshaped toward better outcomes?
- Meanings that could be redefined?

We could also check if the options we being influenced by the identity picture, labels or other aspects within the conditional field?

It can be useful to take your time and consider what other options there might be, including how subtle changes in these options could create a range of different potential outcomes. As you take time – pay attention to any thoughts or feelings that come up to indicate if you're defending your identity rather than moving toward your goal. This can absolutely clarify the decision that you're making.

Doing nothing is sometimes a valuable option – and sometimes it is not.

Often one of the options at our disposal is 'business as usual' or 'do nothing.' In some cases, this is a valuable alternative to consider. In medicine, for example, there are several conditions where 'watch and wait' is the best strategy, as acting has consequences (like side effects) that may not be better than living with the condition for the time being. However, if you want to overcome where you're stuck, then doing nothing will only keep you right where you are.

Please be aware there is a big difference between *choosing to do nothing* and using a defensive, avoidant strategy. One is taken as a logical, well-thought-through position, whereas the other is simply a reactive response driven by your conditional field. When you find yourself not deciding, or not acting, it can be useful to check in – was that purposeful, or avoidant?

Evolution not revolution

Making a decision between options often requires change. Sometimes, when we consider each option at a decision point, we can see that they may require 'revolutions' (complete changes) in what we're doing. When you notice this, perhaps you can also ask yourself what the 'evolution' (small change) would be that you could take first, or is the revolution required? Sometimes it's the small adjustments that change things the most, as revolutions often require major changes and can be just too big to tackle all at once. Can you identify small steps to make the change path easier?

Cost and benefit of the options

Every option has costs and consequences. Once we identify the options available, it can be useful to define the costs and consequences of taking that option. Some may seem like great value; others may suddenly appear too expensive. Sometimes we look at the options, and both seem too 'expensive.' We don't like either option. When this happens, it is a recipe for staying stuck. Perhaps the question to ask is 'which is the better of these two options', and 'once I make the choice, which has the better upside?' Seeing beyond the initial investment to what can emerge can make a choice between difficult options more palatable.

What are the criteria?

A key question is: How do you decide how you will decide?

Imagine we come up with three really great options around a decision. How do I now choose between the three?

Consider Chris, who was on the board of a small company, but nothing seemed to get done when they had meetings. I was asked to sit in and observe, and it quickly became apparent that the group had no decision-making process or rules. They all 'thought' they knew when a decision was being taken, and how it was taken, but the truth was very different.

I ran a session about 'how would they decide'? – in particular, how would they know when a decision was required, what was their process, what would happen afterwards and which new processes were introduced. We immediately implemented:

- When someone thought a decision was due, they would make a proposal. "I propose…" This created the new language to be used.
- The group would then consider the options and expand on them as necessary.
- The board decided it would be majority vote, with the chair (major shareholder) having veto.
- The decision would be written in the minutes and the action items delegated to the appropriate board member to oversee and report back.

More decisions were made in the next 30 minutes than had been made in the last 3 years. The board were thrilled that they were making so much progress.

Unless you know how to decide, it's easy to get stuck.

A great way to help make a decision is to decide what is important to you in the decision, use these as the key criteria for the decision, then order these in importance.

Let's return to the first example of Andy, selecting a university to study at. When I asked him 'HHow will you decide between the options?' His response was 'I don't know.' We explored what was important to him about going to university and discovered his order of importance.

These being:
- Quality of the program on offer
- Reputation of the program and the school in the industry
- Opportunities for a scholarship
- Where his friends were going
- Distance from home (local or international)

For someone else, their order might be very different. As Andy worked through these factors, he discovered that some of his choices ranked highly on some factors, and lower on others. In the end, he was able to see how two of the three options were really close on the top 2 factors, and it came down to third and fourth level criteria to separate them.

Imagine if Andy had simply 'trusted his gut,' and based it on something unconscious like the quality of the brochure developed by that university, or how he 'felt' about being accepted there?

Deciding how to decide – and how to evaluate the criteria or factors in the decision are really important skills. Once you've worked out your criteria, it's important to source high-quality information so you can evaluate your options in valuable way.

Information or insight?

One of the most common places that people get stuck in decision making is confusing information and insight. Information is data that's available for us to process. Insight is what we learn from the data – it's the meaning we make from the data that informs our actions. Information helps us look critically at the criteria we set, whereas insight leaps past all of this to offer an answer.

The Validity of Your Thoughts

People so often trust something because it has come from a thought they've had. Often this thought is intense, or they've had the thought repeatedly. Does this make it valuable, or even true? Does this mean that the thought offers insight and meaning, or simply information? If it's only information, what is it providing information about?

Unstuck Exercise #94: Information or insight?

Take a few moments and answer the following questions:
- What thought should I pay attention to?
- What feeling should I trust?

Understanding that thoughts – regardless how often you have them, or how intense they seem are only one source of information allowing us to use in our decision making. Making the error of believing that any thought has 'insight' is a sure way to get yourself stuck.

One of the most common areas that cause people problems is that they don't know that their thoughts are only information. They believe that their thoughts have special meaning, and they have no valuable strategy to decide whether to pay attention to the thought, or not. Often, they simply respond to the thought because it is repetitive or intense. Yet, like any other piece of information, you get to choose how, and even if, you process it to create insight.

Unstuck Exercise #95: Five minutes of freedom

Take a moment to sit quietly to do this exercise. Imagine you can be an observer of your thoughts. Stand back and watch as thoughts pop into your head. Just watch – don't do anything with them. Let the thoughts float on by and dissolve as other thoughts arrive. For any thought that arises, simply say to yourself, 'That's interesting.' Be curious about what might come next rather than the need to know. Take some time and if a thought wants to be 'grabbed,' then again, just notice this. Continue this exercise for five minutes (or longer if you wish).

What did you notice?

Often, simply realising that you have the choice over which thought you pay attention to can be a powerful trigger for gaining relief from overthinking, intense thoughts and rumination. To put all of this into perspective, it can be valuable to understand a little more about where thoughts come from.

A primer on where your thoughts come from

The information processing model of the brain[10] has proposed that a thought is created as your brain attempts to 'connect the dots' between experiences, imagination, emotions, our conditional field drivers and what's currently happening. Many factors come into play in creating a thought: what you're focusing on, what's relevant, what it connects to your memory, what other thoughts are occurring and much more. The thought that is produced could be about anything, including being completely disconnected from what's actually going on right now. It could be about something real, like an apple, or something completely imaginary, like a superhero eating a banana.

Whatever 'thought' that's created through this non-exact 'join the dots' exercise drops into your working memory. This is part of your short-term memory and acts as a register to hold information that might be important to process. The working memory has a limited capacity, holding just seven (or between five and nine) 'chunks' of information at any time.[11] A thought can either be processed (used to create insight), rehearsed, or else it simply dissolves in less than half a second. Information that's not actively maintained through processing or rehearsal simply fade from the register to make room for other things.

A popular myth is that we have 60,000 – 90,000 thoughts every day. Whilst this has not been scientifically proven, it speaks to the understanding that people are very busy in their heads. With the short-term register rapidly turning over thoughts – including letting them dissolve – this number gives

---

10 Baddeley, Cowan and others
11 Miller, 1956

us at least an insight into the nature of thinking. Our brains create a lot of thoughts, most of which we simply do nothing with. We just let them go.

Think of a situation where you're driving down a busy street, and you see all sorts of different shops, people, dogs, cars, etc. These can trigger any number of different thoughts. However, if we don't do anything with this thought (rehearse or process it in some way), it vanishes and makes room for whatever comes next. For example, if you try and remember driving to work, you might find it's not possible to remember everything you saw or the thoughts you generated on the way. Thoughts that you had on that drive, if they weren't relevant, simply dissolved away. Thoughts that provided useful information could contribute to the process of thinking, whilst useless thoughts can just fade away.

Have you ever realised that any thought could just be garbage?

Thoughts Versus Thinking

There is a massive difference between thoughts and thinking

Thoughts are the random bits of information that drop into your working memory. Thinking, on the other hand, is actively processing information (including thoughts) based on a known goal or purpose. When you are 'thinking' about something, it implies that you are actively using your cognitive processes in a positive, goal-oriented way.

If you're thinking, you possess the capability to notice thoughts as information and to determine if they fit with the goal you're are trying to reach. You retain the capability to let 'junk thoughts' or irrelevancies simply dissolve and to grab onto thoughts of value as they occur. On the other hand, if you're not thinking but simply responding to each thought as if they were real, meaningful or powerful, can you see how this is a recipe for getting stuck?

Unstuck Exercise #96: Five more minutes of freedom

Return to Unstuck Exercise #91. This time, however, as you relax observe your thoughts, recognise that your 'observer' has control. They can choose to notice the thoughts and just let them go. They can choose to see a thought from a distance and simply find it interesting. They can choose that a thought might be valuable and start a process of thinking. Take a few minutes to observe your thoughts. Recognise and play with the control you now have.

What did you notice?

When you allow yourself to view thoughts as simply 'information' available rather than some sort of powerful internal directive, it can create a sense of freedom – and the choice to stop being immersed in thoughts. Recognising that thoughts may or may not add value to your thinking means that you get to decide if they provide meaningful data or simply repetitive, intrusive nonsense that interferes with your ability to move toward your goal.

Feelings as information

If thoughts are just information, then can we interpret feelings in the same way? Previously we've seen how the gap between what we want and what we're experiencing often creates 'feelings' that drive our behaviour. When we allow the feeling to drive behaviour, rather than to use it as a source of additional information, we're setting ourselves up to get stuck.

Unstuck Exercise #97: Feelings as data points

- How do you decide which feeling to pay attention to?
- How do you decide which action you should take based upon your feelings?

What did you notice about your responses?

Often people are unaware that they have the capability to make choices regarding paying attention to feelings, or not. This can serve as a challenge – and sometimes a revelation to them.

Feelings are produced by thoughts we have. We can have particularly strong feelings when we are driven to protect our identity picture, or when something in our conditional field (like our beliefs) are challenged.

If you misinterpret your feelings as insight – if you use your feelings to take important decisions – then you are likely to get stuck. The process of 'emotional reasoning,' a term first coined by Aaron Beck, the father of Cognitive Behavioural Therapy, is where you use your feelings to make your decisions.

I love the idea that 'courage is not the absence of fear, but feeling the fear and taking a well-chosen action anyway.' Courage is the opposite of emotional reasoning, where 'how I feel determines the actions I take.'

Let me be clear from the outset: how you FEEL has almost nothing to do with making the best decision in a circumstance. Allow me to demonstrate this it to you.

Case 1: Callum has to have a knee operation. These days, knee surgeries are like a production line. The patients are queued up, sedated and operated on one at a time. The nurse says to the surgeon, 'This is Mr Smith. We're doing an arthroscope on his right knee.' Imagine if the surgeon replied, 'Hmmm, I have done six knees this morning. I don't *feel* like doing another. In fact, I haven't removed a gall bladder in a while. I *feel* like doing one of those. Pass me the scalpel!'

In the case, it's critical that how the doctor acts is *completely separate from how he feels*.

Case 2: Sally is driving in traffic when all of a sudden—another driver cuts in front of her without indicating. Sally has to slam on her brakes to avoid hitting them. She *feels* incredibly frustrated. If she acts on her feeling, she would likely toot her horn, engage in aggressive behaviour, maybe even follow the driver and get out of the car. A classic road rage incident.

In this case, Sally could also choose to *act* in a way that serves her goals. She can stay in her lane, stay on the speed limit and keep driving to her destination safely. Therefore, how she *acts* needs to be completely independent of how she *feels*.

Case 3: Krishna wants to secure a good job. He has landed an interview but *feels* like he's not good enough for the position. If he trusts this 'feeling,' he might decide that he shouldn't go to the interview. This would be a sure-fire way to guarantee that he will NEVER get what he wants. On the contrary, if he recognises the feeling but chooses to go to the interview and present himself in a competent and professional manner to the best of his ability, he has a chance of securing his dream job.

As can been seen, how you *act* has to be completely different from how you *feel*. Taking action towards your goals allows you to move forward, learn and evolve. Acting from your feelings only reinforces and increases the negative feelings that you experience, rather than relieving them.

In each of these cases acting from 'feelings' not only gets the person stuck but amplifies the issues and the negative feelings. However, allowing your feelings to be 'information' provides data on what's going on inside of you, and in particular your identity picture, labels, and conditional field.

Unstuck Exercise #98: Tuning in and observing

Take a moment to find a comfortable place to sit or lie down.

- When you're comfortable, allow yourself to remember a time when you had strong feelings – anger, frustration, excitement or whatever.
- Take time to observe yourself having those feelings. What if you could allow the feeling to emerge and to just note it – perhaps saying to yourself 'that's interesting' and simply be aware of the feeling.
- If that feeling was information about something going on in your conditional field, what might it be?

What did you notice as you performed this exercise?

Consider David. He was really struggling with his work. It was taking such a toll on him that even driving to the office was a terrible experience. In a session, I suggested the 'that's interesting' observational technique. Hypnotically, we tracked his journey to work, identifying all of the markers that gave him intense, negative feelings. For David, there was a certain sign on the highway, a particular bridge and swiping his card to get into the carpark. We practiced the 'that's interesting' stance. In the next session, David said he had almost turned it into a game – he noticed when approaching the markers on his journey, he felt completely different. As he repeated it, he noticed how he could observe the feeling and be OK. Then he started looking forward to the markers, knowing that he could quell the feeling by not being taken over by it. The change in David was incredible – he had a strategy for allowing feelings to be only information and this completely weakened their grip on controlling his experience.

Intuition: The shortcut to emotional reasoning

Earlier in the book we discussed the unconscious processes known as heuristics. These shortcuts are valuable to help us get to the 'nearly right' answers, most of the time. As a specific type of heuristic, Daniel Kahneman researched the value of intuition – and importantly where it causes issues for those relying on it.

Intuition is rarely valuable. It's unlikely that if you're using intuition to guide your choices, you should be. Only a very small percentage of the population have a useful intuition, and it's not about the person, but the circumstance and experience.

Intuition has been extensively studied. What we know about it is this:

- Intuition is the process of detecting small cues from the environment, often in ways out of our conscious awareness.
- Intuition relies on the summation of a bunch small cues to accurately predict a future event associated with those cues.
- Intuition relies on heuristics and biases – in particular, what cues are predictive of a specific outcome, and which are not.
- The person needs extensive experience in both receiving the environmental cues and the predicted event for the value of the intuition to develop.
- The activation of the intuition relies on the subtle cues summating and triggering an accurate 'prediction' of an event – often represented in a feeling or thought that they then act on.
- Most intuition is difficult to break down into its component parts and happens in the heat of the moment.

There are clear examples where intuition can be developed, such as:
- A firefighter who has an intuition of a building collapse because they have detected a range of cues from the burning building. Having been to identical circumstance many times, the detection of cues is left to unconscious heuristics. The predictive value of the cues is high, and the context-specific.
- A police officer that detects cues from a dangerous circumstance is able to take action, based upon extensive experience and training of such events.
- A mother who knows that their baby is going to cry. They may not consciously know why, but the physical cues or small sounds are strongly predictive that crying will shortly follow.

Unstuck Exercise #99: Intuition

Consider your intuition. Ask yourself the following:
- How strong do you believe your intuition is?
- How much do you rely on your intuition to make decisions?
- What evidence do you have of your intuition working for you?
- What are the boundaries in which your intuition should be listened to? That is, what repeated situations are there where you are expert at picking up cues that matter?

One of the ways people attempt to justify using their feelings to make decisions is to call it 'using their intuition.' However, this is simply creating an excuse for using poor decision-making processes and employing a range of low-quality heuristics that often lead to unhelpful outcomes. The problem is that people rely on emotional reasoning – dressed up as 'intuition' – far too often. It is a key reason why people get stuck.

Context: The key to making intuition work for you

Intuition is only valuable in context. Take the three cases listed above and move the players to other circumstances. Would it be reasonable for the fireman to predict the crying baby? Or the policeman to predict the building collapse?

Or the mother to predict danger in a crime scene? In fact, take a mother and give them a different baby. The truth is, the mother has a far smaller chance of predicting crying in a stranger's baby than in their own child. The predictive abilities of each person drops to the same as the rest of the population – even to the same as pure chance, when not in their specific 'knowledge zone' and context.

This is the key problem with intuition. Unless you're operating in the very tight and repeatable contexts in which your intuition was trained, it is useless. In fact, it may even become dangerous as you rely on it to make decisions that you simply shouldn't. What people will often do is develop a 'reasonable' intuition in a narrow band of expertise. Part of this process will rely on 'having a feeling' relating to the situation. The problem arises when they have a feeling (the same, or only similar) during *other* decision-making processes. They then 'believe' that their intuition is working for them and start making decisions based upon this.

Rather than making a logical decision or using reasonable cues for predicting outcomes, they simply forego this for a reliance on an illogical, ill-formed and incorrect belief in intuition. Previously they may have had a feeling which led to a good outcome, however now every time they get that feeling they believe it predicts a great outcome in whatever they're doing. Can you see how this is a recipe for making poor-quality decisions?

What makes this even worse is the heuristic of confirmation bias. People will review what happened in a circumstance, and those events that confirm their belief — 'I got a great outcome. I had that 'intuition,', and therefore it worked!' is remembered. Examples that don't confirm this belief are ignored. Often, where intuition failed it's often ascribed to another cause – such as being someone else's fault. In this way, they build up a false picture to the benefit of their intuitive sense.

Consider Sarah, a senior executive who believes she makes great decisions. She thinks that her intuition serves her well. Instead of using a decision-making process and focusing on the facts or data in the context and specific scenario, she searches for that 'feeling.' If she feels it, she makes the call. Sarah is making an 'emotional reasoning' judgement and calling it her 'gut feel' or 'intuition.' As the circumstances change, her ability to make a good decision using this approach reduces to pure chance.

When Sarah became frustrated with her performance at work, I taught her how to decide how to decide – that is, a high-quality decision-making process. Once she saw how she was delegating a critical business decision to a 'feeling,' she realised that she was actually putting the business in jeopardy.

At best, intuitive feelings are no more than additional information. If the person doesn't ask *why* they're feeling that feeling, and blindly trust it—the quality of the decision will be unreliable, and likely deliver poor outcomes.

Not knowing

An important part of decision making is that it often happens when we don't have all of the facts, and often can't discover them. We have to make decisions under the pressure of uncertainty. We simply cannot know all of the information, or how the decision will play out.

Being comfortable with uncertainty is a key skill that everyone needs to operate in the world. With so much that we're not in control of and cannot know; there's always going to be uncertainty. Uncertainty often drives a feeling of fear, which feeds back into emotional reasoning (and often leads to avoidance and other strategies to remove the uncertainty). Being clear on what you can know and what you can't – and how much information is enough to make the best decision – are critical parts of good decision-making processes.

Unstuck Exercise #100: Uncertainty and you

Think of something that is uncertain in its outcome. Perhaps something that has a big impact on you. Consider the following:
- Notice the feelings, thoughts, and questions that it raises within you.
- Where do you feel these things?
- Out of ten, how would you rate the level of discomfort this creates?
- In what ways does this uncertainty impact your actions, thoughts, and decision-making?

What do you notice?

By mapping the way that uncertainty affects you, you can become aware of the drive and discomfort it creates. By recognising this, it's possible to understand yourself and see when you're falling into the trap of seeking 'magical certainty' within yourself to remove this discomfort.

What if you can sit with the discomfort and still make a high-quality decision?

What will happen next?

What would happen if you took that decision? Once you have made a decision, it can be valuable to stop and reflect on that decision. Take the time to imagine 'what if' you had taken that decision and were acting on it? As you do this, you may notice things you missed on the first pass or information that wasn't included in the initial decision-making process. If you need to, you can feed that back into your process and get an even better decision. Once you can look ahead and see the path that leads to your goal, it's time to get moving.

Taking action

A decision without action is a waste of effort. If you have decided how to decide and used a high-quality decision process, then perhaps what emerges is the best decision possible for you at that time. We don't have the ability to know the future. We can only make the best decision in this moment relative to where we are and the goals we want to achieve. Once that decision is in, then all that is left is action.

Sometimes regardless of the decision we take, we still may not have the capability to act. I draw your attention back to the behavioural outcomes formula and the 12-step goal setting process – are you really prepared to take the actions that make the decision real?

Toward Better Decision Making

High-quality decisions come from deciding how to decide. By having a great process and consciously making decisions in service of your goals you can shift away from the fundamental errors that humans make and free yourself once and for all.

Unstuck Exercise #101: Better decision making

What you should do when you're stuck:

Start by defining a great question, or even make a 'proposal' to yourself on the issue.
- Write it down

Take the time to explore all of the options
- What have you already considered?
- What options seem 'bad' – how can you change them up to make them better?
- What would someone else consider?
- What happens if you do nothing?
- What small changes could you make in what you are already doing?

Write down the options that emerge.

Next, consider what is important to you in the decision.
- Can you write down and put in order of important factors you want to make that decision?
- What information do you need for the criteria, so the answer now presents itself?
- What information can you not know (and be OK in the uncertainty?)
- What thoughts and feelings are coming up?
- Are these thoughts and feelings valuable, or indicating some pressure to act from your identity picture?

What decision now emerges?

Explore what would it be like to take that decision – what do you learn?
- What actions are you now going to have to take? Can you test that they are possible and probable for you?

Decision making is a learnable skill. When we make decisions based upon defending our outdated identity picture, we're likely to get stuck.

The ability to make great decisions – and to know that you're able to make decisions – leads many people to moving forward in their lives.

Chapter 13

Discriminations That Matter

In his book *The Discriminating Therapist*, Dr Michael Yapok suggests that *'One good "how" question can bring into sharp focus what the person doesn't know that is hurting him or her.'* When we make decisions or discriminations, we often do so without knowing *how* we're making that choice. We often don't consciously know that:

- We're even making that decision or discrimination.
- That the choice is one we have control over.
- That *how* we are making the decision is learned, and that we can shape this learning, or learn something else to replace it.
- That the decisions and discriminations are often unconsciously based on non-valuable beliefs, processes, and rules from our conditional field.

What if you could consciously change the decisions that cause you to be stuck? To follow Dr Yapko's advice, first, we have to bring them into sharp focus.

A workshop with Michael

One of the most valuable moments of my learning journey happened in the first workshop I attended by Dr Yapko. He invited a participant in front of the group and in a matter of three minutes, completely changed the way I wanted to work with people. This all happened through the way he asked the person questions. Instead of 'why' and 'content', Dr Yapko went straight after the 'how' and process-oriented questions. They weren't the questions you usually hear in therapeutic encounters, and they served to highlight the areas where the person was making choices that were immobilising them. It highlighted that it was *how* the person did it, rather than *why* they had the issue. It showed me that there's a path for everyone to get out of being stuck, regardless of any 'why.'

These questions teased out the ineffective or uninformed decisions the person was unconsciously making and identifying where the person had no strategy or criteria for making such discriminations. What I also learned that there are relatively predictable areas where people's discrimination and decision making gets them into trouble, and therefore predictable questions and lessons that could be introduced to help them improve their experience.

Good or Bad?

It's raining outside. Do you think that's a good thing or a bad thing?
- Imagine that you had a day on the beach planned.
- Imagine that you had just planted in a new garden.
- Imagine a monsoon, flash flooding and mudslides.
- Imagine there had been a drought and farmers were worried about keeping their crops.

From these four cases, the correct answer to the question 'is it good or bad' should be '*it depends.*' Every time we make a decision or discrimination, the context becomes critical to understanding the quality of the decision.

If a discrimination is the way we decide between two similar things, then it's the process of looking at the two (or more) options and making fine distinctions between them. Enough to be able to make a decision in context about them, relative to each other.

The Importance of Context-Specific Responses

We have a lifetime of moments that require us to make decisions and act upon them. Some of these are so easy that we don't even seem to make the choice – we simply act. From our lifetime of experience, we learn what works for us and what doesn't. This allows us to have a repertoire of high probability choices that we can fall back on, without needing to put any effort into the choice. We can simply revert to an old rule that we learned along the way – one that may have served us in the past, regardless of how relevant it is for the current situation.

Imagine that you were going to put on a pair of underpants and had no decision rules for doing this task. There are three holes in the garment – a hole at the waistband and a hole for each leg. However, if every time you went to put on your underpants you had to experiment and define a valuable way to approach 'putting your underpants on' imagine the difficulty it would create. How would you make a decision about which limb goes in which hole, and in what order? Imagine the range of possibilities that actually exist. Consider if you had to use trial and error every morning to select how you would put your underpants on.

Instead, we develop unconscious rules and a clear process for what is 'right' and what is 'wrong' in putting on underpants. This allows us to get the result that we want with minimal effort. It's the consigning of learned patterns of behaviours to our unconscious – the removal of any need to think or do something different to the established pattern – that gets the useful result.

In our conditional field, we develop processes, decision rules and beliefs from such learning that make the repetitive tasks in our life—simple. These are invoked without thought or effort – which is great until novelty appears.

Novelty means new decisions are required

As we have learned a repertoire of processes and responses and stored them in our conditional field, things go well... until we hit a situation, we've never encountered.

It may be that something changed, or that we're seeking to do something completely new. Either way, the context of our decision has changed, and this implies that we also need to adapt our decision rules and discriminations.

Consider Freya. She changed jobs. What made her successful in her last job was not appreciated in the new company, it was getting her into trouble. The choices that she had developed at her last job were completely out of context for the novel circumstances. When she did 'what had always made her successful' it caused massive problems. Instead, Freya had to stop doing what she was doing and consciously make new decisions and instil new behaviours. Doing this allowed Freya to adapt successfully to her new job.

Consider Benji, who broke his arm skateboarding. He would find himself trying to do things with his plastered arm without thinking. He now had to stop and work out how to do simple things like getting dressed, shower and write.

People are adaptable, and the world is forever changing. The decisions and discriminations we believe are valuable may even become obsolete, as other things change.

In novel circumstances, we don't have the experiences accumulated to have developed a set of high-quality rules for deciding and discriminating. We may have never had to think about decisions in this area before. Therefore, we often think our way through it or simply apply an old habitual rule that may be unfit for the task.

Unstuck Exercise #102: Experiencing novelty

With your dominant hand (the one you write with) get a roll of sticky tape and tape your fingers together. For the next hour, pay attention to:
- The times you automatically go to use that hand for something.
- What you have to do differently to accommodate the 'novel' situation.
- What was harder to achieve because of this change.

What did you learn from this exercise?

It's also how we interpret the world

We not only make decisions and discriminations in choosing actions, but we also make them in how we interpret the world. By choosing what to focus on, what to expect and how to assign meaning, a series of decisions and discriminations occur deep within your conditional field which impacts how you experience the world.

Consider the following three scenarios:
- June is an out-and-out optimist. She sees the good in everyone and everything and believes that what happens to her is a result of the universe 'manifesting' her desires.
- Megan is a pessimist. She believes that she is responsible for all of her misery and she creates misery for everyone around her.

- Sacha sees the world as risky. She is scared of bad things happening and worries about what will happen next.

Think how all three people view the same situation very differently. What they focus on, what they expect, what they believe and the actions they take are all modified by the decisions they make in how they interpret the world.

This speaks to our fundamental belief structures and in particular the cognitive and attribution styles we choose to make those subtle decisions and discriminations.

Attribution and cognitive styles:

Attribution styles[12] show up in the way that people attribute what happens to them. Any event that occurs can be seen to be attributed to three frames – is it personal, is it permanent and is it pervasive? That is, a person will be seeing an event as:

- In my control *or* something that happens to me
- Something fixed *or* something changeable
- Something global *or* something specific

At any time, an event that happens can be treated with a mix of these three attributions. Some things are at one end of a spectrum, and some things exist at the other. For example, you cannot control the weather, but you can control what you wear. Having a leg amputated is permanent, but twisting an ankle provides pain which will reduce over time. A problem can ruin 'everything,', or it can cause a specific hindrance.

Problems arise when we have a fixed, global approach to attribute meaning – when we see everything through the same fixed lens and are no longer able to discriminate the specificity of the situation or engage in valuable decision making.

This is where the problem with attribution occurs – when an attribution is taken without looking at the context. People get themselves into trouble when

---

[12] Abramson, Seligman and Teasdale, 1978

they take an attribution style and apply it across all elements of their experience. Consider again someone sprains their ankle. With the wrong attribution style, they can blame someone else for it happening (litigation, anyone?), believe the pain will never improve and think that when they walk down that same set of stairs, the injury will happen again.

Think about someone who has been bitten by a dog – with a global, fixed lens they might say "All dogs bite, there's no way of controlling them." Imagine how they now act around dogs. On the other hand, someone who says, "Some dogs bite, particularly if they're scared or provoked. Dogs that are restrained or showing friendly behaviours can be trusted." How will they act in comparison?

Our cognitive styles – how we choose to think about things – play a huge role in our experience. If we have a situation and seek to think about it through the lenses we have learned then we might:

- Think something is 'black and white' rather than recognising it has many shades of grey.
- Focus on the past, present or future more than we should.
- Look for similarities in things, or focus on differences.

These are just three of many different examples of how we might think about things in different ways. Once again, applying our cognitive style is not a problem, unless when we do so in rigid, non-effective ways.

Consider Raj. He has summoned to his boss' office. As he sits in the waiting area, a lot of questions pass through his mind – often without him even applying any conscious effort to them. As he's waiting to be called in, he might be asking himself:

- Am I safe?
- What am I in control of?
- What do they think of me?
- How do I judge my performance?
- How assertive should I be?
- What thoughts and feelings should I pay attention to?
- What should I expect?

In truth, most of these questions, ideas, decisions, and discriminations are managed unconsciously. If we have healthy processes for the context, then we move forward. In any moment, we discriminate between options and initiate unconscious processes around our decisions about how to operate. Yet if you're unaware of how you decide or avoid deciding, these decisions can get stuck in old, unhelpful patterns. For example, perhaps Raj's reference for going into a superior's office is like being called into the Principal's office to get a thrashing with the cane. If he cannot separate the current experience from others in the past, he may reference outdated constructs to answer these unconscious questions.

Regardless of how much self-awareness you have, responding to emerging or novel circumstances requires a set of skills that have the ability to discriminate between options and make choices in valuable ways.

When you find yourself stuck, perhaps you can consider these ideas:

- It's not you; it's how you've been going about it.
- You may be invoking a decision or discrimination that's not appropriate for the context.
- Check if you're using a rigid attribution or cognitive style?
- Are you aware of the questions you're asking yourself?
- Can you describe *how* you are deciding?

Which brings us back to Dr Yapko's quote:

'One good "how" question can bring into sharp focus what the person doesn't know that is hurting him or her.'

Because once are able to understand *how* we're making decisions and distinctions, we can suddenly identify where to focus on learning new ways to get unstuck. It may be that a whole new understanding and process needs to be developed, or only small adaptations are required to break you out and get you moving forward.

The skill of defining the process that gets us stuck is sometimes difficult to apply to ourselves. We think we're making good decisions, but not getting the outcomes we want. Or we believe that the way we see the world (our beliefs, attributions, and cognitions) are all appropriate and justified. By paying attention to where you're stuck, you can look for rigidities in how you approach things and use this as a basis for digging deeper. As you become aware of some of the deeper decisions and distinctions you apply, it can give you the chance to update them and get a better outcome.

Chapter 14

Deeper Discriminations

As we find ourselves applying old decision rules, old attribution or rigid cognition styles, novel circumstances can become the landscape of ineffective behaviours and poor outcomes. Based on the work of Michael Yapko,[13] this chapter explores these some of these deeper choices that often contribute to people getting stuck. Across a wide variety of clients and circumstances, working with these underlying discrimination processes often help people find new and more valuable adaptations to move ahead in their lives.

Each of the discrimination issues in this chapter starts with the question. Take a moment when you read it to see how you would answer it. Then dive in and see how it impacts your experience and perhaps find a different way to answer it, one that may be more valuable to you.

How do you figure out when you should keep going, or when you should give up?

Consider a situation where perseverance is required. How do you decide when you should keep going or when you should give up? At one end of the spectrum, you give up early and 'keep your powder dry.' At the other end of the spectrum you adopt the notion that, 'when the going gets tough, the tough get going.'

Deciding whether to give up or keep going makes huge impact on what you achieve. Neither of these polar responses is always right. However, if your internal rule is rigidly 'give it up early' there will be achievable outcomes you will not reach. On the other hand, if you never give up and always fight on, you will invest energy in lost causes and not be able to attend to other goals that are achievable.

---

13 Yapko, Dr Michael, *The Discriminating Therapist,* Yapko Publications

In any circumstance, it's valuable to know a few things that may influence your decision. These include:
- What have you achieved so far?
- Is the goal something that you or someone else have achieved before?
- Do you have the skills and resources to make it happen?
- What is the benefit in completing the goal, versus the effort required?
- What other benefits do you get from continuing to pursue your goal, e.g., learning or achieving outcomes on the way?

How else might you better be using your efforts and resources?
- At what point is it reasonable to question and test your progress against the goal?

By determining the elements that add value to the overall decision of 'whether to give up or keep going' an objective and thoughtful approach can be taken to answer the question, rather than simply allowing all the 'stuff' in your unconscious conditional field to determine this for you.

Allowing your actions to be driven by automatic decision-making can be directing your actions away from your goal to something else. If you are operating to support your identity picture, for example, the value of what you are working towards might be less than you think. Evaluating the goal consciously can allow you to determine if it valuable to you.

Unstuck Exercise #103: To give up or keep going?

1. Think of a situation where you gave up before you reached your goal.
    - What was the situation?
    - How specifically did you decide to give up?
2. Think of a situation where you kept persevering to achieve your goal.
    - What was the situation?
    - How did you decide to keep going?
3. Think of a current goal you want to achieve.
    - How will you decide when to give up and when to keep going?

- What specific considerations will you use?
- What measures will trigger a 'give up' or a 'keep going' decision?

What did you learn as you did this exercise?

How do I know if my outcome is valuable or if it's easy?

Sometimes in deciding to give up on a goal, people will trade off what is valuable for what is easy. In any circumstance, there is an easy path – it may be easier to give up than put in effort toward an uncertain but valuable outcome. If we ask ourselves in any circumstance what is valuable as opposed to doing what seems easy, we may find that it is in our interests to make a different decision than we're automatically inclined to do.

This idea of easy versus valuable plays a massive role in weight management. People will select what is comfortable or easy, rather than what is difficult and valuable. There are many more aspects to this, but in that moment, whether it be in front of the chocolate cake or when the alarm goes off to get you out of bed for the 6am gym session, there will always be an easy choice or an alternative choice that is more valuable. In this context, shifting the decision from the unconscious to the conscious, and consciously working through the discriminations is better and more valuable decision can be made.

In truth, every big goal is made up of lots of little decisions – with each of these little decisions adding toward achieving the outcome. If the decision to keep doing what is valuable was made in every moment, imagine the outcome that you would get?

- How do you decide that it's valuable?
- When does it stop being valuable?

How do you determine what you're in control of, and what you're responsible for?

Consider a situation that didn't go the way you wanted. Ask yourself: 'What was I in control of?'

I was once working with a group of actors and musicians and set them a small exercise. I asked the group, 'If you are going for an audition, how much of the outcome – you getting the coveted role – is based on you, and how much is based on the audition panel?'

In this situation, the results in the group varied wildly. Some believed that the outcome was based 100 per cent on the artist 0 per cent on the panel, while others believe it was based 90 per cent panel and 10 per cent artist. This variance says a lot about how each individual in the group faces the prospect of going for an audition and what they specifically do to get the role.

Consider Mitch, who believes he's in 90 per cent control of the outcome. What if he gives his greatest performance but the panel decides that he's too tall, too light-haired or in the wrong singing range for the part? Or, if he gives his best performance, but someone is just slightly better?

Consider Steph, who believes that she only has 10 per cent control of the outcome and 90 per cent is based on the director and the audition panel. Her belief is that regardless of what she does almost everything is out of her control. Consider how these different beliefs will impact Mitch and Steph's preparations when they receive the acceptance or rejection letter.

Let's look at another example. Think about what you're wearing right now. When you get up in the morning, do you do a rain dance and wish for a certain temperature and wait for it to arrive? Or do you look at the forecast, see what the weather will be and dress to suit the temperature? The truth is, you cannot control the weather, but you can control how you dress in response to it. You cannot decide when it will rain, but you can decide if you carry an umbrella and when to open it. There are so many things you can't control – the weather, the future, what someone thinks of you or what someone else does. As we have seen, you can't even control the thoughts your brain creates or what feelings you generate.

What Do You Control?

You only ever get to control your response to the situation you find yourself in. In any moment, you get the choice of response. That is all. In fact, your ability to respond is your only responsibility (response-ability). Each time you respond, you create a subsequent circumstance that you can respond to. Life is a series of responses to circumstances that happen, and that we create.

When we believe we have control of things that we don't, it gets us into trouble. We can spend a lot of effort believing that we can control stuff that's simply uncontrollable. On the other hand, when we believe we have no control, we often resort to magical thinking and shift toward helplessness and hopelessness. Think again about Mitch and Steph and their auditions. If they allowed themselves to see that what they were in control of – that is, their response to the circumstance – then the way they prepare would change. They might consider the criteria that they'll be judged against and prepare specifically for the role. Other changes include:

- How they respond to the internal voice saying, 'You're not good enough' may change.
- They'll recognise the role of the panel members and perhaps consider what they could do to appeal to their needs and wants in the role choice.
- They're able to do the best they can in the audition, looking for cues and interacting with the panel to provide the best opportunity to evaluate them.
- They will realise that regardless of how well they do at the audition, there may be other factors that influence the panels choice. For example, the panel may be after a specific look or have to consider how the person fits in with the cast.
- They get the choice of how to respond to the call-up or knock back.

Each of these moments in the process has within it a circumstance and a decision choice of possible responses.

The only thing that we can ever control is how we respond. There's no way to change the circumstance, however the choice of response is entirely ours. When we believe we have no control, we essentially delegate the decisions and choices to our unconscious, which can get us into trouble.

Realising that we can respond through choice to our best ability in every moment gives us a true sense of control. As life provides us with a series of such moments, it's up to us to face these circumstances and choose the best and most valuable response.

On the other hand, when we have a false sense of what we control, we either expend effort trying to control the impossible or simply delegate control of our responses to the unconscious. In some circumstances, the automatic response may be effective, but you're really leaving it up to chance.

Consider Rhonda, who had a huge fear of flying and needed to undertake a 14-hour international flight. On discussion, she reported she did not know what she controlled, had no valid process for determining risk and focused excessively on recent air incidents. She felt 'completely out of control' when she boarded a plane. However, when Rhonda learned that she could only control her responses, the concept of emotional reasoning and how to evaluate risk, we were able to move on and discuss control in relation to the flight. I suggested to Rhonda that she had more control than she realised. In fact, that she was in control of who she delegated control of the aeroplane to! It would be crazy for her to delegate control of the plane to the person who was the biggest control freak on board – perhaps Mr Smith in seat 7D. However, she could choose to control the fact that she delegates control to the pilot and the cabin crew, who are extensively trained and the best people on the aeroplane to fly it to its destination safely.

By responding to the feeling of being out of control, Rhonda now consciously told herself that she was 'delegating control' to the flight crew. If she saw anything before she boarded that would logically challenge that, she could simply choose not to delegate control and control her choice not to board. Then, once Rhonda had boarded, she could then focus on what she was in control of while on board – the entertainment and what to eat and drink. She accepted that she could leave everything else that was not in her control to the crew she had delegated control to. Rhonda later reported that she had an excellent flight and a wonderful time at her destination.

Unstuck Exercise #104: You and control

Think of a time that you feel out of control.
- Take a moment and describe in detail, the circumstances of the situation.
- Consider the response you currently make to the situation – for example, creating a feeling of being out of control.
- Make a list of alternate actions, regardless of how small they are. How could you respond to this situation in future?
- For each alternate, consider what would now change in terms of the outcome?

What did you notice and learn?

How do you know when to feel guilty, and when to feel ashamed?

Even more importantly, do you know the difference between the two?

Shame

Shame can be such a powerful driver of self-recrimination. Shame is learned process of evaluation and attribution, particularly in how we relate to things that we've done in the past.

To feel shame, a person has to:
- Reflect on a situation in the past where they behaved (perhaps even 'thought') in a particular way.
- Compare that behaviour or thought to a standard or expectation they hold or have been taught. They have to believe that their response was not up to that standard.
- Believe that the gap between what they did and the standard they attained was realistic, possible and something they *should* have been able to do.
- Feel negative feelings or engage in negative self-talk because of this 'failure'
- Believe that if other people knew about this gap, they would think badly about them.

- Potentially revisit this 'failure' and the self-recrimination, even when the event is over.

Guilt

The process of guilt is constructed differently.
- A person performs a behaviour in a particular situation.
- The action is judged as not up to a certain standard, either by the person or others.
- The person makes corrections to the behaviour or makes reparation for the outcome caused by the low-standard behaviour.

Importantly:
- The person does not add a component of 'worrying about what others think.'
- Being 'guilty' leads to taking responsibility for the action and from this, a change in future behaviour.
- This responsibility can lead to reparations (if required) and moving on from the circumstance to more informed ways of acting in future.

There are clear differences with these two processes. Shame is a process without end. It's driven by internal feelings and a belief that revealing the actions would lead to negative judgement. Shame has no learning or recovery built into it.

Guilt, on the other hand, is a natural process of learning. It involves action, measurement against a standard, correction and recovery. For example, a person who breaks the law is guilty of not acting in accordance with the legal standard. They are hauled before the judge, who passes judgement on the action. Remedial steps are taken (learning or punishment) to ensure that the future behaviour will now meet the standard. Once the person has served their penalty or undertaken the learning, they're free to resume their normal place in society.

Consider the fact that I couldn't ride a bike when I was four. I could feel guilty of not knowing how to ride a bike. However, I could judge this against the standard or take corrective action and learn. Should a four-year-old feel shame for not knowing how to ride a bike? When I had learned how to ride the bike, I was now on the other side of the learning. I was no longer 'guilty' of not knowing how to ride a bike, I was off racing around with the other kids.

Think of what happens when a kid learns the shame process. How does this differ from when they learn the guilt/learning process? If we personalise the actions as being part of our make-up rather than something that happened, then we create the perfect framework for the shame process to be kick-started.

Guilt is specific to a time or context. Shame is more like a stain that someone carries in their identity picture from that moment forward. To carry shame is to carry an outdated picture and over-responsibility for a past event.

So how do you determine when you should feel guilty and when you should be ashamed? What if you didn't have to feel ashamed, but instead were allowed to feel guilty? What if you were allowed to reflect and learn, knowing that you were doing the best you could in the circumstance? What if you didn't need the internal judgements or to create feelings and thoughts about past events?

Unstuck Exercise #105: Shame and guilt

Consider something you're ashamed about.
- What is your process for generating shame? Does it mirror the path outlined above?
- What if you could view the action and the expectation as separate from you as a person?
- Ask yourself, 'What did I learn from that experience?'
- Ask yourself, 'What if I told people what I did, how would they really judge me?'
- Ask yourself, 'What if I told people what I had learned from the experience, how would they really judge me?'
- What if you could admit to being guilty of acting a certain way, at that time?

- Change the language of how you view the situation. Instead of saying, 'I am ashamed of...', say to yourself, 'I was guilty of...'. Notice what happens. Allow yourself to see how you were guilty then, but not now.
- Consider being on the other side of the learning moment. Reflect on how you were guilty, but the situation has been consigned to the past. What did you learn?

Think again about the situation you were ashamed about. What do you notice now?

How Do You Determine When You Are Safe?

If you cannot determine when you're safe, or the way you determine that you're safe is flawed—it makes it very difficult to take action. At our most primitive levels, the feeling of safety is a critical driver of behaviour.

So how do you know when you're safe? Is it because of a feeling? Are you trusting your intuition? Is it because you're somewhere familiar with a particular person that makes you feel safe?

Unstuck Exercise #106: Safety

Think for a moment about the following circumstances:
- You are attempting to cross a busy road
- A three-year-old child is attempting to cross a busy road
- You are in a dark alley late at night in a bad district
- You're in a crowd of people in a shopping mall
- You're in a crowd of people at a protest where rocks have been thrown at police

For each circumstance, write down how someone should determine if you (or the person in the situation) should evaluate if they're 'safe' or not.

What did you notice?

There are a number of factors that will determine if the person is safe, each one specific to the situation and the person involved. None of them relate to the feelings they generate or the thought the person has. Instead, how safe the person is in the circumstance depends upon:

- The external cues available to indicate if there's danger or a reasonable prospect that danger is emerging.
- The skills and capabilities the person has to respond to the circumstance.
- The experience the person has had in similar situations.

Let's take a look at some of these.

To cross a road, you need to be able to judge the speed and distance of cars, have appropriate line of sight and know when there's enough time for you to cross. While this would change if you were an Olympic sprinter or elderly, the cues that you pay attention to are the same.

For a three-year-old, regardless of how confident, there's every likelihood they lack the skills and capabilities to know which cues to pay attention to –even the skill of negotiating the curb without falling over. As they lack the experience to make the judgements and predictions, they should not be considered safe to cross the road.

If you're in a dark alley in a bad part of town, what cues of danger are you looking for? How vigilant are you? What are you predicting may occur? How are you evaluating risk? Do you have experience in judging if the alley is safe or dangerous? Do you have skills that you could use if something dangerous started? What about if you're in a crowded shopping centre? How is this different from the dark alley? What cues should you now pay attention to that may indicate danger?

As we covered earlier in the book, the 'feeling' of danger is only 'information' about how you feel and may have nothing to do with what's going on. It relates to internal cues, rather than important external cues we need to pay attention to. However, it may be a useful cue to encourage you to be vigilant regarding your external environment, and encourage you to take a logical approach to safety assessment.

We all have the fight or flight[14] response – where we don't get the chance to think before we take action. Most of the time this is a valuable response – yet people get stuck when they apply it out of context, or forget to evaluate the true level of risk in their environment.

Consider Raymond. He presented with agoraphobia. When I asked him, 'How do you determine when you're safe?' his response was "when I am at home." In a way, this was actually a very nuanced answer for someone stuck. The most common answer is "I don't know" – they haven't even realised that they're making a decision about this, and haven't considered that it's something they can change.

Imagine how the world looks to Raymond. He wants to get out and enjoy his life but only feels 'safe' when at home. Every time he thinks about leaving home, the feelings of danger and not being able to cope overwhelm him, and he stays home.

As part of a therapeutic approach, Raymond worked to redefine 'safety' in a more reasonable and practical way. Providing Raymond with a more nuanced view of safety and giving him the space to develop a natural learning adaptation, he was able to better see himself in the world.

The following week I received a text message from Raymond – he was up in a winery region having a picnic lunch with his wife, and loving it. It was such a fantastic event for the two of them, as it had been years since they had time out of the house together. When he was stuck, he didn't know that some simple learning was going to completely change his life.

Unstuck Exercise #107: Unsafe; why?

Think of a circumstance where you feel unsafe but others may not. Ask yourself the following:
- What cues do others look for in the environment to determine if they're safe?

---

14 Flight or fight response: *a response to threat to danger that is marked by physical changes, including nervous and endocrine changes, that prepare a human or animal to react or to retreat. The functions of this response were first described in the early 1900s by American neurologist and physiologist Walter Bradford Cannon.*

- How are these different from the cues you pay attention to?
- What additional skills and capabilities do others have that you don't?
- What would you need to experience to confirm that you have the right skills and experience to be safe?

What did you notice or learn?

How Do You Know What to Expect?

Are you 'Mystic Meg'? Can you tell the future? Of course, you can't. We can't see the future, but we can have a realistic expectation or prediction of what might happen. Like Raymond, it would be reasonable to predict the way he was getting stuck was his inability to judge safety. It's reasonable to predict that someone drink driving at great speed will have an accident. Some things are highly predictable.

An important discrimination is how you determine what you can expect. Some people almost have a hardwired automatic response to expect the worst in a future situation. They might be the type of people referred to as the 'glass half-empty' types. On the other hand, there are those who, regardless of how bad a situation is, remain ridiculously over-optimistic. These are the 'glass half-full' types. In truth, neither response is good nor bad – it's only when we automatically and unconsciously respond to every situation with a fixed approach that it leads to trouble.

Consider Jesse, who wants to ask a girl out on a date. If he believes that she's going say 'No,' how will this change his behaviour? What if he believes that the only thing she will say is 'Yes'? The truth is, until Jesse asks he won't know. Both possibilities exist. If he was to predict which possibility was more likely, how would he do that? Should he trust his feelings and intuition? Should he listen to his critical voice? Should he worry about what other people might think about him?

In fact, none of these are useful. The cues that Jesse needs to observe are not internal, but external to him and specific to the young lady in question. Consider the following, some are useful and some are not.

- She already has a boyfriend
- She has recently broken up with another young man and believes she's not ready to go out with anyone
- She seems to seek out Jesse and talks to him regularly
- She has a cat
- She seems to avoid Jesse and has been quite rude to him in public
- She and Jesse spend time together and share some interests
- Jesse feels that he's not very handsome.

Unstuck Exercise #108: Predicting Jesse

Run through the list of cues regarding Jesse.
- Identify which ones are relevant in helping Jesse better predict the outcome of asking this girl out on a date, and why they might be of value.
- Identify the cues that provide no value.

What did you learn?

When we allow our expectations to be generated by our feelings, our thoughts or old unconscious beliefs or rules they're likely to create a fixed and incorrect view on what may happen. Taking the time to examine the actual cues that really contribute to a prediction is an important thing to do.

The idea that in any moment there exist multiple possibilities – even if one or more of them are quite unlikely – is a valuable idea to consider. Being open to the fact that regardless of the certainty we have about how things will go, there's a possibility that we can be surprised by what occurs. We can consciously believe that the most likely thing will occur, but in truth there are always possibilities. If you have an unconscious bias toward believing that 'only bad things will happen' then you automatically close off the possibilities that don't conform to this belief. By believing things in the future will be bad, people generate anxiety as they predict bad things, they then spend time trying to work out how they'll cope with them.

Allowing yourself to see possibilities and use external cues to work out probabilities can significantly reduce this anxiety. Equally, being a 'realist' and not believing that everything will end perfectly is important. This will help avoid unreasonable disappointment when what you magically believe will happen just doesn't come true.

Life is neither a fairytale or a horror movie. It's simply a mix of different possibilities. Knowing what to expect – what may be possible or probable – can allow you to make better choices in your actions and create more valuable outcomes. It is *how* you respond and use the expectation that is important, not just that you have it.

Unstuck Exercise #109: The future you

Think about a number of things that may happen in the future.
- Take a moment to consider whether your view on the event will be positive or negative.
- For each event, consider some alternate possibilities. If you automatically think negative, take the time to imagine a positive outcome or a neutral outcome (or vice versa).
- Out of 100%, what is the probability of each option?
- Consider each outcome. Which would you prefer? What could you do to help that happen?

What did you notice?

How Do You Determine What Is Possible for You?

Each circumstance comes with a range of possibilities, so how can you determine what is possible for you?

What is reasonable to expect of yourself? What are the upper and lower limits? Once again, the development of unconscious processes for making this discrimination can often be the cause of why someone gets stuck.

Consider Soo, who had a personal expectation that she 'should' be able to deliver perfection in everything she did, particularly at school. This perfectionist ideal is very common, particularly where expectation is built up around the person over time. For example, 'Soo is so clever' or 'Soo wants to be a doctor'. These sorts of statements were present over her lifetime, so Soo adopted the belief that she *should* get perfect scores at school. Instead of understanding that there are a range of possibilities – from failing the subject through to achieving a perfect score. Soo's conditional field had unconsciously formed a set of rules about what she 'should' be capable of. So, consider what would happen if Soo were to take a new subject and struggle with it. Imagine the internal tension this would create due to the gap between her expectation and her reality.

Consider Gabe, who thinks that he's 'bad at school'. He has been told all his life that he is 'stupid' and 'dumb'. What do you think Gabe believes is possible for him?

The truth for both Soo and Gabe is that there are a range of possibilities available to them. Some however, are more likely than others based upon:

- The specific circumstance
- What is possible for other people in this situation and the range of possibilities
- The skills and capabilities they have
- The strategies they have and choose to deploy
- The effort they are prepared to put in
- What they consider valuable.

None of these relate to how they feel, what they have been told or what their critical voice is busy yelling at them. What is possible instead, is based upon what the person can do, wants to do and the effort they're prepared to engage in in order to achieve it. Taking the time to explore the idea of what's possible through conscious reflection is important. It often allows a completely different outcome.

Knowing when something is 'good enough' sets you up to do what is needed to achieve the outcome you want. Getting this wrong has dramatic consequences: Setting the bar too high creates perfectionism and anxiety about not being able to reach those expectations. On the other hand, setting the bar too low will ensure that nothing gets done up to standard.

The key understanding is how to set the expectation correctly based upon the specific circumstance.

There are times when you want as close to 'perfect' as possible – consider a surgeon or a pilot. There are other times that a lower standard, like only needing 50% to pass a test, is adequate.

Knowing what you want to achieve, what you should expect and what's possible for you all provide a powerful 'reality check' on your personal performance.

Unstuck Exercise #110: Possibility

Think of where you're stuck. Ask yourself the following:
- What expectations do you have about what should be possible?
- What do you believe is possible for you in that circumstance?
- What is the basis for that decision?
- What if you could allow yourself to see the range of possibilities that others might achieve? What might these be?
- What skills and capabilities do you have in the field? What additional skills could you learn?
- What strategies are you using? What other strategies could you consider?
- How valuable is the outcome to you?

Take a moment now and reconsider – what might be possible for you in the circumstance?

What did you notice doing this exercise?

How Do You Choose Whose Advice You Should Listen To?

When we enter a situation where we're uncertain, we often look to others to help us make decisions. You may notice that a large number of people will happily offer all sorts of advice to 'help' you. However, how do you decide whose advice to listen to? We can gain a great deal by learning from others, particularly where they have achieved an outcome that we value in a similar circumstance. Whilst a lot of advice is well-meaning, a key discrimination skill is determining exactly which advice is valuable, and which isn't.

Consider the following elements that may make advice valuable:
- The person can offer specific steps, actions, skills and strategies that you could consider
- The person has been through a similar situation, or has expertise in that field
- The advice is current, relevant and isomorphic
- The advice is based on skills and resources you have at your disposal, not on 'fantasy' things which are unavailable to use

Consider the following elements that do not make advice valuable:
- The person has not been in the circumstance or has no experience in the area
- The person is selling something
- The person uses the giving of advice to make themselves feel good about themselves
- The advice is non-specific
- The advice is based upon 'should' or 'must' statements rather than as options for you to choose from
- The advice is based upon resources or skills that are not available or learnable by you
- The person only has 'charisma'

So, take a moment and consider where you get advice from. On some topics, the advice of your friends will be more valuable than your parents. One other topics, your parents will have much more valuable advice to offer.

Remember, that the 'advice' is only ever information that you add to your own process. It has the same value as a thought or a feeling, until you evaluate it and take its value as useful to you.

Receiving advice hopefully expands the range of options you have to select from. From there, you can then use your own high-quality discriminations and decision-making strategies to apply the advice to your circumstance. This will afford you the responsibility of taking your own specific course of action. Blindly following advice of a 'guru' is a poor way to make decisions. Similarly, using mantras or listening to the internal critical voice is a common way for people make poor decisions. When your inner voice says, 'You're not good enough, why should you try?' or your mantra says, 'The universe will manifest whatever I want,' you might want to check that before proceeding.

With advice, it's also useful to watch out for the halo effect. Just because someone is great in one domain, does not mean they are experts in all domains. For example, Elizabeth Taylor was a great actress, but would you really take marriage advice from her? When we take advice from people because they are 'famous' we can often miss the fact that the advice they offer is not actually valuable to us.

Unstuck Exercise #111: Advice

Take a moment to consider the following:
- When have you received well-meaning advice that wasn't useful?
- When have you not followed advice that would have been valuable if you'd have used it in your decision-making process?
- How do you decide who should offer you advice and when?

What did you notice?

How do you work out when it is OK to say 'No'?

When someone asks for something from you – be it time, resources, emotion or whatever – how do you decide whether you should agree to that, or say no? This is a really important question to consider. If all you do is say 'Yes' to everyone, you may often give up things that you don't want to, or can't really afford. However, if your social driver is 'to be liked,' it can be very difficult to say 'No.' When the drive to be liked is linked to being agreeable, then saying yes to almost every request seems like the only option. So how do you determine what requests you should say no to?

Unstuck Exercise #112: The power of yes and no

Think of a time recently when you said 'Yes' to a request when you would have preferred to say 'No.'
- What did you think would happen if you said 'No'?
- What feelings were generated?

- What did you consider before agreeing to the request?

What did you notice?

When someone makes a request, there are some logical questions we can ask ourselves to determine our response. These include:

- Am I capable of doing it?
- What is the cost to me, in doing it? In particular, if I do this, what does this mean I cannot do for myself?
- Who is asking? How valuable is that relationship?
- What will it mean to the person I am doing it for?
- Are there other ways for the person to get this done that is better for them, and me?
- What value will I get out of doing it? (Even 'feeling good for helping' can be a worthwhile reason).
- Do I lose face, prestige or political power by saying no?

One of the biggest issues is that people don't know how to say 'No.' We have been conditioned by society that it's not nice to say no, and it can be associated with uncomfortable feelings.

Consider Stella, who worked as a personal assistant to a group of senior executives. Each senior executive would often rush into her office and ask, 'Can you take care of this please?' In her position, Stella felt that she couldn't say no. The biggest issue was that she had an in-tray overloaded with things to do, but didn't know where to start or how to get through them all. Meanwhile, the company was considering moving her on for lack of performance because she simply couldn't do all of the things that she was saying 'yes' to.

For Stella, we developed an approach to make the interaction with the senior executives less 'black and white.' Instead of saying yes to everything, Stella practiced saying, 'Of course. I currently have six things as an urgent top priority to get done and these other 20 things to knock over. Can you please let me know its urgency, so I determine where to place it in my workflow?' This made the senior executives consider the urgency of the task and what had to be de-prioritised for their task to be completed. Stella was also encouraged to say, 'I am already doing X for Peter, can you have a chat to him to find out if I should drop that and do this, or if this can go later in the queue?'

Stuff has to get done. In Stella's case, it was teaching her about prioritisation and finding ways to empower her and get the requesters to determine the real value of what had to be done.

Often, when challenged, the executives would respond, 'That's a low priority Stella,' or 'As long as it done by Thursday.' In the end, this approach was a way to qualify the importance of the request, but also make it clear that there was a cost for each request. With a new strategy in place, Stella was able to have her inbox sorted by priorities and a clear set of tasks in order. She found that rather than saying 'No,' clarifying the request changed the nature of the interactions with the executives, including the power balance from 'do this' to a conversation about priorities. As a result, Stella received an excellent evaluation on her following performance review.

If you're the sort of person that finds it difficult to say 'No,' how can you show empathy and interest by deepening your understanding of the request? Perhaps you can say something like, 'I am currently doing X and also want to get Y done before 4 pm. I would love to help you, but can it wait until after then?' Just because you say 'Yes' to doing someone a favour, does not mean you have to agree to do it on their time schedule.

Unstuck Exercise #113: What would you say?

Think of the following situations and how you would respond. Would you say yes or no, or deepen the request?

- Your partner asks you to pick up milk on the way home
- Your child asks you to read them a story
- An untrustworthy friend asks to borrow $100
- Your boss wants you to work overtime
- A salesman wants you to buy some add-ons
- You want to go to the football, but a neighbour wants help cutting up trees.

For each situation, how did you respond? What was your initial reaction? If you operated from your feelings, what would have been your responses?

Learning to say 'No' – where it's as an active decision and you're clear on the value and consequences to both parties is a critical life skill. Allowing the unconscious rules of the conditional field to kick in, may well get you stuck. However, by being more nuanced and thoughtful, there are times that saying 'No' (or 'Yes') may be in your best interests.

How do you work out what other people think of you?

One of the greatest lies we tell ourselves is that we know what someone else is thinking.

It's natural for us to use the heuristic of isomorphism to believe that other people will think like we do, or even be motivated like we would. When we are in the habit of thinking bad things about ourselves (especially through our critical voice), it's not a hard stretch to believe that everyone else is thinking bad things about us, too.

Consider Roy. He entered a café one morning and noticed an older man lower the newspaper he was reading, look at him and sneer. Roy took this as a personal attack. However, when working with Roy, we took a step back and looked at the scenario from a different perspective. To do this, I asked Roy to consider a number of options:

- What if the old man had read something in the paper about a politician he disliked?
- What if the old man was thinking about something disagreeable he had to do later in the day?
- What if Roy reminded the old man of someone who he didn't like. Perhaps seeing Roy reminded him of that person and thinking of that person, made him sneer.
- What if the old man was a stroke survivor and that was his normal facial response?

Out of all of these options, which one do you think Roy thought was most likely? The answer is he didn't know – and simply could not know. Whilst we can observe the action of another, we have no way of knowing the motivation or meaning. By immediately leaping to 'he doesn't like me' is a defensive and inaccurate reading of a simple social circumstance. Whilst it may be possible to influence what people think about us; we can never control or know what they think.

Consider if you were to ask 10 people the question, 'What do you think about me?' How many would be honest and how many would socially filter their response and tell you what they think you want to hear? The bottom line is: you can't know what other people are thinking – and in truth, it's none of your business. There are far more rational and valuable things to focus on.

A better question may be, 'I wonder what they think of my actions?'

You can control your actions; your actions deliver outcomes and these outcomes may have an impact on other people. Rather than judging yourself ('I'm not good enough!') or considering that you are being judged ('They think I'm not good enough!'), what if you could change to asking, 'What do I think of my actions?' and 'How do they perceive my actions and what impact could it have on them?'

In the end, you cannot know what meaning other people ascribe to anything. You cannot know how they'll judge. But by shifting the focus to behaviours – that which you can change – you get to judge based upon outcomes, rather than imagined feelings.

Unstuck Exercise #114: Relationships and you

Think of someone who you think doesn't like you'. Consider the following:
- How does this belief change the way you interact with them?
- How do you know that they don't like you? What specific things do they think about you?
- Why should you care what they think?
- Shift your language to, 'This person may not like some of my actions or behaviours. As I choose my actions and behaviours, is there anything I would do differently to change the impact on that person?'

What do you notice?

The Big Questions in Life

So, now we've reviewed some areas where we see common 'experiential gaps', we can now come to your 'big life questions.'

As you consider where you're stuck, you may become aware of some ideas that are difficult and cause you distress. You may even notice where you feel rigid in dealing with a problem, or a belief that doesn't serve you. Imagine if you could now turn that into a 'how' question?

For example:

How do you know when…

How do you decide between…

How do you work out…

How do you know what…

This unlocks the process and allows you to see the discriminations and decisions running in your conditional field. Learn to draw out the question, then find valuable ways to answer it.

Unstuck Exercise #115: Your big questions

Take a few moments and write down the 'big questions' that you're challenged with.

It might be "How do I get happy"? or "How do I know when I should leave this relationship" or whatever it is for you.

- Now take your time to see if you have a valuable answer to that question.
- What criteria will you use to decide?
- How do you know what your options are? Can you find more?
- What attributions and processing styles have you been applying to them? Are these valuable, or perhaps rigid or outdated?
- If it wasn't your question, what would you offer as advice for the options and solutions for someone else?

What did you learn from doing this exercise?

Chapter 15

You Are More Than You Know

Until now, we've been focusing on where you've been stuck; we have 'dug in' and studied it in detail. Sometimes when we do this, it's easy to get consumed on the problem and forget everything else.

If you cast your mind back to the chapter on 'Labels,' you may recall that as we accept a label, it provides a 'lens' through which we see ourselves and the world. Just as you have always been more than your label, you're always more your problem.

When we have a label – or focus strongly on something– it's easy to allow 'confirmation bias' to kick in. That is, things which fit our view of the world are selectively recruited, and anything which challenges such views get rejected.

You may notice it when you have a sore finger or toe – you always seem to bang that very spot. The likelihood is that you bang all of your fingers and toes. However, it's just the fact that it hurts that you remember the times you bang it.

If you believe that you have depression, imagine what that does to the way you see the world – and more importantly, how you see yourself.

When you stop diminishing yourself by only seeing yourself through your label or your problem, you may just start to see other areas in your life where you're not only OK but actually capable and resourceful. Areas where you may have a skill, capability or aptitude that's valuable to you and even of significant value to others.

In this chapter, we're going to expand on the fact – that you're so much more than your problem – because sometimes the most elegant and surprising solutions are already within us. We perhaps have simply failed to notice.

Buried Treasure

Earlier we discussed how the conditional field is like Milton Erickson's idea of a vast storehouse of all of your learning, experiences, and processes. Regarding self-awareness, we looked at how sometimes we had to shine a light into dark corners of this storehouse, to find and review outdated 'automatic processes' that are perhaps getting you stuck. This vast storehouse is also like a hidden treasure trove – because there's so much in your conditional field that is working well and serving you perfectly. You have far more things of value than things outdated. All of the things you've learned and experienced that serve you now, all of your processes, all of your valuable beliefs, decision rules, and discrimination skills. You even have some buried treasure that you perhaps just don't pay attention to anymore.

The things that are working for you completely outweigh the things that aren't, even when things look their bleakest.

Utilisation

Milton Erickson was regarded as an entirely unconventional practitioner in the mental health field, but he seemed to get astounding results in ways that other therapists found difficult to understand. There are now many books discussing his approach, with authors looking at what he did in so many different ways. At its core, Milton Erickson seemed to get his results through what he called 'Utilisation.' In a way, this can be summarised as:

The person with the problem already has the answer within them.

Some of Erickson's cases seem to make no sense until you see the generosity of his spirit toward the people he helped. He saw the person as more than their problem and understood they had a wealth of resources to be 'utilised' to help them move forward. As we saw from Erickson's case reports, it's often not what you expect that will help you. Being open to surprise is a great frame to shift from being stuck.

When we get stuck, we often screen out everything else and project our problem forward and backward in time. We imagine it existing in the future and remember instances from the past. We amplify it. If the answer is within you, perhaps it's time to step back and truly appreciate that you're so much more than your problem.

Appreciation – seeing the more

Unstuck Exercise #116: A moment of appreciation

Find somewhere peaceful that you can come to rest for a few moments. Sit or lie comfortably, and as you read each phrase below, shut your eyes and take a minute or two to simply sit with the idea and explore what it means for you. Only when you're ready, take the time to open your eyes and move on to the next phrase.

Imagine if you were free of all constraints, pressures, and rules. You were able to now simply exist, comfortably and at ease. Perhaps you can even remember a time, like a holiday, where you were able to enjoy not doing anything for a while.

Imagine from this place of comfort watching a 'highlights reel' of your life. It's not about fame and acclamation, but a personal film that has been made just for you. As it runs, there are many small forgotten moments where you acted your best. There may be moments when you overcame challenges. There are times when you were surprised by things that were unexpected. As the film runs, it shows you moments from hobbies, friendships and times that have past, and times that are here now.

As you sit in a comfortable nostalgia, you can simply enjoy remembering things that perhaps you haven't remembered for a while. The small things. The things you learned. The things you allowed yourself to just enjoy.

When you're ready, allow yourself to tune back into the world around you. Bring with you any good thoughts or feelings about those magic moments, and appreciate that you're so much more than you've been focusing on.

What did you notice during this experience?

Compartments

Another way to consider utilisation is to think that we live our lives in 'compartments'. We have different rules, cultures, processes and routines that we associate with different parts of our lives. Whilst we may be doing great in some areas, we might be struggling or stuck in others. Imagine if we were able to see all of the processes, skills, learnings and attributes from across our many compartments, and to see if anything from outside the problem space could actually be a 'hidden treasure' that we could utilise to set us free?

People have a range of skills and resources they employ in all sorts of areas and they have demonstrated the ability to learn and cope with so many different things. These things, however, are often diminished, forgotten or overlooked when they're stuck.

Consider Toby. In one part of his life he was a surfer. In another he was a businessman. In another he was a husband and father. In another he was an amateur antique car enthusiast. Toby had a series of compartments in which he saw himself. In each compartment, which came with its own label, Toby had an assessment of who he was and how he saw himself – his very specific identity. These were separate to the way he saw himself in each of the other compartments – and the skills and resources he had in each specific area were only considered specific to each.

Unstuck Exercise #117: Roles you play

- Take a moment and write a list of all of the 'roles' or compartments you have in your life. For each one, describe how you refer to yourself.
- Write the strengths and skills that you have for each compartment.
- Now, describe a place in your life where you feel stuck. Describe how you see yourself. Describe what are your weaknesses or deficits are in this area.
- Compare the place of being stuck with the other compartments. What do you notice?

Toby was really struggling and felt stuck in the compartment he called 'work'. There were things that happened at work that he felt out of control of. He felt that he could not perform at his best, felt anxious and he lacked the ability to make good choices under pressure. He struggled with negotiating and felt that he let his team down. For all of this to be true, Toby had to completely overlook the other areas of his life. He had to ignore all his resources and strengths – including his discrimination strategies in the other compartments of his life that he could bring to bear at 'work'. What if all the great ways that Toby made decisions, acted and reacted in the other areas of his life would be valuable to him also to apply at work?

For example, when Toby surfed, how did he know which wave to catch? How was he OK in letting waves go and not catching every single one? When he was at home, how did he work out what was the right set of rules and boundaries for his kids? When he was doing up his old cars, how did he know what was a fair price for a part and how did he haggle at swap meets to get what he wanted?

From the outside, you can see that there are a number of highly developed skills and resources that Toby uses whenever he's in one of his other compartments, but not in his work compartment. What do you think would happen if Toby would shift the resources (or allow himself to access them) in the place where he felt stuck? What happens if we all allowed ourselves this?

Perhaps you have guessed that in doing so, people find new and valuable skills and resources that allow them to move forward from being stuck. Sometimes it's not the compartments of your life – it is simply in the small things you love doing. By simply considering those things in your life you love doing, you can find a whole series of rich and valuable resources that can be applied in places you're stuck – to immediate benefit.

With Toby, we took time to explore these adjacent skills. When we used surfing, car meets and being a parent as metaphors for his situation at work; Toby was able to see how some of the decision-making processes and resources that he used unconsciously could be incredibly valuable in the place he was stuck. Working with this, we created some tangible plans for actions and responses he could take using these metaphors as the basis. As a result, Toby felt in control and capable of making a huge difference at his workplace and permitted himself to experiment with the new ways. At our 12-week follow-up, Toby reported a complete change in his work experience and had even forgotten how stuck he felt before.

Toby is a typical example of compartmentalisation of resources and skills. Resources are such a valuable part of our conditional field. However we're not often conscious of the 'buried treasures' we have accumulated in other 'compartments.' We focus on being stuck, look at the problem and miss seeing the 'whole person view.' We miss appreciating all the awesome stuff that people do without thinking. It can be such a nice and generous way to approach ourselves – and those that we work with – to start with the premise that everyone is so much more than their problem. That area where people are not stuck, they have so much of value which may be the key to unlocking them from where they are stuck.

Unstuck Exercise #118: Doing what you love

Write down something you love to do (or something you loved to do but don't do very much of now). This can be a sport, an activity or even a hobby.

- For this thing, take some time to consider what about if you really love, or loved?
- What skills did you have to learn and what decisions did you have to make, to be competent at that thing?
- What did you get or achieve by doing this thing?
- What behaviours did you demonstrate that helped you in this area?

Take your time and repeat the exercise with any other things that come to mind that you love – or loved – to do.

Review your list. What do you notice?

An additional benefit of exploring what people love doing is that gives them a 'rest' from experiencing their problem. The shift you see in people's faces when you ask them "what do you love doing?", or "What did you used to love to do, that you don't do so much anymore?" is incredible. To spend a few minutes discussing and exploring what they love doing shifts their whole state, gives them a 'break' and also subtly teaches people that they're so much more than their problem.

What Are You Not Seeing for Your Problem to Be True?

If our conditional field is full of 'buried treasures,' then what are you *not* seeing for the problem to be true? Stop for a minute and consider this. Where you're stuck, what do you allow yourself to overlook, diminish or forget for your definition of your problem to be true? This is another example of how, in the compartment of where we're stuck, we can't see outside that compartment. Often, as soon as we raise our eyes, the 'rules' that we set up in look incongruous and can't be maintained in light of everything else we know and believe.

When we're stuck, we usually get stuck in limited thinking. We make up stories, we diminish our self-value and resources and use this as a place of self-judgement around our particular problem or issue. We also draw on labels or identity pictures that may be specific to this compartment, and definitely out of date in terms a 'whole of person' view of ourselves.

Remember Terry who 'had depression.' When I asked him how often he had been depressed in the past year, he was adamant that he'd been depressed 100 per cent of the time. So, we did an audit and found that over the last 12 months, his son had graduated high school, his daughter was married, and he had attended some social events. When I asked him about these events – about how he felt about them – he replied that he had felt proud, excited, scared, happy and relaxed during these events. But according to Terry, they didn't count. He had dismissed these events when he decided how depressed he was. In a way, how he maintained the definition of his problem was overlooked.

Healthy competition between compartment identities

Sometimes we have two or more conflicting beliefs or values. These can be a reason we get stuck, as well as a way to overcome them. We want to be the person in 'Compartment A', but also need or want to be the person we in 'Compartment B'. This can either be a recipe for getting stuck (as we are caught between the two) or an interesting 'utilisation' to challenge the contents of one of the compartments and grow. In a way, pulling back and seeing both compartments (including their identity pictures and labels) allows us to update what needs to be updated, and potentially create a more nuanced and holistic view of ourselves, integrating the hidden treasures of both.

Consider Iris. She was a mature lady with an aged mother and grown children of her own.

She was stuck between two roles – needing to be the 'good daughter' to her mother and 'standing up for herself'. These different self-assessments were highly prized by Iris. The problem was her mother was just plain mean. Regardless of what Iris did, the old crone would be dismissive, rude and downright horrible to Iris, whilst demanding that she be a good daughter. She would 'remind' Iris of all of the sacrifices she had made and how this burdened her life. Iris felt compelled to visit her mother, but would walk away seething. It led to her having a breakdown, as it started to affect her ability to look after herself. She was hospitalised in response to this clash of 'compartments' within her.

Consider Sophie, who we met in the chapter on goal-setting. She wanted to stop her cocaine addiction. The leverage for her was found in the compartment relating to 'wanting to be a good mother'. By contrasting what she was doing with the role/image she wanted to have as a mother, we were able to build significant leverage for her to go after her goal. Getting her to imagine what sort of mother she would be if her young daughter was found and snorted her stash, was enough to create a massive visceral reaction – and a huge motivation to achieve her goal. The truth was that this compartment was always there, she just conveniently overlooked it whilst engaging in cocaine activities.

When we become aware of two or more identity stories that are incongruent together – we can either get stuck or use it as leverage to empower change.

Returning to Iris, take a minute and think what might have been a way for her to resolve the situation? Whatever you suggest could work perfectly well, even if it not what someone might have done to help her.

Here are a few thoughts:
- Iris could modify the definition of herself as 'daughter' in the relationship to break open the rules and conditions she is setting. What if she was now the mother figure?
- What if she could employ the skills she used dealing with her own kids when they were upset or angry, with her mother?
- Iris could leverage the desire and history of being a great role model to her own kids. How would she want to role model 'looking after herself' to her kids through this relationship?
- She could redefine the nature of 'care' – perhaps the best thing for her mum would be to receive care from others, as obviously she does not respond well to Iris?
- What if she could use the skills of not taking things personally that she had demonstrated in a lifetime of work and apply them to this specific context?

Hopefully it's clear that there are so many different aspects of Iris' experience that can serve as powerful levers to get her unstuck. Once she had the chance to step back and see the different opportunities for her to leverage different skills, capabilities and even identities, she was able to apply new skills to her problem and help move herself forward.

Your solution often lies in your exception. It's what you are *not* seeing that can set you free.

Consider William, a childcare worker that was addicted to pornography involving young people. He knew it was wrong and against his values, but 'couldn't stop.' To explore the problem deeper, I asked William what he saw when he watched porn. He replied that he was highly focused on the 'obvious' parts, plus the power and risk involved in the stories. To try to shift his perspective, I suggested that William see what was really there. The look of distress on the faces of the performers, the blank stares in their eyes, the fake nature of their interactions, the lack of respect for the women involved, the trafficking of people and drugs who made money from him watching. I posed the question, 'How can you watch it and not see it all? How can you watch it and not be aware of everything it represents?' The result? William could no longer watch his videos without connecting what he was seeing with all these other aspects. Viewing in its entirety, it was completely against everything that he believed in.

By 'not seeing,' he had created the space for watching porn to be OK and therefore the space for his addiction to take hold. But now seeing what he was *really* watching, he could no longer be OK with watching it – and his being stuck collapsed. Obviously, this was only one part of helping moving William forward. However, until he became unstuck from the porn, there was little opportunity to teach him other, more valuable skills.

By seeing what is actually there, we find that what often looks like a problem is not as bad as we think – and what we think is great may actually be pretty awful. As William was able to compartmentalise his viewing from the rest of his values, and even 'screen out' anything that didn't fit with this narrow view of the world, he was able to maintain his problem. Once he had to step back and really see what was there, the compartment and what it contained came into massive conflict with his values. We then had leverage to move forward.

Humans are great at lying to themselves. We are great at overlooking that which is known – or could be known – to build a 'truth' which suits us. In fact, the omission blindness is how many people go through their lives. Growth happens when we can see the exception to our beliefs and find a framework in which it can be integrated. Ignoring exceptions and dismissing different opinions keeps us stuck. You may be reminded of politics or social media as two real-time examples where fixed, narrow views and ignoring 'everything else' happens on a daily basis.

Being fixed in your beliefs or opinions provides certainty. It can be uncomfortable to have what we believe challenged. We will even use biases – such as the confirmation bias – to screen information and ignore or reject what doesn't fit our fixed views of the world. By overlooking information that challenges what we believe, we stay safe in the comfort that our belief can give us. Creating cognitive dissonance – getting people to challenge their belief with non-supporting information – can be one way to help them break out of where they are stuck and create a more integrated, nuanced understanding of what's going on.

Find Your True Resources

Consider Tex. Tex reported massive problems with anxiety. He has a lot of thoughts in his head about bad things that will happen. He looks for all of the 'black linings' in every cloud and has a series of Obsessive Compulsive Disorder (OCD) type behaviours and rituals he believes keeps him safe. When asked, Tex reported that he loves ocean swimming. In fact, when he is swimming, he is highly relaxed and feels great. He is exhilarated and feels connection to nature. He likes the way the weather changes and how the conditions challenge his skills.

Consider what you have just learned about Tex and his two spaces – we could call them 'daily life' and 'ocean swimming.' How different does Tex behave in these two different states? What skills are resources is Tex not using in one space, that he uses in the other?

Let's consider Tex's skillset. When Tex is swimming, he knows how to monitor the conditions before and during a swim. He knows which external cues are relevant to determining what might happen, like tide, wind, waves, rain, etc. He looks forward to the surprising way the conditions change things, where it pushes his skills, and he feels exhilarated when responding (managing with, feeling excited by, and responding to uncertainty). He connects to 'nature' and feels peace (creating a desired feeling and ignoring unwanted thoughts and feelings). He has learnt to co-ordinate his actions, pace himself and to build his stamina. He knows how to make small course corrections to keep going towards his destination.

Imagine if Tex was able to shift the incredible resources that he applies to ocean swimming toward his anxiety? Imagine Tex, in the face of uncertainty (the basis of anxiety), saying:

'I know what to focus on and what to let go of. Thoughts pass like waves that I can just swim through, and I can let them crash on the shore. I know what to pay attention to that will help me predict how things will go by looking at the forecast and the water conditions. I can't know what the future will bring, but I have learnt the skills to monitor and adjust course as I go – and still reach my goals. I am exhilarated by not knowing what will happen and look forward to the 'perfect swim.' I love shutting out the world and feeling at peace – regardless of where I am.'

Teaching Tex how to access his resources in his problem state meant that he had valuable and productive ways of dealing with the things that caused him anxiety. He had the skills and discriminations to make it a thing of the past. When he finds himself feeling unsure of what will happen in the future, he has developed the skill of stepping back and viewing where he is at in a bigger context, noticing the 'hidden gems' from his ocean swimming to help him respond more valuable to what he is facing. The more that Tex did this, the more he learned these skills in daily life and was able to move on.

Play the Exceptions Game

When we are stuck in a compartment, we can develop very rigid views and 'certainties' to describe our experience. As we do that, we screen out everything else. We omit all of the hidden treasures from the rest of our experience. Exploring these 'certainties' and finding exceptions can be a powerful way to open your vision to the possibilities of what else may be possible for you.

Sometimes it is called 'out-of-the-box thinking.' It's often in this exception that the hidden treasure actually lies.

Play the exception game with yourself – every time you hear a fixed, rigid or definitive statement, challenge it by adding 'except when I'm not.' When you hear yourself saying, 'I'm depressed' immediately say to yourself, 'Except when I'm not' – and look for the exceptions where this is true. When you say, 'I'm not good enough,' immediately say, 'Except where I am' and look for the exceptions. This can be a powerful tool to expand your vision to more than your problem, and open the possibilities of discovering what may be your path forward from being stuck.

Unstuck Exercise #119: Except when I'm not

Take the time to consider the following and how you can implement these strategies into your life.

- Listen to other people. When they make a definitive statement, rather than accept it, look to the exception. Where is it *not* true?
- Get close friends to challenge you. When you make a definitive statement, give them permission to say, 'Except where it's not.' Take this as a cue to look for the exception.

Learn to challenge your own thoughts and beliefs. Where you are rigid, global or limited, asking, 'Except where it's not,' and looking for the exception can open out a world of possibilities.

When you find an exception from any of these exercises, take the time to see what you can learn from it. What does it tell you about the belief? What skills or resources are you overlooking? What are you omitting?

You are more than you know. Often the path to getting unstuck already lies within you. Finding a way to expand your view to your hidden treasures – all of your positive resources – can be a powerful way to find the key to getting you unstuck.

Chapter 16

Moving On: Becoming the Next Version of You

From Stuck to Unstuck… To What's Next?

We have covered a lot of ground – approaching what gets and keeps people stuck in many directions and at many levels. I wonder what will be the 'thing' that helps you on your way to becoming unstuck?

Change may happen at any time.

Once you have learned what you need to learn, you may decide to act differently immediately, or you may just choose to wait until the right time presents itself. You cannot be forced to 'change.' In fact, this book is about giving you the tools to be able to change in the ways and in the timeframe that suits you. I expect nothing of you, except that you have the capacity to learn and adapt when you choose to. I offer you the tools and the possibility – the rest is up to you.

Change

When we exist in our 'problem', we feel entirely stuck. When we have been stuck for a long time, it can start to become familiar, even something that you label. This familiarity can sometimes provide a strange sense of comfort when comparing it to what happens when we become unstuck – we move into a place of uncertainty. This can even be scary because it means entering new and unchartered territory. This is the nature of change.

This circles back onto the question: "Are you acting towards your goal or in protection of your identity picture?" If you're open to the possibility of letting go of your old identity picture and setting out into the unknown in the direction of your goal, there's so many different outcomes that might be achieved. Often, we haven't considered what it might be like on the other side of this 'uncertainty gap.'

Unstuck Exercise #120: Moving on

Consider what it would to be like on the other side of your problem or issue.

- What feelings or thoughts do you generate?
- What information do they provide?
- How do you know which thought or feeling adds value?
- How do you reasonably know what to expect will happen as you move beyond your problem?
- How specifically will your labels or identity picture change for the better as you move forward?
- What are the 'ripple effects' (positive and negative) of making the change?
- How would you succinctly and positively describe your goal?
- If you could be beyond the change moment already, what would you be noticing?

What did you learn from this exercise?

Unstuck Exercise #121: Crossing the bridge

Take time to find somewhere quiet to sit or lie down. Below will be a series of ideas. For each idea, take a few moments – as long as you need – to absorb the idea. Perhaps after reading each statement, close your eyes and become absorbed in the idea and perhaps explore it in interesting and meaningful ways.

Imagine that as you become unstuck you're crossing a bridge. As all of the bridges that you have crossed in your life, you can imagine that the bridge can take you further on your journey into new and interesting places.

All of your life you have been on one side of learning, and then on the other. When you learned to walk, to talk, to read. There has always been the unknown of what happens after. But each time that you learned, changed and grown, you've adapted and moved forward. From walking to running. From speaking to communicating. From reading to understanding. As you explore being on the other side of your learning, take time to imagine how the new skills can enhance your experience.

In moments of learning, the unknown is like a birthday present. It's wrapped and waiting to be opened. Think of how a child approaches a birthday present – with excitement and wonder. They rip off the paper and dive into the present to discover all of the joys that will exist in their future.

What did you notice as you experienced this exercise?

The next challenge

As you move from the place of being stuck, you flow until you encounter the next roadblock. This roadblock is where you might next get 'stuck' and will have to go through the same processes of learning your way forward, adapting and overcoming this challenge to move ahead again. When you do, perhaps you can simply use the skills you've developed as you have worked through this book – or even pop back and dive into the chapters that seem relevant.

In a way, this is a description of life – rising above one challenge and then stepping up to face the next. A different way to consider this is to think about all the things in your past that are no longer obstacles to you now, but simply things that you had to learn from, or cope with?

We never truly exist in a world without challenge. The true mark of how you live your life is how you face and respond to each challenge and create a learning and growth opportunity to continue moving you forward. So, while we become unstuck from the current scenario, we may find ourselves being stuck in other areas and in new ways. For each challenge that you have, remember that you only need to find one viable solution in that situation to create the space for learning and getting unstuck.

Who Are You Going to Be When You Have Become 'Unstuck'?

As you change, your labels and identity story should be revised and updated. Sometimes this means that who you thought you were – and in what groups you thought you belonged – may also need to change.

Consider Terry, who for the last 30 years has seen himself as a 'not good enough' victim. On his change journey, he shifted his label to 'survivor,', and his identity picture is far more valuable for moving ahead in his life. Terry hit an immediate 'next roadblock' – he had changed, but still lived in the world of 'old Terry.' A lot of the groups and people around him were relevant for who he *was*, not who he *has become*. For Terry, deciding to 'trade up' to new groups, and redefining who he was in other groups was an important step in him being able to live the changes that he wanted to enact.

Remember the discussion on 'ripples'? As one part of a system changes, it can have a range of positive and negative consequences on the person changing, as well as those in the system. As Terry thought about these changes, he had to make some clear decisions about moving on from some groups of people that actively held him back, and redefine how he interacted with other people and groups. For some people, the change in status quo was a challenge, but as Terry consistently demonstrated the 'new Terry,' people got the message and became supportive. Having the right cheer squad can be really important to help through times such as this.

As you shift up, you may have to find a new tribe. And if you can't find that tribe? Perhaps create one.

Unstuck Exercise #122: Your tribe

Take the time to consider the following. If you made the changes you wanted to make:

- What labels and identities associated with where you were, would no longer be relevant?
- How would you describe the new tribe that you want to become a part of?
- What tribes, groups, individuals, experiences, and ideas no longer fit, and will need to get left behind?
- How will you be different in the groups and tribes that you already belong to?

- What else will you have to learn to fully fit into this new tribe?

What did you notice doing this exercise?

What Next?

So when you've decided to move beyond where you're stuck, all that is missing is *taking action*. No one will do any of this for you. When you discover that something is not working for you and you're stuck, the choice of how you respond is entirely *up to you.*

While some of the processes of self-awareness and self-insight can be challenging, the choices are to experiment with something different or to stay stuck. Once this choice is made, then taking the steps to learn what you need to learn so that you can appropriately adapt can begin. But it takes *action*. I hope that by now the idea of reviewing what needs to be reviewed, learnt and adapted is clear for your path forward. Otherwise, you can do nothing differently – and guess where you will be?

Life is a process of continuous learning and adaptation that emerges as you take action.

Just as you have grown out of being and doing so many things throughout your life, you can continue this process with new challenges that you face. It takes a combination of 'inspiration' and 'perspiration.' Insight leading to action leading to insight.... is really the circle of life.

This book has been packed with exercises for a reason. Each exercise, in its own small way, encourages you to take action regarding what you're learning. Taking action beyond this book is up to you – and it's what will put you on the other side of being stuck and actively implementing your new learning.

Life Is About the Quality of Your Learning

A common theme throughout this book has been about how the process of getting unstuck is actually a process of learning. Once we have learnt something, we seldom dwell on how we were stuck on it in the past but instead get on with enacting the solution in our lives. Think about the metaphor that I shared earlier about the kid that cannot ride a bike. The frustration of not being able to ride (including feelings of shame and fear) evaporates the moment that they learn how to ride. A child that learns to ride a bike does not sit and dwell on all of the reasons they couldn't ride a bike before – instead, they are simply off riding their bike.

Knowing that we must outgrow sets of behaviours, beliefs, goals, and attitudes we've had previously allows us to create space for everything that we are yet to grow into. We outgrow not being able to ride a bike and into being able to ride it. In the split second that this becomes true for the child – as they cross some mythical threshold from non-bike-rider to bike-rider – they unconsciously outgrow one state with all of its associated problems, feelings and implied meanings and create space for something completely different to emerge. What may emerge is the next challenge that has to be overcome.

Consider how we have explored goal formation and outcomes, behavioural processes and the unconscious 'conditional field' that establishes the rules, discriminations, and distinctions that determine what we do, and what we create. Growing out of old patterns, rules and decision-making processes requires that we become aware of them, become insightful about their impact, and make the conscious decision to learn and utilise new, more valuable versions of these. As we can become more nuanced in our approach, and adapt what isn't working for us at any of these levels, we cannot help but move forward.

After working your way to this point, my hope is that you have already gained some insight into how problems or issues are generally constructed (and maybe more importantly, that it can be 'reconstructed' into something else…). The aim of this book has been to break down the barriers that have been created that keep your 'problem' rigidly supported, and you stuck.

My hope is that it has encouraged you to engage in self-reflection and therefore gain self-awareness around what and how you do what you do. In doing so, it would be great if you are encouraged toward a self-accepting view that where you're stuck may be only a small learning step from where you might want to be.

Remember to be kind to yourself and generous in the possibility you offer yourself for growth. As you re-define quality goals and ensure your best behaviours are employed to move you toward (or beyond) your desired outcome, it's the opportunity to reflect that this is the human power that we all have. As the book has highlighted, your problem is not 'you' – rather, it is how you've been going about it. Doing your best from where you're at.

Finally, I hope that this book has encouraged you to move forward and inspired you to see that such moments are just a part of life. Take what you have read here to help you and those around you.

I invite you to return to this book as often as you need to remind you of where to look or how to look. To check in on how you've been doing and where you're going. To remind you to be easy on yourself and for being great at learning and adapting. When you learn what you need to learn, being stuck is no longer an option.

Unstuck Exercise #123: Moving on

Go out and be fabulous. Take action and create the life you want beyond being stuck.

Afterword

This book has been written to help you help yourself and get unstuck. If you were to ask what my purpose is in life, it's to help others do this; in any small way that I can. It's about empowering others and teaching them to find ways forward and create a better way of doing things. This is reflected in my two businesses: My clinical business — Reflective Resolutions: **Reflectiveresolutions.com**, and my corporate coaching, facilitating and consulting business — The Bigger Game: **TheBiggerGame.com.au**. Both hold this premise at their hearts.

As part of my purpose to help others, a portion of profits from my businesses and this book, is funnelled into projects, helping people in disadvantaged communities who want to change but lack the skills or the infrastructure. Through the giving platform B1G1.com, a percentage of profits from this book will go directly to projects to build skills (training programs) and infrastructure (food, water, medicine and transport).

These small giving actions will be the difference for these communities to get unstuck and change for the better.

So, thank you. As you step up and take action to help you, you've already stepped up and facilitated others to be able to help themselves too.

Free Resources for You

As part of your journey in getting unstuck, you may be seeking other support or resources. Once again, I encourage you to reach out to others who may be able to support or help you. To help you further, there are two specific resources associated with this book you can also access: The first is the workbook mentioned at the start of this book. This workbook is available for free download and can provide a framework for you to work through the exercises in each chapter. Download the workbook at **gettingunstuck.com.au**

The second resource is a specially developed application for you to listen to audio courses and segments on your mobile device. You can download in the app store or from **mindsetmaestro.com**. These additional materials and approaches help you get unstuck and shift and enhance your mindset.

This book is also **Interactive!**

To learn more from Philip about how to get Unstuck and set yourself free — go to: **deanpublishing.com/books/philowens** for free videos, audios and much more.

Acknowledgements

A book like this takes a lot of effort and attention from a number of people. I would like to offer a heartfelt thanks and appreciation to everyone who has helped me on my journey and assisted in the book you are reading now.

I would like to acknowledge a number of teachers and experts, from whom I have learned much and shaped into how I view the world:

Dr Michael Yapko
Gordon Young
Rob McNeilly
Judith Bell
Roy Childs
Paul Dunn

I have been fortunate to have Natalie Deane as my editor. She has helped craft this work into what it is today through her sharp editing, all of which made this book significantly better. She has worked tirelessly with passion, good humour and commitment; and I greatly appreciate her efforts.

To my early readers – Dr Michael Yapko for the early first draft read through and comments, which lit a fire under me to create this book in the best way that I could. To Rob Daniel, who provided a critical read through and feedback as we approached the finish line (and ongoing support throughout the process). This book is so much better because of you both.

To my family and friends – who heard I was busy with a book and wondering what it was all about – thank you for your ongoing support and patience. Here it is. I hope it is helpful. Enjoy.

ABOUT THE AUTHOR

Philip Owens has spent his career helping people, teams, and organisations get unstuck. He has worked with individuals and organisations in over 50 countries, helping them to 'shift gears' and move on in their lives, their careers and fields of endeavour.

From his clinical practice —delivering strategic therapy to individuals seeking help with conditions such as anxiety, depression or addiction, through to his highly successful coaching and consulting work in the corporate arena. Phil sees what needs to change and helps people change it.

Training and working with the best in the world, Phil is highly qualified and experienced in creating deep and lasting change. His strategic approach draws on the very best and latest in the science of human performance and change, and his pragmatic approach ensures that it hits the mark.

Now based in Melbourne after living in Berlin, Germany for six years, Phil consults internationally. Married with 2 young adult sons, a Maltese Chihuahua cross, a bearded dragon, and about 50,000 bees, Phil is passionate about his family, sailing, Taekwondo, travelling and continuous learning.

www.reflectiveresolutions.com
www.thebiggergame.com.au

www.ingramcontent.com/pod-product-compliance
Lightning Source LLC
Chambersburg PA
CBHW071224080526
44587CB00013BA/1493